Alsager and District in the Second World War

Dedicated to the Royal British Legion and its work,

and to my wife, Alison Ruth Blaney, for her support and assistance in this project.

© Copyright Rob Blaney. Rob Blaney has asserted his right under the Copyright, Designs and Patents Act 1988 to be identified as the author of this book. By the same author: *Alsager in the Great War*. Amazon Books, ISBN 9781530324088

Every effort has been made to acknowledge copyright for photographs and references in this book. The author is grateful to the individuals, archives and libraries who have given permission to reproduce pictures and documents. All proceeds from this book go to the Royal British Legion Poppy Appeal.

The Royal British Legion, Alsager Branch, would like to thank the following sponsors of this publication:

David Wilson Homes Ltd

BAE Systems

The Rotary Club of Alsager

Joseph Edwards & Sons

Sandbach History Society

Anonymous Sponsor

Mr H. & Mrs E. Pinkney

The Horseshoe Inn, Alsager.

Manor House Hotel, Alsager

The Lions Club of Alsager

Ev & Peter B.

Front Cover: Harry V. Lynam (ARP Officer), sitting, centre, with Alsager Civil Defence personnel. Photographed outside the Alsager Council offices, 1940.

Table of Contents

Preface 4
Simplify Me When I'm Dead – a poem by Keith Douglas (1920-1944) 4
.... 6
Introduction: Alsager and District before the War 7
1939: Prelude to change in Alsager 15
    Air Raid Precautions (ARP) 15
The Declaration of War 3rd September 1939 49
Alsager in 1940 - the dark days 62
    Timeline (history) 62
    In Alsager and District 62
    Alsager LDV (the Home Guard) 74
    The Evacuation from Dunkirk: Alsager and Rode Heath men 80
    The Battle of Britain: 10th July - 31st October 1940 82
Deaths of Servicemen in 1940 84
Alsager in 1941 93
Deaths of servicemen 1941 108
Alsager in 1942 119
    Timeline of the war in 1942 (history) 119
    Captain Charles William Kennerley Potts - Alsager's 'Fighting Padre' 132
Deaths of Servicemen in 1942 139
    In Alsager 164
Deaths of Service Men and Women in 1943 187
Alsager in 1944 207
    Timeline of the war (history) 207
Deaths of Servicemen in 1944 237
Alsager in 1945 281
    1945: Timeline of the war. (history) 281

- VE Day 283
  - Service Personnel who made the news in 1945 290
- Deaths of Servicemen in 1945 299
- Radway Green Royal Ordnance Factory 1940 to 1947 320
  - 327
  - Bombing Raids over Radway Green and Alsager and district 338
  - Working Conditions at Radway Green 345
- The Story of 'Heathside' Hostel for Munitions Workers, Alsager 356
- The Royal Naval Training Establishment, and The Brunds Hostel 376
- (Excalibur) 1942-1947 376
  - Excalibur Displaced Person's Camp 382
- The Acquisition of Milton House in Alsager for the War Effort 385
  - Milton House during the war 390
  - Milton House after World War Two 396
- Conclusion: The Post War Years 399
  - Appendix: Awards to Alsager and District men and women during the Second World War 405
  - Index 406
  - Note on the Author 409
- Citations and Sources 410

Preface

Poetry is often associated with the Great War, but I begin by quoting a great poet from the Second World War, Keith Douglas.

Simplify Me When I'm Dead – a poem by Keith Douglas (1920-1944)

Remember me when I am dead
and simplify me when I'm dead.
As the processes of earth
strip off the colour of the skin:
take the brown hair and blue eye
and leave me simpler than at birth,
when hairless I came howling in
as the moon entered the cold sky.

Of my skeleton perhaps,
so stripped, a learned man will say
"He was of such a type and intelligence", no more.
Thus when in a year collapse
particular memories, you may
deduce, from the long pain I bore
the opinions I held, who was my foe
and what I left, even my appearance
but incidents will be no guide.

Time's wrong-way telescope will show
a minute man ten years hence
and by distance simplified.
through that lens see if I seem
substance or nothing: of the world
deserving mention or charitable oblivion,
not by momentary spleen
or love into decision hurled,
leisurely arrive at an opinion.

Remember me when I am dead
and simplify me when I'm dead.

(Captain Keith Douglas, Royal Armoured Corps, was killed in the battle for Normandy 9th June 1944)

As Keith Douglas says in his 1944 poem, we *'simplify'* the lives of the men and women who have died and they become dates, records, impressions. Douglas does not object to this simplification process, he welcomes it. It is important though not to trivialise biographies. I hope I can do justice to the people described in this book by honouring them and putting down as accurately as possible what I have found out about their lives. To praise them where possible but not exaggerate their achievements. Following the publication of my book *Alsager in the First World War* in 2016 there was unfinished business. I wanted to complete its sequel about the Second World War. Less than twenty years after the cessation of hostilities the town and local villages were faced with the hardship of war again. Interviewing the last surviving soldiers and citizens from this generation and uncovering the story of what happened locally has been a moving experience. I am grateful for the opportunity of being able to share their memories. In 1947, Dorothy Harpur, Alsager Councillor, addressing a special reception for them, said to returning servicemen and women; *'No book would be large enough to record the deeds of valour performed by the officers and men of the various services, and of the women who left their homes to do jobs it was never before thought fit for a woman to perform. We wish you many happy days ahead. We hope you have come home to the ideal job.'*

Sometimes I have found only snippets of information about people, though in a few cases I have been lucky to interview survivors, or the descendants of Second World War veterans about their recollections. There are some amazing stories to recall. The years 1939 to 1947 saw Alsager and the surrounding area in south east Cheshire fundamentally changed by war. This book deals with the changes in the town and the villages around it, provides biographies of service men and women, tells the stories of ordinary citizens who died or survived. It describes events, incidents, and the decisions which permanently or temporarily altered the district. All communities in Britain changed because of the social and economic demands of wartime. Our local story contributes towards the national history of the War. It is a story worth preserving.

Rob Blaney, October 2017.

Pilot Officer Robert Harold Rigby 1915-1940

Battle of Britain Pilot from Alsager.

Painting from family archive

Introduction: Alsager and District before the War

Alsager before the Second World War: Little traffic. Children played in the middle of the road. The town and nearby villages were largely unchanged from the end of the Great War. Photo FHS Archive Crewe

Before examining how Alsager and district and its people were changed by war it is important to describe the area and how it prepared for the threat of war. Alsager and local villages: Hassall Green, Thurlwood, Rode Heath, Church Lawton, Scholar Green and Barthomley, the area covered by this book, were quiet, sleepy places in 1938. The area was governed by a complex and fragmented structure of local government. Alsager was an Urban District Council, while most of the local villages were in Congleton Rural District Council. Barthomley was in Nantwich Rural Council. The Cheshire County Council covered functions such as Education and the Police service, but the District councils were principally self-governing even though they shared responsibilities with the County Council. Local politicians could be aloof and detached from their electorate. An illustration of this insularity from the public came in the Alsager Urban District Council (UDC) meeting of June 1939. The Clerk to the Council, J.J. Nelson stated that Council Minutes were *not* public property. Members of the community only accessed the democratic decisions with difficulty. Councillor Clowes asked if the Council would pin a copy of the minutes on a public noticeboard and send a copy of them to any ratepayer who requested them. Nelson said Alsager ratepayers could only inspect the minutes on payment of a shilling. Mr Clowes demanded the council state how the income from this payment was going to be spent and deplored the lack of accountability to the Alsager public.

In June 1939 Alsager's Medical Officer, Dr Henry Harpur, gave his annual report to the Council. Alsager had a population of three thousand and thirteen people, based on the Registrar General's estimate. Alsager was composed of nine hundred and forty-one inhabited houses according to the rate books, and the rateable value was £17,123 based on a penny rate of £65. There was no slum housing as defined by the Housing Act 1936 and overcrowding was virtually non-existent. Alsager had no largescale industry and agriculture was still important to the local economy. Principal occupations of residents lay outside the town in the pottery and mining industries with workers travelling to North Staffordshire, or to the railway works in Crewe. Agriculture and the railways were important local employers. The London Midland Scottish Railway line came through Alsager from Stoke to Crewe. Smaller lines connected Church Lawton to Middlewich. A branch line connected Keele and Alsager. Another passed through Odd Rode north to Congleton. The villages of Rode Heath, Scholar Green and Barthomley were principally traditional agricultural communities, though according to the 1939 register many in Mount Pleasant and Scholar Green worked local drift mine coalfields. In 1939 Barthomley farmers still employed men like Peter Timmis and Tom Astley in pre-mechanised occupations like *'horseman on farm'*. Other local traditional industries in the villages were associated with the canals, haulage and, blacksmithing. In Alsager, Church Lawton and Scholar Green there was a sprinkling of professional people who travelled to work in Stoke-on-Trent. The lorry manufacturer, Fodens in Sandbach, was another source of local employment.

The government's census of households in 1939, the 1939 Register, (1939Reg), demonstrates most married women did not work but remained at home undertaking *'domestic duties'*. The occupational changes brought about by the Great War where women did men's jobs had been reversed.

Alsager's population, just over three thousand people, had only grown by three hundred since the 1911 census. The Great War had caused Alsager to stagnate and the lack of housing opportunities for working families had caused families to move to areas where council housing was constructed. During 1938 Dr Harpur reported there had been forty live births in Alsager, twenty-two males and eighteen females, and a total of twenty-eight deaths. It was a relatively healthy place to live. There had been an outbreak of diphtheria in July to August 1938 but no other general sickness in the town, and the water supply was '*adequate*'. In August 1939, the cost of water supply to Alsager was metered and set at two shillings per thousand gallons. There had been frequent inspection of the farms and dairies and Harpur confirmed an improvement in cleanliness. However Dr Harpur complained that heating and drainage was inadequate in the Alsager infant school.

Alsager farms were traditional and modern mechanisation was largely absent. Alsager and local villages were good places to live compared to the nearest urban centre, Stoke-on-Trent, beset as it was with pollution, high mortality rates, and poor housing. But there was an impression amongst younger residents, borne out in some of the correspondence soldiers sent back from abroad, that the town was too slow in attracting new industry.

A photograph of Oak Farm, Alsager, from the Sentinel newspaper shows the traditional nature of Alsager farming in the war years. Horses were still used, and hay wains brought in the harvest. Fuel restrictions increased the need for horse power during the war.

Transport

Local villages were quiet places without the hubbub of traffic. Alsager was not located on a trunk road, though car ownership was slowly increasing. In Lawton Road, Holland and Hollinshead Ltd operated a garage business. Another garage was opened by Mr Jones in Crewe Road. Cooke's garage was situated in Sandbach Road. In 1939 the railways were more important than cars; transporting increasing numbers of workers to North Staffordshire and Crewe. Blue collar workers caught the 7 am and the white collar the 8:30 am, all returning at 5:30-6 pm in packed trains. Alsager station had its own newsagents, WH Smith.

W H Smith newsagents, Alsager Station. In the 1930s the trains were packed with workers from Alsager.

A private charabanc was owned by Mr Whitter, of Station Road, Alsager who used to remove the flat coal body of his vehicle and turn it into a bus. A hoist would lift the lorry body up in his coal shed and the charabanc body was lowered to replace it. The top was canvas and could be folded back in summertime. Whitter organised trips to Sandbach market, and further afield to Blackpool in the 1930s. The first regular bus service through Alsager started in 1935 between Alsager and Hanley, the Hanley to Crewe service started soon after. In 1935 milk was still being delivered by a horse-drawn milk float driven by Mr Beswick and pulled by his red roan horse. The first motor-driven milk van was owned by Stan

Dean of Bank Top Farm; an old car with a milk churn on the back seat. He sold the milk loose ladling it into customers' jugs. Ice cream was delivered from a green Morris Cowley van by Robert Hurst of Congleton, who blew a bugle to attract customers. Other deliveries by horse and cart were still commonplace. Phillip Lea and his assistant Dolly Moores, a weather-beaten lady who wore Victorian-length skirts, clogs, a sackcloth apron and several cardigans, sold fruit and vegetables from a horse and cart. Sometimes ice was still sold from a cart.

John Ogden, milkman and smallholder, walked his cows through the streets in the late 1930s. They grazed at the other side of Fairview Park, (site of ASDA 2017) and were taken down Brookhouse Drive, Cedar Avenue, to Well Lane. Other smallholders would drive sheep or cattle down Crewe Road to the abattoirs. An oatcake seller, Mr Bowler, used to walk from Sandbach to sell his oatcakes in Alsager from a large basket. There were other old-fashioned households. Two sisters, Annie Jane and Theresa Taylor, of *Manor Cottage,* Taylor's Lane, ran a smallholding in Oakhanger. They wore white nineteenth century-styled headwear, which covered their ears, and their property had no electricity. They had no toilets except the use of an earth midden, the contents of which they used to sell as manure! Annie died in 1972 aged ninety-two.

Alsager was commercially well resourced having seventy shops such as drapers, butchers, a Co-operative store, and *Hancock's*, a popular food retailer at Bank Corner. Residents did not need to travel outside the town for provisions, they could buy what they needed in Alsager, though the new department stores in Hanley were attracting south Cheshire customers.

Mr. Barker, photographed in his orchard this week, and his grand-daughter Madge gathering part of the apple crop.

Congratulations have been extended to Mr. John Barker, of Ash Bank Farm, Audley-road, Alsager, who was 90 on Thursday.

He is the G.O.M. of Alsager, where he has lived all his life, being born in the same room as his father was, and having lived only in two houses.

He is in excellent health, and when a *Weekly Sentinel* reporter called to see him he was busy in the garden. Although he has had three operations since he was 60, he says that he feels better now than when he was 70!

He did not consider that reaching the great age of 90 was a matter for congratulations, and said with a smile: "Come and see me in ten years' time."

He has never seen the sea, and has no desire to do so; has never been to a picture house, and does not intend to go; has never seen a football match, and is not interested in seeing the game played.

When it is fine he spends most of his day in the garden and tending his cows. He regularly goes to Crewe market alone; but when the weather is bad, he sits by his fireside and reads. He has read the Sentinel as long as he can remember.

His secret for longevity is "regular habits." He goes to bed at 10 p.m. and rises at 7 a.m. daily.

Pointing with pride to his cows in the adjoining field, he said: "I drink plenty of what they give—with a little whisky occasionally. I used to drink ale when it was home brewed, but I don't like the modern stuff. I don't smoke and I don't worry."

Old Alsager; old fashioned farms in 1939. Mr John Barker, born 1853, Ash Bank Farm, Audley Road, had never seen the sea or been to a cinema, or attended a football match. It is interesting that opportunity and expectations were so much lower in the 1940s. Mr Barker claimed his long life was because he didn't smoke. There was no accepted view in the 1940s that smoking was dangerous though Barker obviously thought it was. Peter Barker, born in 1932, (no relation) remembers old John well. He was 'kindly,' and his sister always used to give him an orange when he called at the farm with his father on business.

Alsager Mill late 1930s. Raymond Barker, standing by the lorry; Mr Finney, Mill owner, standing on ledge, left; Robert Moulton, who was killed in the war, standing right on ledge. The mill distributed corn and feed to local farms.

Council administration in Alsager had changed little since 1918 with the two principal council officers, Harry Valentine Lynam (Surveyor) and James J. Nelson (Clerk) still in their posts twenty years after the end of the Great War. There had been no industrial development in the inter-war years and little desire for Alsager to change. Alsager was populated by middle class owner-occupiers in their Victorian and Edwardian villas, with areas of working class housing predominantly in Audley Road, Talke

Road, and the smaller cottages in the town centre. Alsager did have its railway engine sheds which employed over a hundred local men. It also had *Settle Speakman Ltd*, a firm which built railway trucks and operated the transportation of coal. The railway sheds had been in business from before the Great War. No new modern industry came to Alsager between the two world wars.

When Sir Francis Joseph, from *Alsager Hall*, wrote to the *Sentinel* in May 1939 suggesting Alsager might be a good location for a coal fired power station instead of it being located at Barlaston, Staffordshire, Alsager councillors were quick to scotch the plan. Joseph had vast financial interests in collieries in Staffordshire. It is likely Joseph's suggestion was tongue in cheek. He knew that Alsager was unpopular as a location for the new power station. He preferred the Barlaston site as he had considerable mining interests nearby.

Ironically, when the proposal to build a Royal Ordnance at Radway Green was recommended by government in 1939 Sir Francis was the most prominent voice in trying to stop the building of the factory which was to be less than a mile from his home in Alsager.

Fairview House (site of Alsager Library 2017) Note the cage for the air raid siren on the roof. Fair View was used as a Council office in the war with the Fire Service equipment stored in the yard behind the building. It was previously the home of the Band family.

1939: Prelude to change in Alsager

Alsager and district like all communities in Britain was already being prepared for the possibility of war well before the hostilities broke out in September 1939. Local councils were responsible for civil defence in their areas. Organisation of civil defence was taken seriously. Prominent members of the community led the way to develop Air Raid Precautions, and the Red Cross, Auxiliary Fire, and welfare services.

Air Raid Precautions (ARP)

In Britain the national Air Raid Precautions Department (ARP) was formed in March 1935 to supervise civil defence measures throughout the UK. ARP posts were initially set up in wardens' homes, or in a shop or an office, but later headquarters were purpose-built or requisitioned premises. In the aftermath of a raid, ARP wardens would be the first on the scene, carrying out first-aid if there were minor casualties, putting out any small fires and helping to organise the emergency response. Alsager considered the needs of setting up an Air Raid Precautions Committee in 1938 and appointed Harold Valentine Lynam, the Alsager U.D.C. Surveyor, as Air Raid Precautions Officer. Four members of Alsager British Legion were co-opted to his ARP Committee and he was responsible for the recruitment of volunteers. In an emergency, the U.D.C. was expected to man the telephone twenty-four hours a day if the County Council or others needed to contact them.

What the 1939 Register tells us about Alsager and its ARP

A national census (the 1939 Register) taken on 29th September 1939, provides a picture of the civilian population of England and Wales just after the outbreak of the Second World War. It formed the basis for National Registration. Because the census was updated by handwritten comments we know that throughout the war Alsager had many individuals who were part of the local Civil Defence service. Civil Defence also included fire wardens, rescue workers, and stretcher (or first-aid) parties. There were also many backroom staff working at control centres, telephonists, billeting staff, and even messenger boys. The original telephone exchange was on the site in Crewe Road where Barclays Bank is situated in 2017.

Civil Defence work often overlapped with the fire and medical services and the WVS (Women's Voluntary Service). The St Mary's Church magazine (APM) advertised for women to enrol in the WVS in its June 1939 issue asking for volunteers to report to the U.D.C. offices on Tuesdays between 2:20 and 8pm and the response was overwhelming.

Harry Valentine Lynam sitting (centre) with his Civil Defence staff in 1940 outside the Council Offices. Amongst the staff; Ernest Proudlove, standing behind Lyman, second right (Auxiliary Fire Service.); Mr Price, left in civilian clothes, National Bank Manager; Margery Bateman, standing extreme left, worked as a dispensing chemist; Marcia Webb, standing second right, Ambulance Service; Isa Price, standing 3rd from right.

In Alsager H.V. Lynam organised training courses, purchased uniforms for Civil Defence and paid expenses but according to U.D.C. reports in the *Sentinel* he overspent the budget. Alsager Council was strapped for cash. In March 1939, the ARP wardens were told they could use the Council Offices to assemble gas cartons provided they paid for *'heating, lighting and cleaning'*. The U.D.C., it could be said, were not working within the volunteering spirit of the ARP service.

Some ARP staff were classified as full time wardens, and they were paid to do this work. This caused resentment because their pay was higher than serving private soldiers. Most wardens were unpaid volunteers. The 1939

Register records that over one hundred and forty individuals were recorded in Civil Defence or medical services in Alsager out of three thousand citizens. ARP organisation was split between County Council and Urban District Council staff. The 1939 Register shows how Civil Defence was often a family affair. Men like Ernest Hurd worked for the Alsager U.D.C. Civil Defence ARP. Ernest's wife, Francis worked for Alsager ARP as an *'Evacuation worker'*. Others such as Percy Hardman worked as London Midland & Scottish Railway (LMS) ARP wardens, working for their own firms and not specifically in Alsager. Men like Charles Kennedy were recruited to work as part of the *'Builder and Demolition Rescue Squad'*, who would be on standby to deal with the effects of bomb damage. Others included designated lorry drivers such as Wilfred Morris, who owned a lorry as part of his business but who could assist in ARP transport work when needed. James Palin, a retired army Lieutenant in the Yorkshire Regiment, worked as an Air Raid Warden and his daughter, Eileen, worked as a telephonist at Alsager ARP Control. The ARP set up its wartime HQ at the intersection of Chancery Lane and Church Road on what is now adjacent to Alsager School field. The Home Guard was based at *Grove House*, Church Lawton though a contingent met in Sandbach Road.

Of the Timmis family in Alsager, Richard worked for ARP, First Aid, and his daughters, Jeanne (as an unpaid telephonist), and Mary (in the ARP canteen). His son William, who was a bank clerk, worked for Alsager Auxiliary Fire Service. We can see whole families dedicating themselves to Civil Defence work. Quite often these families had sons serving in the forces. Bill Jones, owner of the garage in Crewe Road, opposite Cross Street, converted an early 1930s horsebox into a makeshift ambulance which was used in the Second World War. The ARP also needed other less obvious roles; John Garlick, born in 1922 and unemployed, worked as a volunteer Despatch Rider probably using his own motorcycle. Councillor Dorothy Harpur, soon to become Alsager U.D.C. Chairman, is recorded as working for the ARP with St John's Ambulance at the First Aid point. The First Aid Point was at St Mary's Schoolroom but later transferred to *Prospect House*, the Council offices. By 1943 *Prospect House* was used by the Food Control Committee. One of the services at Prospect House was to supply special orange juice for pregnant women and children in need.

Olive Palfreyman, both of whose sons enlisted in the services, worked as Transport Officer for Alsager ARP. The Red Cross and ambulance service was an important part of the Civil Defence network. George Cummings, ex-army veteran from the Great War, served as the Corps Sergeant Major for the Alsager St John's Ambulance while his son was a cadet in the organisation. Other husband and wife teams worked for St John's Ambulance; John Davenport as an ARP Instructor, and Alice his wife as *'Ambulance Attendant'*. Women were already playing their part in active transport roles. Mabel Bailey and Elfrida Callon were recorded as *'Ambulance Drivers'*.

In October 1939, the Alsager Fire Brigade practised three times a week. The National Fire Service (NFS) was created in August 1941 by the amalgamation of the Auxiliary Fire Service (AFS) and the local authority fire brigades. One local member was Fred James Moseley, shown in his NFS uniform.

Alsager had its own branch of the Women's Voluntary Service (WVS). Florence Wetherby was a committee member, and John Wetherby, an earthenware factory owner in Stoke, was *'Chief Organiser of Factory ARP'*, presumably at his own factory. Other people had specific functions; Kate Walker was *'Chairman, Alsager Red Cross Supply Depot'*. Other backroom staff working for the ARP included Marjorie Harwood as an unpaid *'Service Clerk'* for Alsager ARP, and Gladys Wilson as *'Billeting Officer'*.

Alsager Police Constable on bicycle during WW2

The 1939 Register also records the men who were working as Special Constables in the town. Some of these were quite elderly and were retired police officers such as Fred Boulton, born in 1888 and Robert Hodkinson, born in 1882. Also amongst them was Edwin Archer Boffey, born in 1892, who had served in the Royal Garrison Artillery in the Great War.

From the 1939 Register and the Nursing Register the number of working medical practitioners and nurses in the town is known, although some of these women may have worked in Crewe or the Potteries.

Dr Henry Harpur was Alsager's Health Officer. Dr John Meiklejohn, who lived in Fields Road, is recorded as *'Medical Officer-Divisional Surgeon'*. His wife Gertrude, a qualified doctor, became prominent in the war years in the delivery of medical services in Alsager. Alice Meiklejohn is recorded as being a *'First Aid representative'* in the ARP and assisting as an evacuation officer with the WVS. Twelve other women are recorded as being nurses and living in the town. Of the Medical Practitioners, Dr George Bates, later to serve in the RAF, from 11 Lawton Road, was a GP, and his wife was his receptionist. Another GP, Dr Mathew Sayers, lived in Alsager. He was in poor health in 1939 and died in 1940. After 1941 and the construction of *Heathside Hostel* for munition workers, nurses were recruited to look after the medical needs of residents. Margaret Begg Rose, who qualified as a nurse in Aberdeen in 1917, worked at the hostel. There were also at least two qualified midwives in Alsager including Florence Mitford.

Dr Mathew Sayers

Helen Dudson 1898-1979

Helen May Dudson was Divisional Superintendent, St John's Ambulance, and Head of ARP Casualty Service for Alsager. Later, she became the Staffordshire Superintendent of Nursing for Staffordshire. Helen Dudson was an important contributor to the war effort and was influential in improving nursing services. Born Helen May Wilkes in Blythe Bridge Stoke-on-Trent on 10th May 1898, she married Hubert Scriviner Dudson in 1921 and they settled in Alsager. She was the daughter of Charles Wilkes, a potters' modeller and artist. She had joined the Wolstanton Division of the Red Cross in the Great War and served in the Queen Mary Army Auxiliary Corps at Southern Command.

The Dudsons lived at *Lynwood*, The Avenue, Alsager. Her husband was owner of *Dudson's* pottery firm, and in the Second World War he was an '*Assistant Ward Warden*' in the Cheshire Association of Air Raid Wardens. (In the Great War, Hubert Dudson had served with the Royal Air Force and was commissioned 2nd Lieutenant from April 1918 and worked at New Romney in 59 Squadron as an Observer. He retired from the RAF in 1919 on grounds of ill health.)

In 1938 Helen Dudson reorganized the Alsager Division and became Divisional Superintendent of Nursing. In September 1941, it was reported in the *Staffordshire Advertiser* that Helen was promoted to become '*Lady County Superintendent of all Ambulance Services in Staffordshire*'. Also in 1941, she became responsible for the setting up and maintenance of local Auxiliary Hospitals as part of the Red Cross and St John's Ambulance. Mrs Dudson started a recruitment drive for women to state a preference to do nursing work, if they had registered for National Service. In June 1943, she was present when four hundred nursing cadets gathered in the Victoria Hall, Hanley, for an inspection. The nurses later paraded to Hanley from Shelton with the Boys Brigade. In May 1944, Mrs Dudson, accompanied Lady Mountbatten, Superintendent in Chief of St John's Ambulance, to an event at *Ash Hall*, Stoke-on-Trent. The venue was a leading auxiliary hospital in the War, a hospital service evacuated from Kent in 1940.

ARP Exercises

The sophistication of the ARP/ Civil Defence structure is impressive but from newspaper reports some resources were badly lacking in 1939. Such was the concern about the level of light emanating from the bottle kilns of North Staffordshire it was decided to test local Air Raid Precautions. On 20th March, 1939, the Royal Air Force flew over North Staffordshire and South Cheshire, including Alsager, to test the effect of glare. Certain factories were being tested by adding special paint to try to reduce the level of light which an enemy aircraft could use to aim its bombs. Factories in the southern part of Stoke-on-Trent carried out their work in darkness and in the northern area using anti-glare plant. Observers reported back to the Home Office on their findings. A Civil Defence exercise took place in these areas at the same time. All street lighting, including Alsager, was turned off during the exercise. Householders were asked to screen their house lighting and motorists asked by police to drive using only side lights. The exercise included nine simulated incidents where the ARP, First Aid, Auxiliary Fire Service and Decontamination Squads were tested in dealing with falling high-explosive and gas bombs, incendiaries, and bursting of water, gas, and electricity mains.

At an Alsager U.D.C. council meeting on 15th March 1939, before the exercise took place, a letter was read out from the County ARP officer informing members a major ARP exercise to test emergency planning, which included the Alsager area, would coincide with the RAF aerial analysis of anti-glare testing in North Staffordshire and South Cheshire. As an example of the loose organisation of the ARP before the war, the local ARP surprisingly elected not to take part in the exercise. At a meeting in Sandbach on the Monday evening the local ARP had decided not to co-operate in holding the event. Moses Corfield, former Alsager headmaster, a Great War veteran, a member of Alsager British Legion, and an ARP volunteer, said the Alsager wardens had no equipment, not even whistles, and the First Aid parties *'had no more equipment than the Man in the Moon'*. Alsager U.D.C. decided to take no action against the local ARP for their decision not to participate in the exercise, but agreed to comply with the County ARP plan as far as it could. The Chairman said all lights in Alsager would be out during the exercise. The blackout would be total. Philip Bailey, Divisional Chief Warden from Northwich Police

Division, whose home address was *Ramsdell Hall*, Scholar Green, wrote to the *Sentinel* about the proposed ARP exercise. The exercise was to be postponed until the 20th March and it would not be necessary to call all Air Raid Wardens resident in the Area for duty. He apologised to members of Alsager U.D.C. for the *'misunderstanding'*. Alsager U.D.C. was compelled to write to the *Sentinel* the following day to say in no way was it trying, because of the decision by Alsager ARP, to prevent the area exercise taking place. It appreciated *'an incident'* might take place in Alsager in future which *'would require'* the local services of a first aid party, action by the repairs and decontamination squads, and by the emergency fire brigade.

On 21st March the *Sentinel* reported on the outcome of the exercise extending over North Staffordshire and South Cheshire. A number of *'surprise items'* were planted for ARP squads to deal with in Alsager. These included, dummy *'high explosive and gas bombs'* planted at the Alsager War Memorial, which required first-aid parties to help with stretcher cases. There was also a mock major fire at the Alsager waterworks (Well Lane). It is interesting that Alsager was chosen for inclusion in this major exercise despite the local ARP being told by the county organizer they did not need to turn out for the exercise. There seems to have been a last-minute decision for Alsager and the County ARP to work together. There must have been some final arm twisting because the ARP did participate in the exercise. *The Sentinel* reported ARP Workers dealt *'efficiently with every conceivable kind of incident'* in the district outside the Potteries and Newcastle-under-Lyme.

Alsager ARP outside St Mary's Schoolroom (post 1940) Photo South Cheshire FHS

Only a month later there seemed to be an improvement in ARP facilities in Alsager. Perhaps after the conflict in March the County ARP tried to boost the confidence of local wardens. It seems that there had been a delivery of equipment to the Alsager ARP to raise morale. In April 1939 Alsager ARP held a meeting to hand out badges and certificates to members. H V. Lynam, Alsager ARP Officer, and Mr Holland, Chairman of the Urban District Council, gave out fifty-six badges and twenty-eight anti-gas certificates. The size of this presentation gives another indication of the large size of the Alsager ARP and Civil Defence before the start of the war. For First Aid work with St John's Ambulance, and for the Nursing Division, eighteen certificates, three medallions and one label were issued to Alsager volunteers. Dr Gertrude Meiklejohn spoke at the meeting and said the local ARP had received equipment *'to carry out all necessary services'*. Mr E. Nixon, representing the Assistant Commissioner, St John's Ambulance Brigade, called Alsager the *'Baby Division'* of the North Staffordshire Area. Alsager, despite being a Cheshire town, was within the organisational structure of the North Staffordshire St John's Ambulance area. Conversely, the Alsager ARP was organised within Cheshire administratively.

In May 1939, Alsager Urban District Council agreed to form an *'Emergency Committee'* composed of Councillors Timmis, Elsby, Corfield, and Clowes, to deal with civil defence matters of urgency. The U.D.C. also agreed that if its employees joined the Forces or joined the full time Civil Defence it would make up their pay so the people would not lose out financially. Employees' jobs would be held open for them when they returned to civic duty.

Alsager's fire equipment was rudimentary. Alsager leased a trailer pump and hose which they stored in the Highways Yard. Alsager's fire appliances were on loan from the Home Office. Alsager's Auxiliary Fire Officers were commanded by dentist, Arthur Norman Fisher, and he was assisted by Phillip Band. They used the council yard behind *Fairview House* as their base. A stirrup pump was used at the *Lodge Inn* for practising fire drill until a vehicle was acquired. Ernest Proudlove was part of the team. Alsager U.D.C. wanted to purchase 61 Crewe Road from a private vendor for use by the Fire Brigade. £700 was due to be borrowed from the County Council to complete the sale but the Home Office said the acquisition of the property, which was next to the Mere's water supply, was unnecessary.

Alsager's Fire Service being primitive, the Council Minutes state Alsager U.D.C. entered into agreement with Sandbach Council for fire protection as the contract with Stoke-on-Trent had expired. There had been a poor relationship with Stoke-on-Trent Fire Service over their level of service for some time. In 1938 there had been a fire at the Alsager L.M.S Railway sheds. Crewe Fire Service attended and dealt with the fire. Stoke-on-Trent Fire Service attended but on seeing Crewe present left the scene. When Stoke-on-Trent Fire Service sent a bill for £12.10s to Alsager Council it was rejected, Alsager arguing they only paid for services when their Surveyor, the Chief Officer for Police, or a *'responsible person'*, telephoned the City Council for assistance.

Sir Francis Joseph with his wife and Civil Defence personnel outside St Mary's Church

The County Council ARP Committee also agreed to pay Alsager council officials an honorarium for undertaking preparation for additional wartime duties; H.V Lynam (ARP Officer) £26; J.B Harwood (Financial Officer) £10, and J. Rigby (Rate Collector) £5.

Despite the problems with civil defence the Alsager Civic Parade of May 1939 was one of the largest for years. It was marshalled by Great War Veteran, Warrant Officer William Harry Horsley, and included the British Legion, the B'hoys, the Rover Scouts, Girl Guides, the Ladies' Nursing Division, Alsager St John's Ambulance, and representative organisations such as Alsager Working Men's Club. Sir Francis Joseph read the lesson and £8. 7s. was collected for the Alsager Sick Nursing Fund. Horsley is remembered as a tall man with a military bearing. He had served in the North Staffs Regiment in the Great War and had risen from Private to Warrant Officer in the 8th Battalion.

On June 28th, 1939, Alsager was treated to a propaganda display organised by the government. Tanks and mobile kitchens, part of a mile-long convoy, were touring the *'North'* country for *'show purposes'*, and it came through Alsager.

Army's Road Show Will Include "Hush-hush" Guns

The convoy comprised a hundred vehicles and four hundred officers and men and the *Manchester Evening News* suggested the new *'hush hush'* 3.7-inch anti-aircraft gun, and the new anti-tank gun would be on display along with Bren gun carriers, mortars, searchlights and three tanks. It was quite a display to watch as it drove through Alsager.

By August 1939 the Alsager ARP were again in conflict with County organisers. Councillor James Clowes reported to the General Purposes Committee of the U.D.C. that the ARP trenches proposed for the *'Recreation Ground'* were *'too wide'*. He recommended the order to proceed with them should be halted. The Council's surveyor, Mr H. Lynam said the concrete foundation for the trenches had been obtained and it was proposed to proceed with the construction of the trenches. Clowes was supported in his views by Mr J. Edwards.

Alsager UDC Councillor, James Clowes. 1893-1954. He was disfigured by mustard gas in the Great War. His brother, Sir Harold Clowes later became Mayor of Stoke-on-Trent.

Both Clowes and Edwards were Great War veterans and committee members of Alsager British Legion. Mr Holland, Chairman of the Council, said the specification for the trenches had been drawn up by the Home Office and there was no reason why it should be changed. The vote to construct the trenches was passed by the Council with only Mr Clowes and Mr Edwards voting against the motion. It seems that the former Great War soldiers were still holding onto their 1914-18 views on defensive trench design. The report does indicate however that Alsager was taking the question of defence and the possibility of air attack seriously.

Meanwhile, in the same month the UDC received a report from the Nursing Superintendent who visited Alsager and reported that the local nurse had made two hundred and twenty-seven visits in the previous month with twenty-seven cases which needed special attention. Health matters were a regular feature of local government meetings in the 1930s and 1940s.

Members of the military auxiliary services mentioned in the 1939 Register

As well as identifying members of the Civil Defence a few members of the military auxiliary services, and Territorial Army reserve (before it was amalgamated into the regular army) can be seen in the published Alsager 1939 Register. Most younger residents are not visible on the Register, their identities redacted under the confidentiality rules of publishing the Register (people thought to be still alive in 1992.)

Thomas Brufnell, born in 1918, is listed as a Sapper with the Royal Engineers (T.A) working on an anti-aircraft gun. Huntley Goss is recorded as a Civil Air Guard Pilot. He was nearly 40 when the war commenced. (Huntley Goss was an extrovert who lived in a ramshackle property at 63 Crewe Road, and who worked as a radio engineer.) The Civil Air Guard, of which Huntly was a member, was established in 1938, comprising voluntary and unpaid pilots recruited from flying clubs. Their aim was to assist the Royal Air Force in a time of emergency. The government offered a grant of £25 to pilot members of flying clubs who obtained an 'A' type licence if they volunteered for the Civil Air Guard. With the cessation of civil flying as the war approached, most members of the Civil Air Guard enlisted in either the Royal Air Force or the Fleet Air Arm; some of the women members went on to join the Air Transport Auxiliary. Other members were used for special duties in both military and civil aviation, or moved on to other non-aviation war duties. Jack Band, a joiner of 61 Audley Road, was in the Civil Air Guard. He went on to be an Officer of the Royal Air Force Volunteer Reserve in 46 Squadron. He lived in *Sunnyside* Alsager and died in 1994.

Jack Band's wedding to Florence Ebsworth, June 1939.

Photographed in the garden of 61 Audley Road, Alsager

Photo: family collection.

George Holdcroft, born 1885, of Talke Road was a pay clerk with the workshops of the Royal Engineers (T.A.) George Holland, born 1898, of Sandbach Road is entered on the Register as *'Anti-aircraft T.A.'*.

Badges -- Civil Defence

Foreign-Born Nationals mentioned in the Alsager 1939 Register

The 1939 Register was designed so the government could identify the pool of potential workers and troops for the expected declaration of war. It also helped identify foreign nationals. Before and during the war the place of foreign nationals in our communities was scrutinised by the authorities. The percentage of Alsager residents who were foreign national was small in 1939 but amongst them were interesting individuals. Dr Michael Ivan Aische, born in 1877, lived at the *Cedars,* a magnificent house at the rear of Station Road in what was known as *Cinder Lane* which later became *Cedar Avenue.*

According to the Register, Aische lived in the house with his son Francis, and a Housekeeper, Roddam Stevenson.

The Cedars (pictured with earlier occupiers before the Great War) During the Second World War the Cedars was requisitioned by the Ministry of Supply and was used for billeting. A Women's Voluntary Service run NAAFI (Navy Army & Air Force Institutes canteen for service members) was located behind the Cedars.

Michael Aische is described as *'married'* but Mrs Aische is not registered at the address. According to records Aische married Sarah Drinkwater in

Yorkshire in 1920. Francis was born in 1922. There were other children. The Register describes Aische as a former officer in the Imperial Russian Navy and an expert in explosives. He gained a science degree from St Petersburg before the Great War and a Ph.D. from Reval, Tallinn. But who was the real Michael Ivan Aische? Can we trust what Aische claimed to be when he spoke to the enumerator of the 1939 census? We can be sure he was a clever scientist. He was an expert in paints and colours. In the 1920s and 30s Aische owned a factory in Stoke-on-Trent specialising in the manufacture of colours for the pottery industry. He specialised in making the colour *Prussian Blue* and other colours for cellulose paints. According to newspaper reports he converted garages at the *Cedars* into laboratories for his experiments and he had *'once held a high position in another country'*. He said he once worked three days and nights consecutively studying new methods of converting lead products for paint. He purchased old lead mines in Derbyshire and tried to develop new ways of exploiting the lead for paint. In the 1920s he developed other products including improvements in soap manufacture, and a process for the reclamation of Plaster of Paris.

Aische converted an outbuilding at the *Cedars* into a Roman Catholic chapel where a priest held services. Newspaper articles stated Aische possessed several original Rembrandt paintings in his lounge said to be worth £250,000 at the time. Local children spread a rumour he was a *'German spy'!* For personal security, he built a ten feet high wall round his property and had three guard dogs. In Alsager, Aische was well known in the Roman Catholic community and the newspaper reports state he was known generally as *'a doctor, well known for his generosity and hospitality'*. If we believe the 1939 Register, Aische was wealthy, and newspaper articles confirmed this. However, in 1942, an article on June 6th appeared in the *Staffordshire Advertiser* titled *'Prisoner's Romantic Career'*.

Aische was convicted for molesting a five year old child in Shelton, Stoke-on-Trent after pleading guilty. His address was given as Clive Street, Shelton, where he lived after leaving the *Cedars*, which had been requisitioned by the Ministry for the war effort. When arrested on the day of the assault Aische was drunk and unable to be interviewed until the following day when he denied the charge. He was found guilty and sentenced to nine months in prison. Aische told the court he had come to

Britain in 1917 after the Russian Revolution and that he was a Doctor of Science as well as a qualified doctor of medicine and surgery. Acting Detective Inspector said Aische was born in Libau (Latvia) of wealthy parents, *'and claimed'* to have entered universities in Leningrad (St Petersburg), and graduated in science, medicine, and philosophy, and subsequently in Estonia, Leningrad and Moscow. Godson said Aische claimed to have served in the British Army in the Boer War and for a short period in the French Army in the Great War. He stated that Aische's ceramics business started in Stoke-on-Trent in 1930 had failed. He had since traded as a paint manufacturer. Since December 1941 he had worked as a *'consultant physician'* to members of the public. Godson said Aische was a *'plausible and heavy drinker'*. Mr Norman Carr, defending solicitor, said Aische's patients were *'standing behind him in his present trouble'*. He had no previous convictions.

According to professional directories after his release, Aische worked as a physician in Manchester towards the end of the Second World War. He died in Lancashire in 1961. We cannot be sure of which information Michael Ivan Aische said about himself was the truth and what was make-believe. He was undoubtedly a clever man who fell from grace after what could have been a successful career.

Alsager's German-Jewish population and internment procedures.

With the persecution of Jews by the Nazis it is interesting to report what Government documents say about Alsager's Jewish population, which in 1939 was limited to a few households. Eileen Kirby, *nee* Taylor, of *Mere Cottage*, qualified as a nurse from Manchester Jewish Hospital in 1937 and she worked as a nurse in the War. There are records for two German Jewish families who had settled in Alsager. Robert Bloch (born 1862) and Frida Bloch (born 1874) lived at 7 Crewe Road. Dr Walter Bloch (born 1900) was a *'Consultative Chemist'*, and his wife Helene worked for the ARP as a First Aid worker. With them lived their daughter, Margaret, and an elderly relative, Augusta Levi (born in 1872). Peter Barker, in 2017, remembering Augusta, says she always wore black Victorian dresses. The Bloch family were popular in Alsager and according to recent interviews suffered no anti-German hostility during the war.

Ilse Forchheimer, born in 1913, also lived in the Bloch household. She is recorded as working as a *'Railway official'*. She later applied for National Service.

German citizens had to apply for exemption from internment and in the case of the Bloch family, Robert was declared category 'C' and free from internment in 1939. He died in 1942. His wife, Frida was also exempt from internment. The Blochs played an active part in Alsager and were involved in civil defence. The family also assisted in community activities at the Working Men's Club later in the war.

Robert Bloch's exemption certificate from internment 1939. (Imm)

Ilse Sara Forchheimer was also exempt from detention as shown in her certificate issued in 1939.

The only other record of a decision on internment for a German born individual in Alsager was for Dora Pfingst born in 1922. She was a student and exempt from internment.

Later in the war, John Francis Maddock, a retired earthenware manufacturer, of *Brundrett House*, a large property near the War Memorial in Sandbach Road South, employed two Austrian women who had escaped from Nazi Austria. *Brundrett House* had a large garden which once abutted Fields Road. The name *Brundrett House* is similar to that of *Brunds Farm* and *The Brunds*, local properties, which came to be associated with Royal Naval Marines *Excalibur*. The derivation of the word *'Brunds'* is from a rare surname.

Brundrett House was often to focus of charity fundraising for the WVS as Miss Grace Maddock, 1884-1964, was their Secretary. Her sister Miss Beatrice 'Bee' Maddock, born 1885, also assisted with the WVS.

1939 – High Society

Alsager and district had its wealthy and influential citizens. Alsager's upper class were not long-established families such as the Baker Wilbrahams of *Rode Hall*. They were mainly self-made industrialists. Despite the threat of war, the social calendar for the wealthy and well-connected in Alsager continued. Sir Francis Joseph rose from being a railway messenger boy in Liverpool to major colliery owner. Joseph was born in 1870 in Liverpool, and was educated at Caledonian School in Liverpool until he was twelve when he left to become a railway messenger, although he continued to attend evening classes. After a number of varied jobs, he became a stockbroker. Later he joined Settle, Speakman & Company and became the chairman and managing director. He worked for the War Office in the Great War becoming an assistant secretary at the Ministry of National Service. He was knighted in 1922 and made a baronet in 1942. He changed the name of his house in Alsager from *'The Hill'* to *'The Hall'* as the latter name sounded more impressive.

Sir Francis organized a dance for his daughters at his London house in Stanhope Gate, London, on the roof garden terrace. His daughter, Cynthia, a debutante, attended many county and national celebrity events like this. Waitresses in Hungarian dress offered a *'picturesque touch'*, and *'all windows were thrown open to the June night'*. All the known debutantes were at the party with their chaperones. Sir Francis was seen partnering Princess Wiasemsky in a dance who was escorting her daughter, Tatiana, also a debutante at the event. It is here that Tatiana possibly became acquainted with Craig Wheaton-Smith, of Milton House, Alsager, whom she married in 1941. Guests at the event danced until dawn and breakfasted on bacon and eggs before they departed.

Sketch of the rooftop dance in June 1939 from the Liverpool Express

Sir Francis was influential in developing plans to increase national saving in the event of war. He had an important part to play in morale-boosting events before and throughout the war. In May 1939, Major Herridge, Deputy Commissioner, National Savings, Cheshire, attended Alsager's National Savings Association annual meeting with Sir Francis. Ten other branches were also represented. He reported that Alsager and district had one member in seventeen members of the total population compared to one in twenty-nine nationally and he complimented the district on their above average participation. National Savings was essential to fund the economy when war eventually broke out. Herridge encouraged members by showing a series of films to the public on the advantages of investing in National Savings.

As well as activities initiated by Alsager's elite, efforts were made to develop community participation through the development of a Parents' Association. In June 1939 Alsager held its second meeting of the association. Its aim was to foster a *'sympathetic and healthy'* relationship between home and school. Mr Owen, the headmaster, announced he was arranging an excursion to London for its members. Parents were shown around the school and inspected where the new playground was to be constructed. Unfortunately, the Association did not function after the start of the war. People were too busy to participate in it.

The Evacuees to Alsager

In the spring of 1939 before the declaration of war, as with many other Cheshire towns, Alsager was selected to receive evacuees from Lancashire. Most of them came from Liverpool.

In *Wartime Britain 1939-1945*, (Gardiner), the problems of the evacuation scheme are analysed. One and a half million people were evacuated under the government scheme in 1939, which anticipated widescale bombing of British cities. In March 1939, the Minister of Health reported to the House of Commons that all children to be evacuated were regularly medically examined. They were not *'scrofulous and verminous children'*, as reported in some newspapers. This proved to be untrue. Many children were infested as they had not been recently examined by the school *'nit nurse'*. The government had long planned to evacuate the vulnerable from cities which might suffer from widespread bombing. Public Information Leaflet No 3 said the scheme involved moving children, their schoolteachers, and other helpers to areas where they could be safe. The scheme was voluntary. On 1st September throughout Britain the operation to get the children away began. Between sixty-one and seventy percent of children from Liverpool left for destinations in England and Wales. The plan was for children, and their mothers in some cases, to be billeted in private homes. The billeting officers and their helpers were untrained. In some parts of the country allocation of homes was haphazard with householders choosing who they wanted. Boys were often chosen first by farming families. Until 1940 and 1941 there were no special facilities provided such as plastic sheets for bedwetters. In 1939 each household was paid £0.8s.6d for each child they accommodated. Evacuation administrators were supposed to reclaim the cost from parents based on their *'ability to pay'*. The true cost of billeting a child is estimated to have been £0.9s.0d a week. There was no national plan on how evacuees were to stay in contact with their parents. In January and February 1939 in

Alsager a window card was prepared for householders who were prepared to take in evacuees. From this arrangement, potential hosts were recruited.

The *Sentinel* included a short report on the local evacuee scheme on 31st August 1939, just days before the declaration of war. Alsager seems to be too small a town to receive seven hundred and fifty evacuees, but the local council was adamant it was prepared for such large a number. The number of evacuees was later halved.

Alsager was very well prepared for the evacuees. H.V. Lynam had taken on the major responsibility for the organisation of the evacuees' needs. As well as being the Council's Surveyor, and the ARP Officer for the Council he was tasked with being the *'Reception Officer'*. One can imagine the scene at Alsager Railway Station with all the organizations waiting for the children to arrive and then took the children to St Mary's Schoolroom, next to St Mary's Church (Sainsbury's store in 2017) which had been seconded to the ARP. The Congregational Church hall was earmarked as an overflow facility for evacuees and for the distribution of gas masks.

ALSAGER

Everything is ready at Alsager for the reception of 750 children from Lancashire. They will arrive by train to-morrow afternoon and will be met at the station by Mr. H. V. Lynam (Alsager Reception Officer), marshals and officials. The children will go to St. Mary's Schools, where they will be provided with refreshments and receive rations. Boy Scouts and Girl Guides are among those who have volunteered to assist in taking the children to the homes where they are to be billeted.

Liverpool Evacuees ready to board the train. Picture (Livecho) *1939*

On 1st September, the *Sentinel* reported a change of plan and four hundred children were now expected to arrive in Alsager. Mrs P.J Palfreyman, Transport Officer, had laid on many cars to move the children. Wright's shop in Lawton Road was used as a temporary medical examination centre and St Mary's Schoolroom was taken over as an equipped First Aid Centre. Councillor Mrs Dorothy Harpur, Chairman of the Council, and Councillor Barber were appointed to the Evacuation Tribunal to deal with disputes concerning evacuees.

Dorothy Harpur: Alsager's first woman councillor, elected in 1939. Photo: Sentinel

On 5th September, the Sentinel reported on the progress of the evacuation scheme. Three hundred and forty mothers and children had been resettled in Alsager. They arrived on a special train at Alsager station on 2nd September at 12.30pm. An appeal was put out for dolls and toys for the children, and for blankets. The Ministry of Health promised to supply beds later. Most of the children were pre-school age. The arrangement had been coordinated by Mr J Harwood, Billeting Officer, and Mr Lyman. Dr Henry Harpur, Medical Officer of Health for Alsager, had overseen the First Aid arrangements. Alsager's Emergency Committee was meeting every day to plan and direct the town's needs. On 5th September, a large air raid shelter was completed in Alsager U.D.C.'s recreation ground. (This was the area which came to be known as Fairview Park, now Alsager's main car park.). A second underground shelter built was adjacent to St Mary's Church of England Primary School (Highfield's School Annexe in 2017).

On 9th October 1939 Dr Harpur gave his report to the Council on the evacuees. With the help of other medical men from the town he examined the children. Many children were *'dirty and verminous'*. Ambulance workers assisted, and some children were segregated and billeted at *Oak Villa*, Station Road. The doctors opened a clinic and treated the children free of charge because the government had not offered payment for the medical support of evacuees - Nurse Garrett had written to the Council to ask if the mothers of evacuee children should be asked to pay for their medical treatment. Councillor Elsby declared that, *'if a woman whose husband was serving in the Forces, and the serviceman earned only £1. 15s a week, how could he pay for the treatment for his wife and children. She could not pay for a doctor. Who was responsible to make up the shortfall?'* (to pay for evacuees' needs)

One of the lucky ones! An evacuee family, from Kirkdale, Liverpool, and staff, enjoying the gardens of Sir Francis Joseph at Alsager Hall in September 1939. They lived in an annexe adjacent to the main house. Some Land Girls were also billeted there. The garden is at the rear of the house looking towards Audley Road in the background. Picture Liverpool Echo.

SIR FRANCIS JOSEPH ON EVACUATION

There is a happy band of evacuated Liverpool families and children in Alsager, Cheshire, and tribute to the efficiency of the teachers who supervised the "trek" is paid by Sir Francis Joseph, who resides at The Hall, Alsager.

He writes: "The teachers had the complete confidence of both mothers and children. I am sure they are similar to the other members of the teaching profession in Liverpool."

He cites one incident as testimony to the gratitude of the visitors. When he told the mother, sheltered in his home, that he was going to church on Sunday morning, her four children said they would go, too. They were ready in good time with clean hands and faces, and their clothes carefully smoothed down. Their behaviour in church was an example for all.

Sir Francis concludes that "as a Liverpool man, he is proud that his home is sheltering some of his native city's children."

Sir Francis wrote in the (Liv 2) about the family he was 'sheltering'.

Sir Francis walked each morning from the rear of his home over the fields to the rear of Alsager Hall via Fanny's Croft to Alsager Railway Station to go to work in Stoke-on-Trent.

Wartime Diary

Mary Morris in *Alsager, the Place and its People* (AP&P, 1999) in the chapter, *Alsager in World War Two*, tells the story of a fifteen-year-old girl in her wartime diary. It is re-printed here because of its value in describing the potential divisions brought about by deprived inner-city children being billeted in a country town.

'On the first September, we were told that the evacuees were coming and we spent the day filling paillasses (mattresses) with straw, and on the 2nd September, that was the day before war broke out, the evacuees came, and we marshalled them into St Mary's Church, and in my diary, it said "Woo ... they were horrid." You saw them to their billets and I was on duty at Oak Villa, and I remember we rocked a baby to sleep on a handcart and we took the bedding round. War was declared on the 3rd September and we spent the day unpacking rations after our return from the Hall, where I was when war was declared, and we took bedding out and dealt with evacuee complaints and there were many complaints. And a lot of the evacuees took off and went to Winsford, they refused to stay here. And all through my diary I have got about stamping ration cards; reporting for duty; taking blankets out on the handcart and all this ...up to 25th November. But I remember the bedding was so filthy of the evacuees who'd gone back, that there were bugs. I'd never seen a bug in my life and my mother was horrified when I went home, and I told her we'd been killing bugs. And we had to burn all the bedding in the yard in the back of the Council Offices.'

Margaret Holland, (later Bebbington), in her own diary was more sympathetic to the evacuees from Liverpool. She was a Girl Guide and responsible for helping the evacuees after they had been transported from the railway station. After their medical examination, the Guides and Scouts were responsible for setting out the rations in the church and telling the evacuees where they must go next. *'It was really a pitiful sight, we the Guides helped these poor mothers struggling with baby complete with gas mask, and helped her mother with her luggage, (two battered parcels and the masks) the mother crying through sheer weariness and her other four children moaning hanging on to her. But nobody bothered, everyone was intent on his or her job of getting them through and onto their billet.'* Margaret Holland acknowledged that some mothers returned with complaints, some of which were spurious, but records some *'evacuees had been turned out by their hostesses'*. By nightfall they were all billeted again. There were two cases of diphtheria and one of scarlet fever. These were isolated and the families with bed bugs separated to an empty house. Margaret returned to this specially chosen house the next day to help the families. One mother had abandoned her child and gone to keep solace in a local pub. A hostess later turned up at the hostel to say her evacuee had *'taken sides with her husband and had turned her out'*. The billeting officer had to *'sort things out'*.

Women wardens inspect evacuees' gas masks after an air raid all clear in North Staffordshire. Photo: Sentinel

Margaret Holland said that all the Liverpool evacuees had left Alsager within three weeks. (This cannot be verified) Other accounts say 8 weeks. In Britain in September and October 1939 billeting officers were inundated with requests from parents to remove their evacuees. The contrast between city and country was probably too much of a shock for them. Many of the evacuees moved on to live in Winsford. There was more of a tradition of Liverpool families living in Winsford, which had already received seven hundred and fifty evacuees from Liverpool. Nantwich Rural Council wanted to turn Crewe Hall into an emergency accommodation for *'difficult'* evacuees. It was a short-lived proposal though the Duchy of Lancaster supported it.

Conscription in 1939 and in following years

At the outbreak of war, on 3rd September 1939, the Military Training Act was overtaken by the National Service (Armed Forces) Act, and the first intake was absorbed into the army. This act imposed a liability to conscription of all men eighteen to forty-one years old. Men could be rejected for medical reasons, and those engaged in vital industries or occupations were *'reserved'* at an age beyond which no one in that job would be enlisted. The Territorial Army was merged with the Regular Army. Although a man could express a preference to join the Army, Navy, or Royal Air Force there was no guarantee this could be honoured especially as it was less popular to serve in the Army. By May 1940 the Act had called up men up to the age of twenty-seven. Those up to forty were not conscripted until June 1941. The government was committed not to send men overseas until they were twenty years of age. Basic training lasted three months. On the Home Front men not engaged in the Services were employed in vital national war work. The reserved occupation scheme included a wide range of occupations from boiler makers, teachers, doctors, but engineering had the highest number of exemptions from military conscription.

Women were not conscripted at the beginning of the war, the aim being to encourage volunteers to work in the essential industries. On 18th December 1941, the National Service (No. 2) Act was passed. All men *and* women aged eighteen to sixty were now liable for national service, including military service for those under fifty-one. The first military registration of eighteen and a half-year-olds took place. The Schedule of Reserved Occupations was abandoned; from now on only individual deferments from conscription were accepted. This made Britain the first country to conscript women. Women had the option to join any of the main Services, the Auxiliary Territorial Service (ATS), the Women's Royal Naval Service (WRNS) or The Women's Auxiliary Air Force (WAAF) or they could be directed into industry or Civil Defence. In practice, most women were directed into the ATS and the munitions industry. Single women between the ages of twenty and thirty could be conscripted into military service, (age nineteen from 1943). Discharge rates from the ATS were high, up to 29%, and as many were unwilling recruits, dismissal was what they wanted! Service conditions improved and by 1943 80% of recruits were retained. Women were allowed to work tending barrage balloons and man Anti-Aircraft guns. Most of work undertaken by the WRNS was domestic or clerical as they were on-shore workers, but their role was extended to coastal mine-spotters, welders, ship repair, radar, communications, and serving on tug boats and harbour launches, though never to sea on warships. The WRAAF were employed in plotting aircraft and radar, packing parachutes, driving and administration. By 1941 women were employed in the Air Transport Auxiliary delivering planes from factory to airfield, and in manning barrage balloons.

Exemption from conscription

British subjects from outside Britain and the Isle of Man who had lived in the country for less than two years were exempt from conscription into the services or national service. The other categories of persons exempted were as follows: *Northern Ireland residents; Students; Persons employed by the government of any country of the British Empire except the United Kingdom; Clergy of any denomination; those who were blind or had mental disorders; Married women and women who had one or more children fourteen years old or younger living with them. This included their own children, legitimate or illegitimate, stepchildren, and adopted children, if the child was adopted before 18 December 1941.* Pregnant women were not exempted, but in practice were not called up. As the war progressed married women with children were directed into part-time work.

In the First World War Alsager had recorded no conscientious objectors but in December 1939 the Sentinel reported Raymond Joseph of Wesley Place applied for exemption to conscription on religious grounds. He was however willing to serve in the Royal Army Medical Corps. It is not known whether his application was successful.

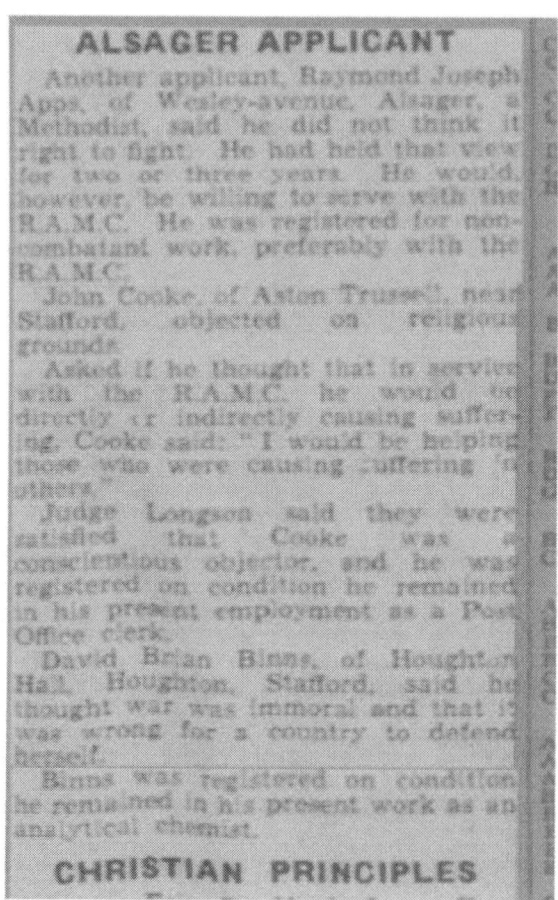

The alterative to being conscripted into the military services for women was to serve in Civil Defence work such as driving ambulances, the ARP service, the Women's Auxiliary Police Corps or the Women's Auxiliary Fire Service, the Women's Land Army or to do factory work; principally munitions work. The Labour exchanges were primed to direct single women into munitions work and move them to anywhere in the country they were required.

The Declaration of War 3rd September 1939

Background to the conflict

After the First World War Germany lost large areas of its territory to other countries. The Nazis wanted to recover these areas with Hitler's aim that all Germans could live in one great and powerful German nation. After the First World War, the Treaty of Versailles prevented Germany from having a large army. The countries which had won in 1918 wanted to prevent Germany from ever starting another war. But Hitler's government built up a large army anyway. Hitler used his strong army as a threat, and demanded the return of the lost German territories. In 1936 the Rhineland, which had been occupied by France since 1918, was occupied by German troops. The Anschluss (*'Unification'*) of March 1938 made Austria a part of Germany. In 1939 part of Czechoslovakia, the Sudetenland, the German speaking part of the country, was occupied despite Neville Chamberlain signing the Munich Agreement in 1938. The Munich Agreement was a settlement permitting Nazi Germany's annexation of portions of Czechoslovakia along the country's borders mainly inhabited by German speakers, for which a new territorial designation *'Sudetenland'* was coined. The agreement was signed in the early hours of 30th September 1938 (but dated 29th September) after being negotiated at a conference held in Munich, Germany, among the major powers of Europe, excluding the Soviet Union. Germany broke the Agreement by occupying other areas of Czechoslovakia. On 15th March 1939, the German army moved into the remainder of Czechoslovakia and, from Prague Castle, Hitler proclaimed Bohemia and Moravia the Protectorate of Bohemia and Moravia. On 31st March, 1939, in response to Nazi Germany's defiance of the Munich Agreement and occupation of Czechoslovakia, the United Kingdom pledged the support of itself and France to guarantee Polish independence. The agreement contained promises of mutual military assistance between the nations in the event either was attacked by some *'European country'*. When Poland was invaded by the German army on 1st September 1939, Britain and France declared war on Germany.

At 11.15 a.m. 3rd September 1939 the Prime Minister, (1939) broadcast to the nation the following statement announcing that a state of war existed between Britain and Germany:

"This morning the British Ambassador in Berlin handed the German Government a final Note stating that, unless we heard from them by 11 o'clock that they were prepared at once to withdraw their troops from Poland, a state of war would exist between us. I have to tell you now that no such undertaking has been received, and that consequently this country is at war with Germany. You can imagine what a bitter blow it is to me that all my long struggle to win peace has failed. Yet I cannot believe that there is anything more or anything different that I could have done and that would have been more successful. Up to the very last it would have been quite possible to have arranged a peaceful and honourable settlement between Germany and Poland, but Hitler would not have it. He had evidently made up his mind to attack Poland whatever happened, and although He now says he put forward reasonable proposals which were rejected by the Poles, that is not a true statement. The proposals were never shown to the Poles, nor to us, and, although they were announced in a German broadcast on Thursday night, Hitler did not wait to hear comments on them, but ordered his troops to cross the Polish frontier. His action shows convincingly that there is no chance of expecting that this man will ever give up his practice of using force to gain his will. He can only be stopped by force. We and France are today, in fulfilment of our obligations, going to the aid of Poland, who is so bravely resisting this wicked and unprovoked attack on her people. We have a clear conscience. We have done all that any country could do to establish peace. The situation in which no word given by Germany's ruler could be trusted and no people or country could feel themselves safe has become intolerable. And now that we have resolved to finish it, I know that you will all play your part with calmness and courage. At such a moment as this the assurances of support that we have received from the Empire are a source of profound encouragement to us. The Government have made plans under which it will be possible to carry on the work of the nation in the days of stress and strain that may be ahead. But these plans need your help. You may be taking your part in the fighting services or as a volunteer in one of the branches of Civil Defence. If so you will report for duty in accordance with the instructions you have received. You may be engaged in work essential to the prosecution of war for the maintenance of the life of the people - in factories, in transport, in public utility concerns, or in the supply of other necessities of life. If so, it is of vital importance that you should carry on with your jobs. Now may God bless you all. May He defend the right. It is the evil things that we shall be fighting against - brute force, bad faith,

injustice, oppression and persecution - and against them I am certain that the right will prevail."

A recollection on the declaration of war (Joan Hamlett, 1939)

On 3rd September 1939 at 11.15 a.m. Joan Bailey, *nee* Hamlett, came out of chapel in Scholar Green where she was a Sunday School teacher and an old lady popped out of her house to tell her she has been listening to the radio and Britain had declared war on Germany. Joan lived in Forge Valley, Scholar Green adjacent to *Boden Hall* where her father worked as a gardener.

'Soon after war was declared everyone had to black out their windows at night and Dad was kept busy making frames to fit the windows and covering them with thick cardboard or brown paper ... dad was too old for this war after serving in the First but when volunteers were wanted for the L.D.V., he was there.'

In 1940 Joan worked at Fodens, Sandbach, in the drawing offices earning 17s.6d a week. Fodens were building tanks. She recalls everyone had to wear an identity bracelet or tag on them with their name and identity number, just in case she was a bomb victim and had to be identified. Gas masks were carried in a cardboard carrier, which had to be taken everywhere. She wore an identity badge in the form of a Spitfire plane. A well-known secret in the district was the visit of Emperor Haile Selassie of Ethiopia to stay at *Rode Hall* after coming to Britain for his own safety. She remembers him as a *'little dapper man with his small figure and black beard, black cloak billowing out behind him'*. He was a familiar figure in Rode Park. He once went with Mr & Mrs Baker Wilbraham to *Boden Hall* for dinner with Colonel Johnson, formerly Lieutenant Colonel of the Staffordshire Regiment. In 1936, Mussolini had invaded Ethiopia and the country was defeated. Haile Selassie fled to England, first to London and then to Malvern. His visit to *Rode Hall* would have been in 1940. His exile lasted five years, 1936 -1941, principally living in Bath.

At seven o'clock at night Joan remembered the *'steady drone'* of the German bombers going over to Manchester and Liverpool and the sound of the air raid siren. If the Luftwaffe decided to drop a bomb or two which they did close to Joan's house she would *'dive under the kitchen table, wait for the thud and the house to stop shaking and breathe a sigh of relief.'* Living in a wooded area they were often mistaken for Byley Airfield. On one occasion, the planes were overhead and dropped incendiary bombs into the woods which started fires. Neighbours knocked on the door and were hysterical and they had to calm them down. The men went out with spades to put out the fires. Joan's father had to jump off his bike and dive into a ditch until things went quiet and he could return to Home Guard HQ. Mr & Mrs Sant from Alsager called to see Joan the next day as people from Alsager had heard about the raid and were worried because there were rumours of people being killed and they were glad to see Joan and her family were *'alive and kicking'*.

Joan remembered the rationing. All eggs were supposed to go to the Ministry of Agriculture packing stations to be graded and stamping but kindly farmers would let her have half a dozen *'on the side'*. Everything had to be kept secret from the Ministry man, so people used the village grapevine to tell each other when food parcels outside rationing could be collected from *'Mr So-and-So'*. Flower gardens were given over to growing vegetables as were many lawns and sports fields. Joan remembered encountering Italian prisoners of war in their brown uniforms cycling to work on local farms and smiling and saying, *'Good Morning'*, in *'probably the only English they knew'*.

Once there was a rumour a German spy had parachuted into Rode Park. The Home Guard were called out to search the park and woods. Only one or two carried rifles and some carried pitchforks, but they found nothing. As all local street signs had been removed or painted over Joan guessed any fugitive would *'not have got far'*.

Joan remembered one terrible Sunday, a beautiful sunny day, soon after the outbreak of war, when the Rolls Royce factory in Crewe was bombed and several people killed, and dozens injured. The Army had a large barrage balloon site near Crewe Station but on that particular Sunday the balloons were grounded. One German pilot came over and noticed the lack of defences and the Rolls Royce Factory was an easy target. At 3pm Joan was sitting in chapel in Rode Heath and heard the sound of the bombing in Crewe.

Rode Heath LDV/Home Guard was only 20 strong. They trained in Rode Park and one occasion arranging a *'mock'* attack on Rode Heath Corn Mill in Sandbach Road. On another the Rode Heath Home Guard defended a position in Brook Bridge from Love Lane, Betchton, but were outmanoeuvred by the attackers led by Arthur Bailey, a Great War veteran, who took the undefended bridge from the Boden Valley direction. (Westwood, 2009)

International Events late 1939 (history)

1 Sept   Germany invaded Poland. First use of Blitzkrieg. Britain and France gave Germany an ultimatum to get out. Blackout and evacuation plans were put in place in Britain.

2 Sept   Chamberlain sent Hitler an ultimatum: withdraw German troops from Poland or war will be declared. The Luftwaffe gained air superiority over the Polish air force.

3 Sept   Germany ignored the ultimatum and Britain and France declared war on Germany.

British troops (the BEF) were ordered to France. The passenger liner SS Athenia was the first British ship to be sunk by Nazi Germany in the war. Carrying 1,103 civilian passengers, including 300 Americans, she had departed Liverpool bound for Montreal. Torpedoes fired from the German submarine U-30, would see 98 passengers and 19 crew members killed.

4 Sept. The RAF raided German warships based in the Heligoland Bight.

9 Sept   The IV Panzer Division reached Warsaw and the city was effectively put under siege. The British Expeditionary Force began moving to France in September 1939. The British assembled along the Belgian–French border on the left of the French First Army as part of the French 1er groupe d'armées (1st Army Group) of the Front du Nord-Est (North-Eastern Front). The enemy did not advance towards them. Most of the BEF spent the 'Phoney War' digging field defences on the French–Belgian border.

17 Sept   Sixteen days after Nazi Germany had invaded Poland from the west, the Russian Red Army attacked from the east. Now facing massive opposition on a second front, Polish troops were ordered to evacuate to neutral Romania.

24 Sept   1,150 German aircraft bombed Warsaw.

26 Sept   The Luftwaffe attacked the Royal Naval base at Scapa Flow. German propaganda claimed they have sunk the carrier HMS Ark Royal, when the 2,000-lb bomb had missed by almost 30 yards! A Skua aircraft from Ark Royal shot down the first German plane of the war.

27 Sept With civilian losses estimated at 200,000 Poland surrendered to Germany. Polish lands were divided between the Soviet Union and Germany, as were 660,000 prisoners of war.

6 Oct Last Polish troops ceased fighting. Hitler launched his "last" Peace Offensive to the Western democracies, but this was rejected by Neville Chamberlain.

14 Oct HMS Royal Oak was torpedoed at Scapa Flow in Orkney, Scotland, by German U-Boat 47. Of the old ship's complement of 1,234, more than 800 men and boys died as result. Still visible, the Royal Oak is a designated war grave.

30 Nov Without a formal declaration of war, Russia's Red Army invaded Finland – the Winter War. The Soviet air force bombed the capital Helsinki, whilst 1,000,000 troops poured across the border.

13 Dec The Battle of the River Plate, the first naval battle of the war, was fought and ended with the German pocket battleship Admiral Graf Spee in flames after being scuttled in the River Plate Estuary off Montevideo, Uruguay.

Coming to terms with war in Alsager and district

Air Raid Prevention Services became officially part of *'Civil Defence General Services'* after the declaration of war.

On 3rd September, the day war was declared, Alsager's social scene continued as normal. An *'American Tea'* was held in St Mary's Schoolroom to raise money for church funds, despite the room also being used to co-ordinate assistance for the evacuees. It was fundraising for parish funds and Miss Barlow of Tunstall contributed songs accompanied by Mr Westlake the church organist on piano. The great and the good from Alsager attended, including Sir Francis Joseph, who gave a talk in the evening on the international situation. The Vicar, Charles Churton Potts, Mrs Wheaton-Smith from *Milton House* (daughter of the late M.P. Ernest Craig), Mrs D'Arcy Ellis, and Mrs Maddocks, all attended. It was Alsager's unofficial elite attending a traditional church fundraising event. This picture of middle class social life soon changed. Fundraising for the war effort took precedence over church and charitable causes.

Soon afterward the declaration of war Alsager began to change physically. Brick air raid shelters were completed in what was Fairview Park, and at the top of Well Lane where it joined Station Road.

A block house and underground shelter was built opposite the Police Station, and sand bags were placed around the Council offices at Bank Corner. Children volunteered to help fill the sandbags at Barker's sand

quarry. All wrought iron railings and gates were removed by order of the government and melted down for the war effort. (It was rumoured by locals that Sir Francis Joseph hid his iron gates in the spinney adjacent to his house to stop them being destroyed.) The railings round the War

Memorial and the Gates to Christ Church, and even the iron railings round the school playground were removed. Sign posts and mile posts had their information removed, vehicles had the town or village they came from painted out. All buses' windows were painted blue, so you could not see through them and it was difficult to know when you had reached your destination. It is possible that route numbers were introduced for the first time during the war as destination signs were prohibited. All windows had tape stuck across them to protect against blast damage. Blackout blinds had to be in place after dark. All citizens were issued with identity cards and gas masks. Mr Peter Barker (Barker, 2017) recalls posters being put up around Alsager, particularly. *'Careless Talk Costs Lives'*, *'Dig for Victory'*, posters, and *'Squander Bug'* posters to persuade people not to waste their money on unnecessary items.

A shelter was constructed at Alsager C of E School. (Highfields annexe in 2017) It was still visible until 1963. This picture from the Sentinel is of a sandbagged exit to a local shelter.

On 4th October 1939 proposals were presented to Alsager U.D.C. for a public air raid shelter in Linley. Councillor Timmis was worried about shelter provision for schoolchildren and H.V Lynam, ARP Officer, said the County Council were making plans for provision for more *'vulnerable areas'*. The Alsager Fire Brigade were undertaking practices three times a week. Also, volunteers had agreed to paint white rings around telegraph poles to improve visibility during the blackout. The Council reported there was a balance of £35.3s in the Civil Defence budget. Health monitoring continued as normal. The District Nurse visited twenty-five seriously ill patients in Alsager in September 1939 and visited two hundred and twenty seven other households. The Local Fuel Overseer Mr Rigby, said that there were *'chaotic conditions'*, on the supply of fuel in Alsager but things were beginning to be clarified. The Council was bogged down in red tape issues. It needed £15 to spend on a First Aid Point and on 3rd September Dr Harpur had committed expenditure of £15 but discovered a few days later he only had permission to spend up to 15 shillings. He had to ask traders to take back some of the equipment he had purchased. Meanwhile the push to persuade citizens to develop allotments commenced. The Council began to advertise to see what the take up would be for allotments and promised to provide land for them.

Certificate of Merit to Mr Dabbs of Alsager by the Allotments Committee

On 10th October, the council reported it had received more applications for allotments and decided to invite representatives of the Allotments Association to come to Alsager to advise them. A large allotment close to Alsager Mill looked after by Mr Raymond Barker was subject to theft and a crop of onions stolen by black market criminals. (In 1941 there were complaints of people trespassing on allotments and damage to the Recreation Ground (Fairview Park), and a demand made the park be locked up at night. This allotment on the site of which is now Highfields was the main *'Dig for Victory'* allotment in Alsager.)

The War Effort

The people of Alsager responded to the commencement of war by more public fundraising events. In October 1939, there was a *'Bring and Buy'* sale for the Red Cross organised by Mr & Mrs Bingham at their house, *Willowsmere*, Alsager. Alsager's leading families turned out for the event, including Mrs Wheaton-Smith, President of the Branch; Lady Joseph; and Mrs D'Arcy Ellis. £13 was raised in conjunction with the Alsager Branch of the Hospital Supply Depot. Lady Joseph also hosted meetings at *Alsager Hall* for the nursing service.

Roll of Honour

On 17th October 1939, Alsager British Legion wrote to the *Sentinel* asking the people of Alsager to submit the names of their sons who enlisted in the Army, Navy or Royal Air Force so they could construct a Roll of Honour of active servicemen. Unfortunately, this Roll of Honour no longer exists. The Legion promised to send each of the men gifts of cigarettes and chocolate in time for Christmas from *'The Boys of the Old Brigade'*.

Savings Campaign

On 13th December 1939 Sir Francis Joseph, who as well as his many other jobs was a Member of the Advisory Committee on National Savings, addressed a meeting at St Mary's School Room to further the cause of National Savings to raise funds to pay for the war. He said that *'unless we won this war there would be nothing else left for us to defend. Our money would be confiscated. The State would be impoverished, and we would lose our freedom of conscience, thought, speech and action.'* He was concerned Britain might run up foreign debt, principally with the United States, on not very good terms.

He said Britain had bought £2,500,000,000 worth of goods from the United States in the Great War. Britain needed to be more self-sufficient. In addition, Russia still owed Britain from debts in the Great War of £475,000,000 (Money it was unlikely to recover from the Soviets). Sir Francis gave details of the latest National Savings Certificate and the War Bonds offer and there was *'no chance of loss'*. Older Alsager residents may have remembered how their War Bonds from the Great War had subsequently become devalued!

Charles Churton Potts, vicar of Alsager 1934 to 1944. Photo: St Mary's Church.

The Reverend Charles Churton Potts wrote in the Alsager Parish Magazine in December 1939. *'It is a strange war. None of us expected that in twenty-one year's time we should be engaged in another world war. Some of us knew all the time that there was going to be another war, and some felt that it was coming, but no one foresaw the deadlock ... The war has come as a climax, the inevitable issue of rivalry, competition, aggression, and loss of faith. For the real Christian believer would today never start a war to gain his own ends: he can only be dragged into it to stem aggression and preserve freedom.'*

Potts gives moral justification for the British people to fight. He goes on to refer to the suffering of the Jews and the Poles and he does not blame God for allowing war to happen, instead blaming the *'free will'* of men.

Sir Francis Joseph, writing in the *Sentinel* in December 1939 gave insight into how he expected the war to go. *'It may be that the final victory in this conflict will not be brought about by the bravery of our men. It may be that the victory will go to the nations who can carry on the longest. In 1914-18 we got used to seeing five thousand, six thousand, up to seven thousand casualties a day. Thank God that after three months of war our casualties are only in minor proportions. Can the stalemate on the Western Front go on indefinitely we ask? Is it likely that attacks will be made on the Siegfried or Maginot lines? Or will the blockade and economic pressure decide the issue?'*

Sir Francis did not foresee during the *'phony war'* the German army going around the major allied defences via a flanking movement through the thickly wooded Ardennes region, mistakenly perceived by Allied planners as an impenetrable natural barrier against armoured vehicles.

Pre-war Crewe Road, Alsager, showing Cartwright's Garage. Note the absence of vehicles. It was not until the building of Radway Green Munitions factory in 1940 factory that the level of traffic increased appreciably.

Alsager Football Club 1939. Most players were soon to be conscripted or if underage served in the Local Defence Volunteers or Civil Defence.

Alsager Football Club.		1939	
1	C. Turner.	12	Fred Wallis.
2	Roy Ledward	13	Mr Barratt MR JACKSON
3	George Morris	14	Bloor.
4	Tom Smith	15	Mr Barratt.
5	Charlie Clarke	16	Eddie Ebsworth
6	Joe Bebbington	17	Fred Beech
7	Sid Bourne	18	Cyril Skerratt.
8	Peter Barratt.	19	Jack Jackson
9	Fred Moseley.	20	B. CONDLIFFE.
10	Ken Cowden	21	Mick Barratt.
11	Bill Mitchell	22	Percy Sherratt.

Alsager in 1940 - the dark days

Timeline (history)

Rationing started in the UK.

German 'Blitzkrieg' overwhelmed Belgium, Holland and France. Denmark surrendered immediately, but the Norwegians fought on - with British and French assistance - surrendering in June only once events in France meant that they were fighting alone.

On 10 May - the same day that Winston Churchill replaced Neville Chamberlain as Prime Minister of the UK - Germany invaded France, Belgium and Holland, and western Europe encountered the Blitzkrieg - or 'lightning war'.

Germany's combination of fast armoured tanks on land, and superiority in the air, made a unified attacking force that was both innovative and effective. Despite greater numbers of air and army personnel - and the presence of the British Expeditionary Force - the Low Countries and France proved no match for the Wehrmacht and the Luftwaffe. Holland and Belgium fell by the end of May; Paris was taken two weeks later. The British Expeditionary Force was evacuated from Dunkirk. British troops retreated from the invaders in haste, and some 226,000 British and 110,000 French troops were rescued from the channel port of Dunkirk only by a ragged fleet, using craft that ranged from pleasure boats to Navy destroyers.

In France an armistice was signed with Germany, with the puppet French Vichy government - under a hero of World War One, Marshall Pétain - in control in the 'unoccupied' part of southern and eastern France, and Germany in control in the rest of the country.

Churchill became Prime Minister and a British victory in the Battle of Britain forced Hitler to postpone invasion plans.

In Alsager and District

In Rode Heath, caves in the valley opposite to the *Broughton Arms* were used originally for stabling canal horses but in the Second World War were used as makeshift shelters. The public shelters in Rode Heath were at Rode Heath School and built of brick and concrete. Today, the caves are bricked up.

As the war effort geared up in January 1940 Alsager U.D.C. was offered *Milton House* in Alsager to be its new Council chambers by the Wheaton-Smith family. Unfortunately, the Ministry of Health wrote to the council to say new borrowing restrictions prevented the council from going ahead with the purchase. Wartime economies were being introduced to stop councils overspending and government agencies such as the Ministry of Supply and Ministry of Health were making decisions which limited the power of local government.

The air raid sirens on *Fairview House*, and the police station in Alsager, were tested in January 1940, but the U.D.C. received complaints that the noise was so *'feeble'* they could hardly be heard. H.V Lynam said the volume depended *'on the direction of the wind'*, but Members were unhappy the sirens were not doing their job. The U.D.C. agreed to contact the Chief Constable to provide more sirens. In an unpopular move, the U.D.C. put up the rate charges to £11s.6d in the pound, an increase of 6d, saying the cost was mainly due to increased ARP costs levied by the County Council. Rate commitments rose to £9,206 as opposed to £8,731 in the previous year. Despite the blackout where £428 had been saved in lighting costs, the council had been *'swamped'* by additional war costs of £312, giving a saving of only £116. It seems the public were expecting a rate decrease because of the blackout. This would have particularly rankled with the people who had been prosecuted for blackout infringements. Ann Hopwood, of Station Road; Florence Gater, of the Avenue; and Charles Bennett, of Fields Road; were all fined £1.10s at Sandbach Magistrates Court for breaches of the Lighting Restrictions Order in 1940.

In January 1940, the government introduced food rationing. The scheme was designed to ensure fair shares for all at a time of national shortage. The Ministry of Food was responsible for overseeing rationing. Every man, woman and child was given a ration book with coupons. These were required before rationed goods could be purchased. Basic foodstuffs such as sugar, meat, fats, bacon and cheese were directly rationed by an allowance of coupons. There was a double ration of cheese for agricultural workers. Many other items, such as tinned goods, dried fruit, cereals and biscuits, were rationed using a points system. The number of points allocated changed according to availability and consumer demand. Priority allowances of milk and eggs were given to those most in need, including children and expectant mothers. Housewives had to register with a chosen retailer.

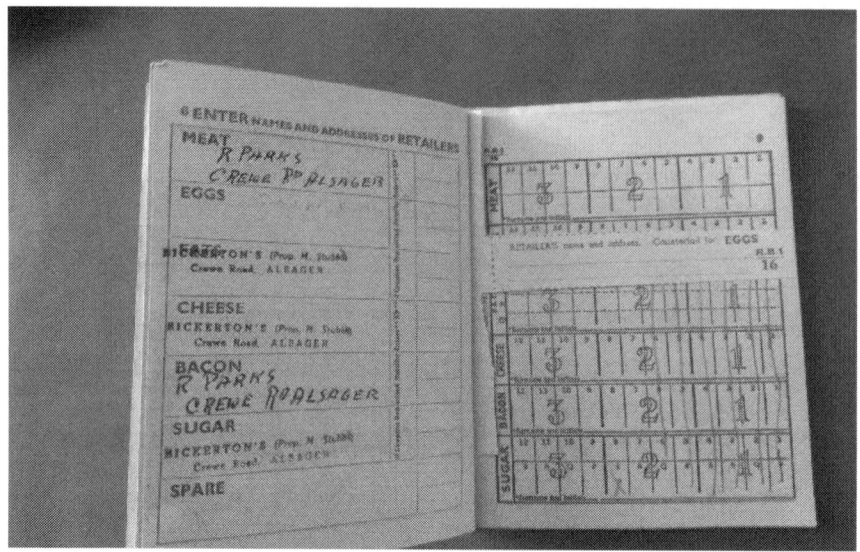

Alsager Ration Book belonging to Peter Barker. (post WW2 book)

In Alsager this would have been shops such as *Hancock's*, *Parks'* butchers, and the *Cooperative*, *Bickerton's*, and *Boyce Adams*. Peter Barker never remembered being hungry during rationing. He regretted Miss Smith's Sweet Shop on Crewe Road was closed throughout the war, except her large jars with artificial sweets remained! He enjoyed getting tinned sausages from the United States. There were two accidents which brought food to the larder. In Rode Heath two lorries overturned on separate occasions, once in at the junction of Townend Lane and the A50 and oranges were gathered by locals after the best had been salvaged by the authorities, but a great deal of the fruit was ruined by over exuberance by the locals trampling it underfoot. On the other occasion, a consignment of biscuits was rescued when a lorry overturned on the A50 by Chapel Lane. Some tea was recovered after a crash by *Odd Rode Rectory*, most was written off, but Scholar Green boys dried some of it and took it to school. There was a trainload of bananas (a consignment rare as hen's teeth) which became surplus to requirements because of a train derailment.

People from Alsager and surrounding villages descended on the train and were invited to take the produce away as it was past its best.

As food shortages increased, long queues became commonplace. It was usual for someone to reach the front of a long queue, only to find out that the item they had been waiting for had just run out. Not all foods were rationed. Fruit and vegetables were never rationed but were often in short supply, especially tomatoes, onions and fruit shipped from overseas. Wartime bread was greyish in colour and unpalatable. Most village residents could obtain real eggs whereas city people made do with dried eggs and milk. Certain key non-food items were also rationed – petrol in 1939, clothes in June 1941 and soap in February 1942. The end of the war saw additional cuts. Bread, which was never rationed during wartime, was put on the ration in July 1946. One Alsager resident remembers having to shop at Boyce Adams for his father, who had fought in the Great War and hated Spam and called it *'dog meat'*. When mindlessly he asked for *'dog meat'*, at Boyce Adams's shop the boy was turned out by the shopkeeper. Rabbits were an excellent source of meat and Mr Mottram in Thurlwood used to sell them at one shilling each. Cereals were a treat for children, *'Force'*, being the most popular with children. Some farmers engaged in black market activities (Westwood, 2009) one local farmer in Rode Heath supplying pork *'under the counter'*, when the word went round; *'He's killing tonight'*.

The demand for allotments in Alsager was not as high as expected. By January 1940 only twenty applications had been made for allotments and land was set aside on the Parsonage Field and Mr Dunn's land in Lawton Road, but land offered by Mr Rogerson near the marl pits was deemed unsuitable for allotments. In 1941 the reason for the lack of demand was put down to Alsager houses having large gardens to grow their own produce.

In January 1940 Sir Francis Joseph was chief guest of the Alsager Christ Church and St Mary's Annual Tea in the St Mary's Schoolroom. Mr T.A Meredith, Secretary of the Trustees of St Mary's Schools said, *'On the outbreak of war social life practically ceased in Alsager. The schools were taken over for a short time by the authorities, who later made other arrangements.'* Meredith was wrong. Social life did not end but it changed. St Mary's Schoolroom and the Alsager Institute remained the main centres for social gatherings. Dances and film shows and concerts continued. Film shows and live entertainment in St Mary's were cold affairs in winter as there was no heating. Peter recalled his father used to take a heated fire brick wrapped in a blanket to performances at *St Mary's Schoolroom* it was so cold in 1940. The recreational clubs such as the cricket and football teams continued but with a smaller pool of players to draw on. The Working Men's Club in Sandbach Road, continued to provide facilities and to entertain local people, sometimes Workers Educational lectures and concerts were held at the WMC.

Alsager Working Men's Club Sandbach Road.

Sir Francis Joseph supported the beginning in Alsager of the *'Sunday evenings socials'* at St Mary's. These socials had been successful in Hanley. He said it was not only young people who had ceased to go to church in Alsager, it was people of all ages. He was concerned about the rise of juvenile crime in the area. Sir Francis said, *'We fight to protect our liberties which mean so much to us. The struggle is to allow us to worship God in our own way. It is to preserve these rights, not merely for ourselves, but for those who follow'*. Peter Barker remembers seeing Queen Wilhelmina of the Netherlands visit Alsager during the war. The visit was censored. The Dutch *Prinses Irene Brigade* was based in Congleton during the war and the Queen visited them several times while she was exiled in Britain. She came to Alsager, to accompany the Dutch Army Band who played on the bandstand on the Parsonage Field during the carnival.

Peter Barker born 1932. (National Service photo.)

'Queen Wilhelmina came to Alsager. She sat apart from us for security.'

Queen Wilhelmina, exiled to Britain 1939

Church attendance was in decline in Alsager but ladies' groups from the churches formed working groups to make woollen goods to send to the Staffordshire Regiment for the troops in France. Lady Joseph formed the

Alsager Working Group and sent money and woollens to the regiment in January 1940. Lady Baker Wilbraham of *Rode Hall* also played her part in the campaign.

An example of the rise in crime can be seen by the break-in at *Home Farm*, Alsager in February 1940. Police Constable Mullins, on seeing a light pass from one room to another at *Home Farm* caught James Brown of Kidsgrove stealing a home safe from the farm. An iron file was found by an open window. Brown was taken to Alsager Police Station and put in the cells. He was later sent to prison at Sandbach Magistrates, Brown asking the magistrate if he could see his mother before being sent down.

Siren of the type on Alsager Council Offices and Police Station

Opening of the refurbished Settle Speakman works

Sir Francis Joseph was Chairman of Settle Speakman Ltd. From 1920 it manufactured and repaired railway wagons. The wagons moved coal from the eight collieries Joseph owned locally and further afield. With the increasing need for coal supplies in wartime he extended the wagon repairing capacity at Settle Speakman during the war. Because of the national pooling of railway wagons in the second world war many other firm's wagons came to the Alsager works for repair. Threatened by enemy bombing Settle Speakman Ltd were persuaded to improve the camouflage of their premises. Sir Francis' colleries and wagon works were nationalised in 1948.

January 1940 saw the death, aged 69, of one of Alsager most revered, but today, unknown citizens. Captain Robert George Smith of the White Star Line (He was not related to Captain Smith of Titanic fame but had an illustrious career as a sea captain.) The *Liverpool Daily Post* gave an obituary. He lived in *'Westwood'* 11 Church Road, Alsager. He retired in 1930 after thirty three years with the White Star Line. He was born in Liverpool and was one of the few men who captained in both sail and steam. He began his sea career in 1885 and joined the White Star Line in 1897 as the Fourth Officer of the *Tauric*. In 1912 he was given command of the *Cevic* and by his retirement had commanded twelve White Star Liners including *Regina, Canopic, Canada*, and from 1927 to 1930, the *Cedric*. He broke the record for the fastest crossing of the Atlantic in the *Cedric* in 1928. He inaugurated *'tourist class'* travel. Altogether he completed 2.5 million miles in ships, two hundred and fifty thousand of these in sailing ships. He left a widow, three daughters and two sons.

The War effort accelerates

In February, Major General Lord Mottistone, Chairman of the War Savings Committee, stayed with Sir Francis and Lady Joseph at *The Hall*, Alsager while he was in the area to promote the War Finance campaign. In a speech Mottistone admitted the Chancellor of the Exchequer could not impose any new taxes on the British people and that the savings campaign was crucial to financing the war effort.

In March Sir Francis Joseph spoke at Crewe Town Hall on the War Savings issue. He said that in the hour meeting the Government expenditure was £44,000 more than it was a year ago. Crewe was benefiting from the government rearmament investment and good wages were being paid. He pleaded with the council to promote War Savings.

In other news, ninety respirators had been received for children under two years of age in Alsager. These were specialist apparatus as normal gas masks did not fit the youngest children.

In February, there was a campaign in Cheshire to employ women as drivers with the Mechanised Transport Corps (formerly called the Trained Women's Driver's Association). Lady Vera Broughton of *Doddington Hall* promoted the scheme which had been successful in London. (Crewe Chronicle)

Lady Broughton. Photo Crewe Chronicle

In March 1940 Alsager British Legion sent 73 parcels to Alsager men serving in the forces. In addition to the B.E.F in France, Navy parcels were sent to Egypt, Malaya. Palestine, and India. Included in the parcels were 120 cigarettes, 1lb of chocolate, tin of Oxo cubes, ½ 1b of gingerbread, and ½ lb tin of sweets. 1 woollen good in each parcel was provided by the Women's Section of Alsager British Legion, the Alsager Rangers and Mrs Reeves. 1940 was the fifteenth year since the formation of the Alsager British Legion which had formed in 1925.

Rode Heath received its first evacuees from Manchester arriving at the Rode Heath Institute in dark buses. They were eight or nine years of age, wore name tags and had their teachers with them. They were fostered with local families, but the increased number of children caused problems at the school where a shift system had to be introduces with the evacuees attending in the morning and local children in the afternoon. Like the Alsager evacuees many of the children returned to Manchester after a few weeks when the bombing over the city decreased. There were problems occasionally when an evacuee's parents turned up and tried to tell foster parents how they should be bringing up their child. Some of the evacuees had to be told not to trespass in the kale fields and how to behave when cattle were around. Only one or two evacuees stayed in the village for the duration of the war. (Westwood, 2009)

In April 1940 John James Nelson, Alsager's longstanding Clerk to the Council, died. He had served the UDC from before the Great War and worked tirelessly to support the war effort in both world wars. Photo: Sentinel

In April a bizarre incident occurred in Barthomley. Mr J. Brassington was visiting Barthomley Parish Church and came across an open bible with blood traced in the design of a swastika shaped backwords. The blood was still wet. It was not sure whether the swastika was done by Nazi sympathizers or by ill-advised youths who regularly visited the church from surrounding districts.

Cynthia and Rosamund Joseph were hardly ever out of the newspapers in North Staffordshire and the North West. The sisters were featured in the (MENews) in June 1940 in a report on the completion of their training as Red Cross Nurses.

During December 1940, the Rev. Potts commented on the changes he was witnessing in Alsager,

'We are becoming familiar with the roar of street traffic. Empty houses are being turned into hostels, and soldiers, munition managers and workers are settling all over the village, while our old residents are overworked and tied down with new duties.'

He knew the war was changing Alsager irrevocably.

Alsager LDV (the Home Guard)

Alsager LDV 1940

On 14th May 1940 Anthony Eden, Secretary of State for War, broadcast on radio an appeal for men aged between seventeen and sixty-five to come forward to enrol in a new force to become Local Defence Volunteers (LDV) to protect local communities in the event of attack. Men flocked to enrol at police stations. Alsager and district LDV set up its base in Church Lawton. Many members were former servicemen from the Great War or men too young to enrol in the services. Nationally, no one had thought how to arm the LDV and initially they were told to use sticks or truncheons and were taught how to make Molotov cocktails and homemade *'sticky'* bombs. Usually the LDV were only as good as the men chosen to lead them, men with good experience of military discipline. (Churchill had the organization's name changed to 'The Home Guard', in June 1941.) In a secret memo of 27th May 1941 communists and fascists were barred from joining the force. Women were also barred from joining the Home Guard. In some parts of Britain women formed themselves into the Women's Home Defence, technically an illegal organisation. Grudgingly the government allowed the Women's Home Guard Auxiliaries to be formed after April 1943. The Women's Home Guard were not allowed to undertake military duties but were to perform non-combatant duties such as clerical work, cooking and driving.

In Alsager, the LDV, later renamed the Home Guard, was commanded by Captain John Swindells. Son of a wealthy silk manufacturer from Macclesfield, Swindells rose to the rank of Captain in the Great War and was invalided out with a Silver War Badge in 1918. He was born in 1885 and attended Uppingham School, Rutland. He won the British Open Golf Championship in 1909. He served in the Lancashire Fusiliers in the Great War. He went on to become a *'Silk Thrower Manager'* in Macclesfield. He married Jesse and they had four daughters. He moved to Alsager and after the outbreak of the Second World War took the role of training Civil Defence messengers and then became commander of the LDV on its formation. Falling ill, he moved to Whitmore and died in June 1944. His daughter, Mary Swindells, was a Section Officer in the W.A.A.F in Yorkshire before her marriage in 1943.

Captain John Swindells, centre front row, with LDV comrades in the Alsager LDV (Home Guard) Photo Weekly Sentinel August 1940. Note: several of these men are wearing medal ribbons showing they served in the Great War.

Alsager LDV marching August 1940: Photo Weekly Sentinel

Alsager LDV with rifles August 1940: Photo Weekly Sentinel

The Alsager LDV (Home Guard) were detailed to protect key buildings in Alsager such as the Council Chamber, Police Station, the water depot, and to safeguard air raid shelters. Members of the Home Guard could earn certificates of proficiency. Jo Bebbington undertook skill training and tests in 1944 in the Home Guard as can be seen in his certificate.

Certificate of proficiency in the Home Guard. Mr J. Bebbington

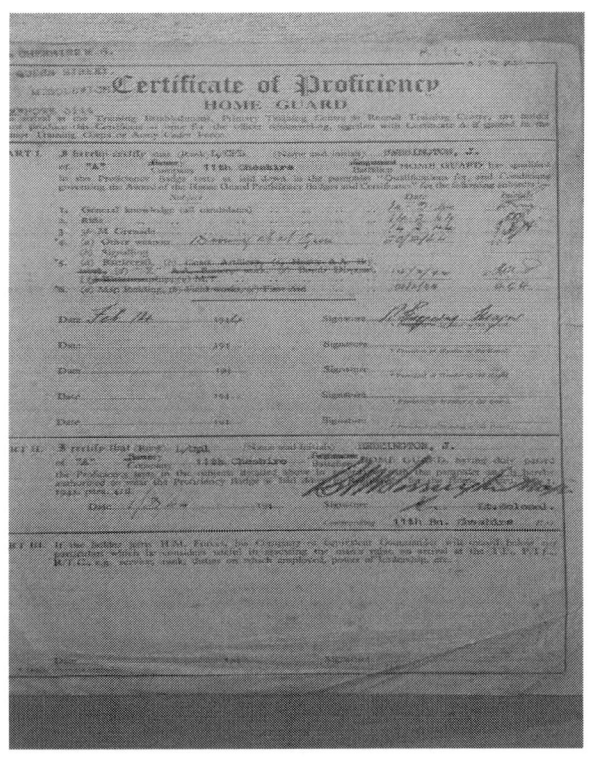

Mr Charles Bourne later commanded the Home Guard in Alsager. In 1971 Charles said, *'even when they (the Home Guard) went off on 'secret manoeuvres,' their wives mysteriously arrived with food and drink. We were never entirely sure whether the Home Guard were protecting the Navy or vice versa.'* (He was referring to the Marines at the Excalibur base)

Charles Bourne commanding Alsager Home Guard 1941-4 (Photo: 1971 Cheshire Life)

There were also regular troops stationed in Alsager. The South Staffordshire Regiment were camped in Mr Cureton's field in Cedar Avenue. One lady remembers how the troops would give her and local children spare food when they passed by. The troops were stationed in Alsager to be on hand if needed to defend Radway Green in its construction and when it went into production. Other soldiers were billeted in houses in Station Road.

Some older men who had served in the Great War managed to enlist in the Second World War as regular servicemen. George Pyatt, born in 1897, and who served in the Royal Marines, joined *HMS Valiant* in spring 1940. *Valiant* was part of a fleet which included the *HMS Ark Royal*. It was engaged in firing near Scapa Flow and in patrols off the Norwegian coast. On 9th June from 23.45 hours to early the next morning the convoy was under German air attack by six aircraft but avoided damage. On 26th June, *Valiant* departed Scapa Flow for Gibraltar as the French Fleet had surrendered to the enemy and the Italians had declared war on the allies. In late July 1940 George was deemed too old to continue in the ranks and was discharged. In 1942, he returned to Crewe Road Alsager and obtained a job as postman in Stoke-on-Trent. George Pyatt died in 1961.

Strengthening Civil Defence in 1940

In August 1940 Alsager Urban District Council approved the Surveyor's scheme to create eleven new air raid shelters for domestic use. At the same time, it deferred a decision to remove the railings from outside the council offices. Alsager St John's Ambulance was encouraged by the council to combine with the Alsager First Aid Depot to make their organisations more efficient.

The following month, September 1940, Queen Elizabeth visited Crewe, and Alsager was encouraged to send a delegation to the reception.

The newspaper report (Ches Observer) stated: *'To Major Quinton fell the honour of being addressed by Her Majesty, who enquired "the whereabouts of Alsager".'*

Alsager's delegation consisted of Councillors Corfield and Elsby, Miss Walker, Mrs Bingham, Mrs H.P Harpur, Mrs Webb, Mrs Ashmore (Nursing Division), Mr J. Davenport, First Aid Party, Mrs Palfreyman, Mrs Pryce, and Miss Collier (ambulance drivers), Major J. Quinton M.C., Captain S.O Stewart, Mr M. Stubbs and Mr Leeson (Air Raid Wardens). The journalist wrote, *'representatives were greatly impressed by the Queen's charm and courageous manner'*.

Joseph Quinton, a delegate to the Royal Reception, was born in 1894. He lived at 80 Sandbach Road, and he was a former Major in the Royal Horse Artillery, later Royal Garrison Artillery. He became Alsager's Chief Air Raid Warden in the war. In 1916, he had been awarded the Military Medal for bravery when he was a 2nd Lieutenant. He was a High School maths teacher by profession.

Joseph Quinton

The Evacuation from Dunkirk: Alsager and Rode Heath men

In May 1940 two and a half million German troops were assembled along Germany's western border. The German army moved through the difficult terrain of the Ardennes into France and simultaneously occupied Belgium. The Allied armies were trapped with the only escape route being then via the Channel ports of Calais and Dunkirk. Between 21st and 23rd May the German army occupied Boulogne and isolated the British garrison of Calais. Dunkirk was chosen as an alternative base. On 25th May Belgium surrendered and on the 28th May began an evacuation of the British Expeditionary Force and allies from Dunkirk. The evacuation was assisted by Hitler calling a halt to the attack on Dunkirk on 26th May which permitted the construction of hasty defences around the perimeter of the Dunkirk area. Hitler rescinded the order two days later. Eight hundred and fifty British ships and small craft were sent to Dunkirk to assist in the evacuation. Three hundred and thirty-eight thousand men including one hundred and twelve thousand Belgium and French soldiers were rescued. Many troops died, as a result of aerial attacks by the Luftwaffe, while waiting to be rescued. The Allies had put too much reliance on defending the positions around eastern Lorraine and the River Rhine. Although the evacuation was described as a triumph many B.E.F troops were killed, and a great deal of British military equipment was destroyed, and Britain was left vulnerable to attack.

On 8th June, 1940 the *Staffordshire Weekly Sentinel* gave the names of men from Alsager and Rode Heath who had successfully been evacuated from Dunkirk.

> Lance-Corporal A. J. Johnson, 76, Harrowby-street.
>
> **ALSAGER**
> Driver James Clowes, Linley
> Gunner T. Kennerley, The Fields.
> Private Robinson, Lawton-road.
> Driver J. Clowes, Linley.
> Gunner J. Kennerley, The Fields.
> Private Stuart Edwards, Crewe-road.
> Private Tom Haywood, Audley-road.
>
> **RODE HEATH AND SCHOLAR GREEN**
> Private Frank Leese.
> Private Frank Lawton.
> Gunner Jack Mottram.
> Private Robert Bateman.

James Clowes is mentioned twice in the list. His home was at *White Rose Cottages*, Linley. The Kennerleys were from military families with strong British Legion connections. Not in this newspaper list of evacuees was Captain George Jacobs of the Cheshire Regiment, who used to live in Alsager and had been a pupil teacher at Alsager school next to Christ Church before the Great War. He also managed to escape from Dunkirk. He had retired from the army but was again commissioned Lieutenant on 27th April 1940, took part in the Expeditionary Force and was amongst the men who successfully returned from Dunkirk. He then took up a position managing British Prisoner of War Camps using his knowledge and experience to good effect. After the war he joined Dover Staff College in the rank of Major until forced to retire through ill health in June 1947. The newspaper (DoverEx) reported on 16th July 1948 that George had died suddenly in Dover. He left a widow Marie G. Jacobs.

The Battle of Britain: 10th July - 31st October 1940

"Never in the field of human conflict was so much owed by so many, to so few." Winston Churchill.

Following the evacuation from Dunkirk and France's surrender in June 1940 the British Empire was left alone to withstand the force of the Axis powers. The British Army was in severely depleted. There were twenty-nine Divisions of the British Army still intact but they were not combat ready. The Royal Air Force and Royal Navy were better prepared for battle.

'Operation Sea Lion' was Hitler's plan to invade Britain. Because an invasion would need control of the sea and the Royal Navy was powerful, Hitler decided the Luftwaffe should first defeat the RAF before neutralizing the British Navy.

The *Battle of Britain* was a decisive air campaign fought over southern England. It was one of Britain's most important victories of the Second World War. It took place between July and October 1940. The Germans began by attacking coastal targets and British shipping operating in the English Channel. The Germans had two thousand eight hundred planes (nine hundred fighters and one thousand three hundred bombers). Against them Britain could only muster six hundred and fifty operational fighters. Britain did have an effective new radar protection system. The Nazis first concentrated on strafing seaports and fighter bases. British Fighter Command came out of this phase of the battle well. The Germans next concentrated on attacking inland bases with large groups of bombers protected by fighters. More than four hundred and fifty British planes were destroyed. London was bombed. Britain retaliated by bombing Berlin and Hitler was so incensed he changed the focus of most of his air attacks to London. Although there was terrible damage to London the Luftwaffe also suffered high losses. On 14th September Bomber Command and the Royal Navy destroyed two hundred German attack barges in French and Dutch ports, nearly one tenth of their total force.

Hitler was compelled to call off *Operation Sea Lion* scheduled for 27th September and then 10th October. In the last phase of the Battle of Britain the Luftwaffe attempted hit and run attacks on the RAF without a breakthrough. Radar was the deciding factor which brought about a RAF victory. In the battle Germany lost one thousand seven hundred and thirty-three planes and Britain nine hundred and fifteen. Without air victory Hitler could not invade southern England. The Blitz of London and other cities however continued unabated until May 1941 with forty-three thousand citizens killed and fifty-one thousand seriously injured.

On 29th June, 1940 it was reported that Lieutenant Reginald B. Holland, the son of Councillor William Holland, of Sandbach Road had been gazetted Captain. Reginald enlisted in the Royal Signals in 1937 and in June 1940 became engaged to Miss Kay Osborne of Swadlincote.

ALSAGER

Local Officer's Promotion

Lieutenant Reg. B. Holland has just been gazetted captain. He is the elder son of Councillor and Mrs. W. Holland, of Belle Garde, Sandbach-road, Alsager. His younger brother is Sergeant Selwyn Holland, who is in an A.A. Unit.

Deaths of Servicemen in 1940

Private Wilfred Ernest Cartwright: Bedfordshire & Hertfordshire Regiment

Date of death: 13th July 1940

Commemorated on Odd Rode War Memorial, All Saints Church

Wilfred Ernest Cartwright was the first local serviceman man to die in the Second World War. He was born on 18th September 1916 in Scholar Green to Walter and Sarah Cartwright. His father was a *'Rural Postman'* according to the 1939 Register. Wilfred was a *'Wholesale Grocer's Packer'*. The family lived at 12 Spring Terrace, Scholar Green. Wilfred's mother had died on Christmas day in 1924.

Wilfred enlisted in the Bedfordshire & Hertfordshire Regiment as a private soldier, service number 5953821 in the 6th Battalion. This Battalion was designated for home defence and was based in 1939 in Luton. The 5th Territorial Battalion were mobilised on 25th August and C and D Companies from the Luton area were immediately separated to form the nucleus of a new reorganised battalion, called the 6th Territorial Battalion. Both would be engaged in extensive guard duties in Bedfordshire and Hertfordshire and have little time for training over the next year. In the summer of 1940 the 6th Battalion was based in Alnwick, Northumberland.

On 13th July 1940 Wilfred was killed in an accident while training with the 6th Battalion in Northumberland.

Army record of Wilfred's death

Wilfred's body was repatriated to Cheshire where he was buried with his mother in the parish church graveyard at All Saints church. It is listed as a Commonwealth War Grave.

 **Pilot Officer Robert Harold Rigby: Royal Air Force**

Date of death: 18th July 1940

Commemorated on Alsager War Memorial

Robert Harold Rigby was born in Alsager on 22nd December 1915 to Howard and Ursula Alberta Rigby (nee Alcock.) His parents were married in Stoke-on-Trent in 1911. His father, who died in 1924, was a *'Corn Factor'*. The family lived at *'Hafod,'* 46 The Fields, Alsager. His sisters were Nancy Ursula born 1918, Pamela, born 1919, and Ethel, born 1922. His mother was well known locally. She bred dogs and trained them and advertised her business in the local press. Robert's uncle, Donald, of 4 Audley Road, was Alsager's Rate Collector before and during the Second World War.

Robert Rigby in childhood, (standing right.)

Robert Harold Rigby enlisted in the Royal Air Force before war was declared. He joined the RAF on a short service commission, with 236 Squadron, Service number 42149, in March 1939.

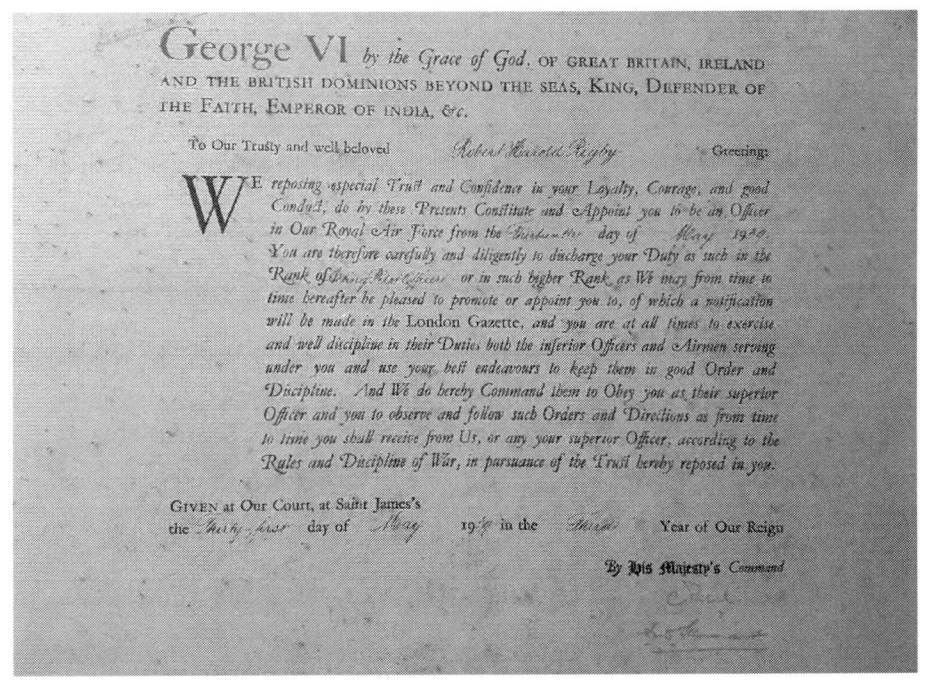

Scroll of Robert's RAF Pupil Pilot Officer appointment

Rigby carried out his initial training at 10 E & RFTS Yatesbury from 13th March, 1939, and moved to 5 FTS Sealand as a Pupil Pilot Officer on 31st May 1939. With his training completed he joined 236 Squadron at Stradishall on 6th November 1939 from 9FTS Hullavington. He was appointed Pilot Officer from 6th November 1939 with a Temporary Commission. He was given a full Commission as Pilot Officer on 13th March 1940 (London Gazette, 9th April 1940.)

236 Squadron

The Squadron was formed in the Great War and closed after hostilities ended. On 31st October 1939, No. 236 Squadron reformed at Stradishall as part of Fighter Command. It was supplied with Blenheim fighters in December 1939. The Squadron moved to North Coates at the end of February 1940 to join Coastal Command, but reverted to Fighter Command in April on arrival at Speke near Liverpool. During May and June 1940, the squadron flew defensive patrols over shipping in the English Channel. On 4th June, the Squadron was based at Middle Wallop, and from 4th July from Thorny Island. On that day, the squadron re-joined Coastal Command for fighter and reconnaissance duties.

RAF Coastal Command also had an important role. It carried out anti-invasion patrols, provided vital intelligence on German positions along the European coast and occasionally bombed German shipping and industrial targets. Aerial reconnaissance was one of the key methods of obtaining intelligence about the enemy and their activities. Photographs provided concrete evidence - fast. Within hours of a reconnaissance sortie, the film could be developed, printed and interpreted.

Allied reconnaissance, for the most part, was classified under two main headings: mapping and damage assessment. Enemy activity was recorded, and new installations were located, so that accurate maps, to be used by the ground forces, could be made. From damage assessment photographs, the exact moment when a target that had been previously hit should be re-attacked could be calculated, and the effectiveness of the enemy's rebuilding programme could be assessed.

Pilot Officer Robert Rigby, Battle of Britain Pilot.

Robert Rigby failed to return from a photographic-reconnaissance operation over Le Havre on 18th July 1940 in Blenheim L6639, Mk.IVF during the Battle of Britain. The weather was bad and intense flak was encountered over Cape de la Hague though it is believed the aircraft was shot down by a Messerschmitt Bf 109. Sergeant Donald Duncan Mackinnon, his gunner, was also killed. Robert Rigby was twenty-four.

Donald Duncan McKinnon, Gunner in Blenheim L6639, with Robert Rigby's mother, Ursula

A description of the action in which Rigby was killed is quoted in *Coastal Dawn: Blenheims in Action. From the Phoney War through the Battle of Britain*, by Andrew Bird, Grub Street Publishing, 24th October 2012.

'The daily forays continued and in spite of the bad weather very few patrols and reconnaissance flights were cancelled. 236 Squadron dispatched three aircraft from Thorney Island led by Pilot Officer Charles Powers who had joined the RAF on a short service commission in June 1937. The aerodrome was awash with water, the top soil could neither absorb neither the drainage cope with the torrential rain. As their tyres lifted off the grass runway and rotated into place at 11.20 hours shards of water droplets darted earthwards. Heading towards Le Havre and Cherbourg on reconnaissance they snaked past the Channel Islands.'

As the three Blenhiem aircraft flew over occupied Alderney, Channel Islands, they were detected by the enemy and the information passed to shore batteries in the village of Auderville close to the lighthouse Cap de La Hague in Normandy. The three British planes were flying in a north-westerly direction. With a deluge of heavy rain and anti-aircraft fire the planes scattered. Planes L6779, L6639 and L1278 lost contact with each other. Robert Rigby, in Blenheim, L6639 was recorded as checking for damage on his plane. The British planes looked out for enemy aircraft. Two Messerschmitt attacked them at 13.15 hours and Messerschmitt JG2 piloted by Major Wolfgang Schellman hit a Blenheim which fell to earth. A second Blenheim was hit by Uffizier Willie Mulched in the other Messerschmitt at 13.25 hours. Pilot Officer Powers in Blenheim L1278 surviving the attack looked around for the signs of the other two British planes. He was unaware his compatriots were shot down by the Messerschmitt.

'The sky was empty. I came to the conclusion both may have been hit by anti-aircraft fire.' Officially it was one year and a month later when their families were notified they were *'presumed killed'* by the Air Ministry.

Robert Rigby's remains were discovered and he was buried in Sainte Marie Cemetery, Le Havre, France, (Division 67 Row D Grave 10). It is a Commonwealth War Grave. A seat in the Alsager War Memorial garden is dedicated to the memory of Robert Rigby. His mother continued to live in Alsager after the War.

Robert Rigby's grave in Le Havre.

The Rigby extended family was particularly affected by other tragedies during the war. Two of Robert's cousins were both Pilot Officers and were killed in the war as described in the *Staffordshire Advertiser*.

Family of Fliers

The funeral took place at Hartshill Cemetery on Monday of Pilot Officer Leonard Terence Jervis Ryan, son of Mr. and Mrs. T. J. Ryan, of New Plymouth, New Zealand, and grandson of the late Mr. and Mrs. J. A. Alcock, of Stoke, who was killed in a flying accident while serving with the R.A.F. A brother, Pilot Officer A. J. H. Ryan, by a sad coincidence was killed in the same month last year, and was also laid to rest at Hartshill Cemetery, while a cousin, Pilot Officer R. H. Rigby, son of Mrs. H. Rigby, of Hafod, Field Road, Alsager, has been reported missing for some time. A third brother is a Pilot Officer in Australia. The funeral was of a private nature, the coffin being brought direct from his active service station to Hartshill, where a service was conducted by the Vicar of Penkhull (the Rev. V. G. Aston).

The Staffordshire Advertiser on 7 December 1940 described the sad news concerning cousins of Robert Rigby who were all Pilot Officers who had been killed.

Terence Ryan left, Leonard Ryan right

Benjamin Conlon: Air Raid Warden

Date of death: 1940

Commemorated on Odd Rode War Memorial, All Saints Church

Benjamin was born on 18th February 1883 in Scholar Green to James and Annie Conlon. His father died when he was a boy and he was raised by his stepfather, William Lawton.

Benjamin married Esther Leeson on 28th December 1919 in the Primitive Methodist Chapel, Congleton. Benjamin was a coal hewer and in 1939 the family lived in Kent Green. Benjamin's son, John, was a motor wagon driver, and his daughter Joyce was a mill hand. In the war Benjamin worked as an Air Raid Warden; the reason he is included on the war memorial. He died in 1940 (July to September.) His grave at All Saints Churchyard is not constituted as a Commonwealth War Grave.

Odd Rode War Memorial

Alsager in 1941

1941 War Timeline

Following the defeat of the Italian dictator Mussolini's armies in Greece and Tobruk North Africa, German forces arrived in North Africa in February, and invaded Greece and Yugoslavia in April.

While the bombing of British and German cities, the Blitz, continued, and the gas chambers at Auschwitz were first used, Hitler invaded Russia. Operation 'Barbarossa', as the invasion was called, began on 22nd June. The initial advance was swift, with the fall of Sebastopol at the end of October, and Moscow coming under attack at the end of the year.

The bitter Russian winter, however, like the one that Napoleon had experienced a century and a half earlier, crippled the Germans. The Soviets counterattacked in December and fighting in the Eastern Front stagnated until the spring. The Japanese, tired of American trade embargoes, mounted a surprise attack on the US Navy base of Pearl Harbour, in Hawaii, on 7th December. Global conflict commenced, with Germany declaring war on the US, a few days later. Within a week of Pearl Harbour, Japan had invaded the Philippines, Burma and Hong Kong starting the Pacific War.

In Alsager

Alsager & District Home Guard held a fundraising dance at St Mary's Schoolroom in January with *Fredalan and his Rhythm Boys* providing the music. Guests included Sir Francis Joseph and his daughters. Plans were discussed early in 1941 in Alsager for the erection of new housing to accommodate munitions workers. The site chosen for this was *Longview Farm*. In January 1941, the contents of the farm were advertised for sale, the Ministry having agreed to purchase the land, the acquisition made easier as the farmer, Herbert Jones, was deceased. He and his wife had been killed in a car crash with a bus in Linley.

FRIDAY, January 31st, 1941, at 11.30 a.m.
LONGVIEW FARM, LAWTON ROAD, ALSAGER.

ENTIRE UNRESERVED SALE OF THE WHOLE OF THE FARM STOCK and EFFECTS, including Milch Cow, Two Stirk Heifers, Two Work Horses, Implements, Vehicles, Machinery, Gears, Poultry Houses and Appliances; 100 GRAND R.I.R. and LIGHT SUSSEX PULLETS; Produce and Mature Growing Crops, also the whole of the Superior HOUSEHOLD FURNITURE & EFFECTS By Order of the Executor of the late Mr. Herbert Jones.

Descriptive Cards from the Auctioneers: —HENRY MANLEY and SONS, Crewe and Branches.

VALE VIEW. ALSAGER

Longview Farm, (on the far side of Lawton Road,) site of the 'Radway Estate'. Picture taken before the construction of the estate shows it before the building of Moorhouse Avenue where it was to connect with Lawton Road.

The plan was to rapidly build four hundred properties for families moving from London. The design was low-cost, the properties being concrete, flat-roofed, with metal windows and open coal fires. A new road, parallel to Lawton Road, called Longview Avenue, connecting to Moorhouse Avenue, formed part of the new estate.

Local residents were unhappy that priority was being given to workers from London rather than themselves.

The completed houses on the estate, which became known as the *'Radway Estate,'* were spacious and had long gardens in many cases, which was to provide workers with land grow their own food. Many of the houses were reinforced and air raid shelters provided

Radway estate houses with flat roofs

If the war wasn't enough to worry about, Alsager, like many other villages in Cheshire, was affected by foot and mouth disease in March 1941. The *Cheshire Observer* reported Mr Herbert Bickerton of *Ashbank Farm*, Hassall Road, Alsager, had been hit by the disease. The farm became a controlled area to stop the spread of infection. Twenty cases had been reported in the county since January 1941. The Alsager case spread the geographical area with foot and mouth to south Cheshire. Most cases had previously been in the north of the county.

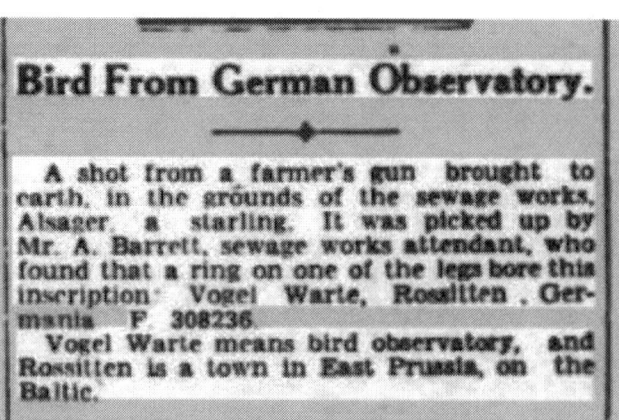

An amusing incident occurred in Alsager in March 1941. The bird shot by an Alsager farmer no doubt had profound symbolic significance for the local population who were still threatened by a Nazi invasion!

Decisions in Agriculture

Cheshire Agricultural War Executive Committee served a notice on Alsager Council that it must plough a field for a crop of oats before March. The Council reported it was difficult to find people to do the work, but the arrangements were in hand. The Committee could impose draconian targets on farmers as to what they should produce and how much was to be harvested. Later in the year the Council set up a Garden Fruit Committee to promote jam making in Alsager. An appeal was made for jam jars and to sell surplus fruit to the centre of operations at *Milton House*.

Blood Donors

Following a campaign to recruit blood donors in Alsager an initial thirty-three people were recruited.

Speeding buses and bathing ban

The Council received complaints in 1941 of speeding buses and *'excessive internal lighting'* in them. The buses were conveying workers to Radway Green and operating to tight timetables. This was another example of how Alsager was becoming busier and noisier. The Council took the matter up with the Chief Constable. The Council also commenced a survey of iron railings belonging to residents with the intention of removing them for raw materials for munitions. The Council also planned a public meeting to advise the public on how to deal with fire bombs. It postponed the call up to the local Auxiliary Fire Service, AFS, for those now liable for military service. A move by women ARP personnel to arrange a committee for comforts for Civil Defence Service workers was proposed. On a separate matter, the Council agreed to ban bathing in the Mere. It was becoming a popular spot for bathing, but local householders were not pleased.

Waterworks

A scheme to bore for water in Alsager to extend the waterworks was agreed by the Council at a cost of £14,374. Congleton RDC wanted to buy water from Alsager.

Alsager W.V.S in 1941

Despite all the hardships encountered in Alsager with new housebuilding, the expansion of Radway Green, and foot and mouth disease, fundraising continued for the war effort. The county of Cheshire participated in the national *'Aircraft Victory Fund'*, its aim to replenish aircraft lost in the Battle of Britain. Alsager raised £425 in May 1941 towards the total Cheshire total of £27,870. Crewe raised £5,549. The money was sent direct to the Ministry of Aircraft Production. County Women's Institutes played an important role in the fundraising.

The Women's Voluntary Service was well supported in Alsager. It was led by Mrs H. Johnson, its Centre Organiser, who was responsible for two hundred and fourteen enrolled members in the town. Centre Organisers had ultimate control over the work they did in their areas; they were tightly scrutinised by the County and Regional offices and Headquarters.

In Alsager, activities included the organisation of two rest centres, a food club, a clothing depot, a store for the distribution of books for the forces, and help at the Y.MC.A. The *'Rest Centres'* provided shelter, food, and importantly, sanitation and information centres to tell people what they were entitled to and how they could obtain the services. The WVS had invented the concept of Rest Centres and in London they were important in helping victims of the Blitz. In June 1940, during the Battle of Britain, the WVS nationally put out an appeal for anything made of aluminium to be collected locally for use to produce aircraft. The WVS centres became collection points for vast quantities of saucepans and tin products. The local WVS was also resourceful operating a *'salvage'* service, a canteen, a first aid point, Red Cross supplies, and a mobile canteen squad. Cookery lessons had been held and another round of these was started in June 1941. The WVS also instigated the *'Meat Pie Scheme'* whereby village bakers cooked pies, containing a pennyworth of meat. The WVS then took the pies, or made sandwiches, for farm workers in the fields. The Alsager WVS had participated in the refugee evacuation scheme in 1939, the Aircraft Victory Fund, the British Legion Christmas Parcels, and the comforts funds for the civil defence workers. They did not stop extending their range of services; offering assistance to the county library (based in the Alsager Institute) and supporting the Alsager Institute's other activities. They undertook jam making schemes. In May, at one of their regular meetings, they reported Ambulance and transport arrangements were *'very satisfactory'*. The immense effort and coordinating work done by the Alsager WVS was mirrored up and down the country. Mr H.V. Lynam attended the meeting and thanked the WVS for assisting the Urban District Council, especially with *'excellent results in salvage and baling'*. The WVS collected bones, tin, paper and rags for salvage. They also collected cotton reels used by the army in telephonic communication systems. On 1st June 1941, civilian clothing was rationed for the first time. The WVS clothing exchange schemes facilitated the swapping of clothes of growing children for the next size up. They also arranged for the mending, and alteration of clothing. Blouses were made from net cloth, and curtains recycled to make dresses, skirts or bras. Blankets were made into coats. The uniform for the WVS was designed by Digby Morton. It was bottle green with touches of grey and dark red. With it came a felt hat. The uniform was not obligatory, as members had to buy their own uniforms, but most members chose to acquire it. Many members were wives of prominent members of the community or women of independent means who were not forced by shortage of money to work for a living. They included some women mobilised into war service, but most leaders belonged to prominent local families. Nationally, the WVS, started by Lady Reading in 1938 grew to a membership of 1.3 million. Its written aims were initially:

(1) the enrolment of women for the Air Raid Precautions Services of the Local Authorities;

(2) to help bring home to every household in the country what air attack may mean;

(3) to make known to every household what it can do to protect itself and help the community.

The WVS was initially seen as a recruiting agency for the Air Raid Precautions services, attracting women to help with the Civil Nursing Reserve and Hospital Supply Depots, or to be ambulance drivers or Air Raid Wardens. The original target had been to recruit thirty thousand women, but by the end of December 1938 this target had been reached and it had become clear that the WVS could achieve much more than the government had originally envisaged. It began to assist local authorities in whatever way was needed and gained the slogan *"The WVS never says No"*. This led to a re-consideration of the name and purpose of the organisation and to encompass its expanding role, it was renamed the Women's Voluntary Services for Civil Defence in February 1939.

The Reverend Potts was also concerned about welfare matters in Alsager. At the May meeting of the Church Council he proposed a welfare worker should be recruited to look after the interests of girls coming to live in the *'hostel'*. He was referring to the new hostels for munition workers.

Alsager Shepherds' Fete August 1941

> **ALSAGER SHEPHERDS' FETE**
> The 22nd annual fete in connexion with the Order of Shepherds took place on Thursday, and was largely attended. A procession was formed in the morning and paraded the village, accompanied by the Stone Military Band and Woodcocks Wells Brass Band. A service was held at the Mission Church, the officiating clergyman being the Rev. J. H. Whitehead. The members afterwards dined together at the Alsager Arms Hotel; the Rev. J. H. Whitehead presiding. The Chairman proposed the toast " Success to the Shepherds of Alsager," which was responded to by the secretary (Mr. Lovatt). The members subsequently proceeded to a field, where a number of amusements were provided, including a cricket match between Rode Park and Audley.

It was almost as if there wasn't a war on. The organization, 'The Order of Shepherds', held their annual celebration in August 1941. At least it provided an escape from the drudgery of rationing and hardship. The organisation is a Friendly Society. Shepherds Friendly started life as a sickness and benefits society, Ashton Unity, which was formed in Ashton-under-Lyne, Lancashire on Christmas Day in 1826. It was later renamed as the Loyal Order of Ancient Shepherds, *"loyal"* referring to the Crown and *"shepherds"* to the Nativity of Jesus.

Also in August, the Home Guard were involved in military exercises with the Regular Army in South Cheshire. The Regulars had supposedly landed from troop-carrying planes and brought mechanised equipment and attacked the Home Guard. The exercise was as realistic as possible with blank grenades, mortars, smoke screens, flares, and machine guns. The Home Guard had to defend from *'tank attack'* and were successful in blocking them. Regular troops were seen to go through local houses to get better attacking positions. The Crewe Home Guard led the defences which were concentrated in Crewe town.

Mock battle with South Cheshire Home Guard in Crewe, August 1941. Photos: Daily Mail.

Service personnel in the news in 1941

Lieutenant Derrick H. Jones

Derrick Jones was commissioned 2nd Lieutenant in the Royal Artillery in 1941. He was previously employed in the Westminster Bank, Alsager. He was the son of the late H. T Jones formerly the manager of the bank.

Claud Herbert Godwin DSO

Hero from the Great War, and a Commander in the Second World War.

On 27th September 1941 Claud Godwin's ship, the *Springbank* was sunk by German torpedoes. It was the third time Godwin had been forced to abandon his vessel because of enemy action

Claud was born in Alsager on 3rd December 1887, the son of Herbert Godwin and his wife, Mary, who lived in Mere Lane (Sandbach Road North). His brother George and sister, Erin, were born in 1885, and his sister Gertrude in 1893. Claud was baptised on 17th March 1888 at Christ Church Alsager. His father, a graduate of Cambridge University, took Holy Orders and in 1902 became curate of Kidsgrove, Staffordshire. Claud went to Ryley's School in Alderley Edge, Cheshire, and joined the navy in 1903 on HMS training ship *Britannia*.

Naval Career

15 Jan 1903	Cadet
30 Jun 1904	Midshipman
30 Aug 1907	Second (Sub) Lieutenant
28 Feb 1909	Lieutenant. Academic class of certificates: Seamanship (1) Navigation (1) Gen, Subjects (2) Pilotage (2) Torpedo (1) Gunnery (1)
28 Feb 1917	Lieutenant Commander
31 Dec 1921	Commander
26 Dec 1933	Capt. (retired)

Recalled for the Second World War: Captain of HMS *Springbank* 1940/1

Lieutenant Claud Godwin had served on *HMS Majestic* (a battleship) under Captain Talbot. In early 1915, she was dispatched to the Mediterranean for service in the Dardanelles Campaign. She participated in bombardments of Turkish forts and supported the Allied landings at Gallipoli. Godwin won a DSO for stopping the Turkish Navy from capturing a grounded British submarine. He destroyed the submarine by firing a torpedo from a boat.

On 31st December 1921 Godwin had been appointed Commander and served on *HMS Royal Oak* from 1919-1921. He worked at the Admiralty in the Department of Torpedoes and Mining from 15th May 1922 to 1924 He then worked on and *HMS Victory* and *HMS Centurion* and *HMS Clematis* and officially retired on 31st December 1933.

However, in 1937 he was recalled to service and served in the Second World War. He was initially based in Kirkwall in the Orkney Isles and then at *HMS Cochrane* (shore establishment) a Rosyth naval base commissioned in 1938.

At 02.11 hours on 27th September 1941 the German submarine U-201 fired two torpedoes at *HMS Springbank* captained by Claud Godwin, which was part of convoy HG-73 north-northeast of the Azores. The convoy was travelling between Gibraltar and Liverpool. Claud Godwin had assumed command of *HMS Springbank* on 18th November 1940 until the vessel was sunk.

HMS Springbank was one of a new type of Fighter Catapult Ship developed to counter the threat from land-based aircraft. Originally constructed for merchant service in 1926, she was taken up into RN service in 1940 and converted into an anti-aircraft ship with a formidable armament including 8.4-inch guns in four twin turrets and two sets of quadruple two pounder pom-poms. In March 1941 she was fitted with a cordite powered catapult amidships mounted with a Fulmar two-seater naval fighter. On 18th September 1941, *HMS Springbank* had launched the Fulmar fighter, which chased away a German Fw200 Condor aircraft and landed at Gibraltar where it was discovered that faulty ammunition had caused all but one of the guns to jam. The next day her AA armament was used to keep a shadowing Fw200 at distance to the convoy.

Completed in May 1926 as motor merchant Springbank was built by Harland & Wolff Ltd, Govan, Glasgow for Andrew Weir & Co, London

At 02.09 hours on 27th September 1941, German U-Boat U-201 fired the stern torpedo at a steamer in convoy HG-73 but missed, so the U-boat turned around and fired a spread of two torpedoes at the same ship at 02.11 hours. Lookouts on *HMS Springbank* (Capt. C.H. Godwin, DSO, RN) on station in the fifth column observed a torpedo passing between her and the *Leadgate*, shortly before the fighter catapult ship was hit on the port side by two torpedoes about four hundred and thirty miles west-southwest of Cape Clear. Most survivors from the vessel were rescued by *HMS Jasmine* (K 23) (Lt. Cdr C.D.B. Coventry, RNR), which went alongside to take off survivors and later scuttled her by gunfire after an attempt to sink her with depth charges failed. One officer and thirty-one ratings were lost. Other survivors were picked up by *HMS Hibiscus* (K 24) (Lt. Cdr C.G. Cuthbertson, RNR), which landed them at Gibraltar and by *HMS Periwinkle* (K 55) (Lt. Cdr P.G. MacIver, RNR) which landed them at Milford Haven. In total, there were two hundred and thirty-three crew (thirty-two dead and two hundred and one survivors).

In September 1942 Claud Godwin went on to serve on *HMS Malabar*, a shore-based role in Bermuda, remaining officially on the retired list as Captain.

He married Jean Hunter Forrester on 6th June 1918 in Ightham, Kent. They had one daughter, Audrey Hunter Godwin. Claud died on the 16th November 1960 in Cattistock, Dorset.

Rev. William Thomas Jones, Alsager's Congregational Minister

William was born on 20th March 1907 in Cirencester, Gloucestershire to William John Jones and his wife Harriet, nee Willavoys. In the 1911 census he was named Thomas Jones. He was ordained, and became the Minister at Alsager Congregational Church in 1937. He also worked for Alsager Scouts as a Scoutmaster. In 1939 he lived at 98 Lawton Road, Alsager with his sister, Doris M. Jones, born on 20th June 1914, who worked as his housekeeper. (She married Norman F. O'Brien in Cirencester in 1941.)

Rev W.T. Jones front row 2nd right. Other WW2 combatants: Robert Moulton, back row second left, killed in the war, and Alec McKie DFC, 2nd left front row.

William enlisted as a Chaplain with HM Forces in 1940 as can be seen in the London Gazette of 14th May:

The undermentioned to be Chaplains. to the Forces, 4th Cl.: —14th May 1940: — Rev. William Thomas JONES, B.A. (127433)

In 1941 Jones was reported as missing in Crete whilst serving as a Chaplain to the armed forces. The invasion of Crete began on the morning of 20th May 1941, when Nazi Germany began an airborne invasion. Greek forces and other Allied forces, along with Cretan civilians, defended the island. After one day of fighting, the Germans had suffered heavy casualties and the Allied troops were confident that they would defeat the invasion. The next day, through communication failures, Allied tactical hesitation and German offensive operations, Maleme airfield in western Crete fell, enabling the Germans to land reinforcements and overwhelm the defensive positions on the north of the island. Allied forces withdrew to the south coast. Over half were evacuated by the British Royal Navy; the remainder surrendered or joined the Cretan resistance. Over twelve thousand allied troops were captured. The following Casualty list below includes W.T. Jones.

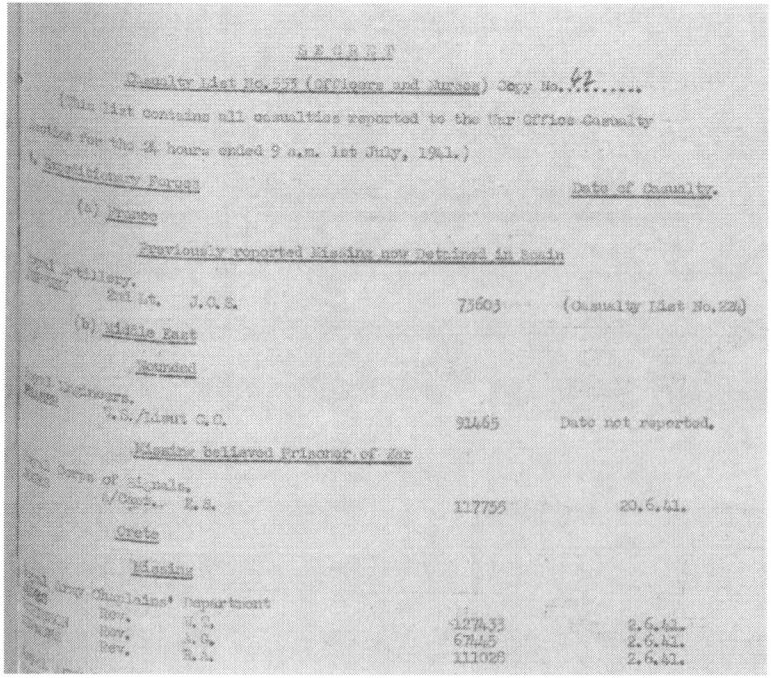

On 15th July some nineteen thousand prisoners, together with eighty five sick and medical officers and orderlies, were shipped from Canea to Salonika. Then on 20th July another two thousand were moved to Suda Bay for embarkation to Greece. The medical officers found the ship of two thousand tons very dirty and lacking water and sanitation. They persuaded the Germans to embark only one thousand four hundred. On 25th July a further nine hundred British and three hundred Greek soldiers were taken to Greece. The *'missing'* category for W.T. Jones was later changed to *'Prisoner of War'* category and in July 1944 is shown as *'repatriated'*. After being repatriated he resigned his commission in June 1945 owing to ill health.

SUPPLEMENT TO THE LONDON GAZETTE, 19 JUNE 1945 3175
ROYAL ARMY CHAPLAINS' DEPARTMENT:

Rev. W. T. JONES, B.A. (127433) Chaplain. to the Forces, 4th Cl. (U.B.) relinquishes his commn. on account of disability, 19th. June 1945, and is granted the hon. rank of Chaplain. to the Forces, 4th Cl.

It appears Jones was either wounded when he was captured or became disabled whilst a Prisoner of War.

Back from Germany he spoke at the Congregational conference on church unity in 1945. He died in Cirencester, Gloucestershire on 24th April 1952. Local people say he died when a bale of hay fell off a tractor trailer and hit him when he was cycling. Probate of £642. 12 was to his father William John Jones.

Deaths of servicemen 1941

Robert Bruce Moulton: 'Wireman', Royal Navy

Date of death: 18th May 1941

Commemorated on Alsager War Memorial

Robert Bruce Moulton. {Interview with Angela Munslow. (Munslow, 2017)} was born in Tunstall, Staffordshire on 1st October 1919, the son of Charles and Maria Moulton. He was part of a large family of four brothers and three sisters. His father was a house decorator. The family moved to Alsager before the War. In 1939 the family lived at *Four Wynds*, 6 Dunnocksfold Road, Alsager.

Robert Moulton with his mother in 1925

Robert Moulton at his wedding to Ethel Joan Barratt 1940

Robert joined the Royal Navy, and was given Service Number P/MX63954. He trained as a *'Wireman'*, or electrician. The rank of *'wireman'* was an attempt by the Royal Navy to utilize the skills of electricians. *'Wiremen'* were usually used in torpedo work but they might work for any electrical need aboard ship.

Robert Moulton married Ethel Joan Barrett in Crewe in 1940. They lived with the family at *'Four Wynds'*, Dunnocksfold Road in Alsager.

Robert was killed on *HMS Jewel*, lost at sea, on 18th May 1941 aged 21. *HMS Jewel* was built in 1908 and was fifty-four feet long. The ship hit a mine in Belfast Lough and sank. It was working as a minesweeper. *HMS Jewel* was a naval drifter, a boat built along the lines of a commercial fishing drifter but fitted out for naval purposes. Drifters were robust boats built, like trawlers, to work in most weather conditions, but designed to deploy and retrieve drift nets. They were generally smaller and slower than trawlers. If requisitioned by the Navy, they were typically armed with an anti-submarine gun and depth charges and used to maintain and patrol anti-submarine nets.

The following is an extract from *Trawlers Go to War* by Lund & Ludlum (Foulsham 1971)

Drifter HMS Jewel, mined off Belfast Lough.

Many Patrol Servicemen were sent straight from Lowestoft to the trawler base at Belfast. Here, trawlers were employed both on Atlantic convoys and on minesweeping. Within, weeks of joining the old Dutch trawler 'Friesland,' Seaman Robert Thomas was involved in the tragedy of a sister ship.

'It was a Sunday, and we were duty ship. At about 2 P.M. the quayside telephone started ringing. The sentry who should have been on the quay was on the mess deck, and the rest of the seamen were in their bunks. An argument started between them and the sentry as to who should answer the phone, which kept on ringing. Eventually a young Scotsman with more imagination than the rest said it might be important and dashed up on deck to answer it. He returned with a message that there had been an explosion down Belfast Lough. As duty ship we steamed out to investigate, but when we reached the scene all that remained on the surface was some floating wreckage and a lifebelt bearing the name of the drifter, 'Jewel', an inshore minesweeper. She had gone up on a mine. In among the wreckage was the body of her young Sub Lieutenant; we found no survivors. Ironically, one of Jewel's Patrol Service crew had only just joined her; he'd been sent to recuperate at a quiet base after harassing time minesweeping at Dover.

Soon after we returned to harbour the quayside phone rang again and this time I answered. A woman's voice asked if she could speak to Sub Lieutenant, of one of our minesweepers. I told her that his ship was at sea, which was true enough. The 'Jewel' would never return, and the Sub Lieutenant was lying on our deck, his broken body covered with a blanket.'

HMS Jewel badge

Robert Moulton's body was not recovered but he is commemorated at the Portsmouth Naval Memorial, panel 57. In his will he left probate of £1,266.10s.6d to his father and his brother in law, Arthur Earle Barratt. His father, Charles Enoch Moulton of 32 Hassall Road, died in 1943.

Robert is commemorated on the Portsmouth Naval Memorial Panel 57, Column 1.

Pilot Officer Harry Brant

Date of death: 6th August 1941

Commemorated on Church Lawton War Memorial, All Saints Church

On 31st August 1941, the *Staffordshire Advertiser* (1939-45) published a report on the pilot Harry Brant who was missing in action. Harry's plane was lost, and he is commemorated on the Church Lawton War Memorial, All Saints Church. Harry was born in Newcastle-under-Lyme in 1917. In the 1939 Register Harry is identified as a *'Grocer's Manager'*, living with his parents at *'The Laurels'*, Church Lawton.

On 7th March 1941 Harry was confirmed in the *London Gazette* as a qualified Pilot Officer. The rank was backdated to 9th February 1941.

Brant's Wellington Bomber took off at 23:00 hours from Driffield, Yorkshire, with ninety seven other aircraft to bomb targets in the Karlsruhe area, Germany. The plane was hit by flak in the target area. The crew of six were all killed.

The

NEWCASTLE
PILOT OFFICER MISSING

Pilot Officer Harry Brant, R.A.F. only son of Ald. and Mrs. F. T. Brant, The Laurels, Church Lawton, who is officially reported missing while serving with Bomber Command, was formerly associated with his father in a well-known grocery business. Pilot Officer Brant, who was educated at Newcastle High School, is 24 years of age. He joined the R.A.F. Volunteer Reserve in 1938, and was called up for service on the outbreak of war. He has taken part in many bombing raids over Germany.

His father is president of the North Staffordshire Grocers' Association, and is well known in public life in Newcastle.

Commonwealth War Graves Commission gives the following information about Harry:

(CWGC) Rank: Pilot Officer. Trade: Observer. Service No: 60834. Date of Death: 06/08/1941. Regiment/Service Royal Air Force Volunteer Reserve 104 Sqdn. Grave Reference: Coll. grave 2. B. 9-12. Cemetery: DURNBACH WAR CEMETERY. The cemetery is near Bayern, Bavaria, Germany.

In his will Harry left £700 to his father, Thomas.

Pilot Officer Colin Tremaine Martyn-Johns: RAF

Date of death: 25th November 1941

Commemorated on Church Lawton War Memorial

Colin Tremaine Martyn-Johns was a nephew of Constantine Bradford Martyn-Johns (1886-1950), Rector of Church Lawton, All Saints. He was included on the Lawton War Memorial for this reason.

He was born in 1914 in London to William Arthur Tremaine Martyn-Johns, a Commercial Traveller, (Constantine's brother) and his wife Lillie. He had a sister, Phyllis. The family lived 27 Dartmouth Road Hendon London in 1937.

Colin joined the Royal Air Force Reserve but was killed in a night flying accident on 25th November 1941 at Oundle, Northamptonshire. He was 27. He was a Sergeant Pilot Officer (- service number 1380362). He is buried in Row 4.
Mill Hill (St Paul) churchyard,
Borough of Barnet,
London.

Able Seaman Alfred Woodward

Date of death: 19th December 1941

Commemorated on Odd Rode War Memorial, All Saints Church

Alfred was born on 3rd June 1920 in Thurlwood to William Henry and Agnes (nee Leech), Woodward. He attended Rode Heath School and Sandbach Grammar School. His father was a bricklayer on the railways maintenance staff. His brother John was born in 1921, Herbert in 1929 and Phillip in 1931. He also had two sisters, Joyce and Nancy. The family lived at 6 Council Houses, Thurlwood, Rode Heath. Alfred worked on the railways after leaving school. He was a talented football player and in 1938 was offered a month's trial with Manchester United. He played for Stoke City 'A' team against West Bromwich Albion in 1939/40. Alfred joined the Royal Navy, service number D/JX 217214 on 21st August 1940 as an Ordinary Seaman and served aboard *HMS Neptune* (NavHist) a Leander Class cruiser which was ordered under the 1930 naval building programme from H.M. Dockyard, Devonport on 2nd March 1931. Alfred trained as a Submarine Detector (Asdic). The ship was laid down on 24th September that year. She was launched on 31st March 1932 as the fourteenth Royal Navy ship to carry the name. The cruiser was completed on 22nd February 1934. In 1939, she was deployed in the South Atlantic.

HMS Neptune 1937

Woodward's last leave home was in April 1941.

The ship's war service in December 1941:

17th   The ship sailed from Malta with HM Destroyers *Jaguar* and *Kandahar* as 'Force B' to support Mediterranean Fleet ships from Alexandria which were engaging Italian warships attempting to prevent return of *HMS Breconshire* bringing fuel supplies to Malta.
This was called the First Battle of Sirte.

18th   After Italian warships withdrew *HMS Neptune* was deployed in search for Italian convoy M42.

Neptune returned to Malta after failing to find M42. On its return it was despatched with HM Cruisers and Destroyers to intercept the supply convoy reported outside the entrance to Tripoli harbour. During the passage, in position twenty miles from Tripoli, *Neptune* ran into an enemy minefield. The ship hit one mine and was disabled. Whilst adrift it hit a second mine which wrecked its propellers and rudder. Subsequently it detonated a third mine which caused further damage aft. Nearly three hours later a fourth mine was struck amidships, and the ship then sank very quickly. Only one seaman survived and was taken prisoner out of a ship's complement of seven hundred and sixty-four. Able Seaman Alfred Woodward's body was never recovered. The sinking of the *Neptune* and also HMS *Kandahar* on the same day was the second most substantial loss of life suffered by the Royal Navy in the whole of the Mediterranean campaign, and ranks among the heaviest crew losses experienced in any naval theatre of World War II.

Royal Navy death record

Alfred is commemorated on the Plymouth Naval Memorial, Devon

Rank: Able Seaman, Service No: D/JX 217214   Date of Death: 19/12/1941 Regiment/Service: Royal Navy H.M.S. Neptune Panel Reference: Panel 49, Column 1. Additional Information: Son of William Henry and Agnes Woodward, of Rode Heath, Cheshire.

On a Pilgrimage to Malta and Tripoli, 21st-29th April 2007, organised by the Neptune Association, by relatives of the crew of the *Neptune*, Janet Edwards, niece of Alfred Woodward, represented the family. There is also a memorial to Neptune at the National Memorial Arboretum.

H.M.S Neptune Memorial, National Memorial Arboretum, Alrewas

Photos: The Neptune Association

Alsager in 1942

Timeline of the war in 1942 (history)

The first Americans arrived in England in January - and in North Africa German Field Marshal Erwin Rommel's Afrika Korps began their counter-offensive, capturing Tobruk in June.

The Blitz intensified in both England and Germany, with the first thousand-bomber air raid on Cologne, and German bombing of British cathedral cities.

In the Pacific, the Japanese continued their expansion into Borneo, Java and Sumatra. The 'unassailable' British fortress of Singapore fell rapidly in February, with around twenty-five thousand prisoners taken, many of whom would die in Japanese camps in the years to follow.

But June saw the peak of Japanese expansion. The Battle of Midway, in which US sea-based aircraft destroyed four Japanese carriers and a cruiser, marked the turning point in the Pacific War.

The second half of the year also saw a reversal of German fortunes. British forces under Montgomery gained the initiative in North Africa at El Alamein, and Russian forces counterattacked at Stalingrad. The news of mass murders of Jewish people by the Nazis reached the Allies, and the US pledged to avenge these crimes.

Alsager and district in 1942

In January 1942 Mr Frederick Frank Evanson from Alsager, was awarded the Royal Humane Society parchment for diving fully clothed into a water-filled disused marl pit in Bradwell to save the life of a three-year-old girl who had fallen in. The pit was sixteen feet deep. Frederick was a fireman/driver on the railway. Evanson, who was born in 1908, was married to Agnes, and they lived at 35 Talke Road. A Royal Humane Society Testimonial on Parchment is awarded where someone has put themselves in danger to save, or attempt to save, someone else. Many of the awards go to people who have swum to the rescue of someone else - in a quarry, a lake, a river or at sea.

1942 also opened with Alsager beginning its *'Warship Week'* a fundraising effort to raise money for the navy. *'Warship Weeks'* were British National Savings campaigns during the Second World War, with the adoption of a Royal Navy warship by communities. A target level of savings would be set to raise enough money to provide the cost of building a naval ship. The aim was for cities to raise enough money to adopt battleships and aircraft carriers, while towns and villages would focus on cruisers and destroyers. Smaller towns and villages like Alsager were set a lower figure. Once the target money was saved for the ship, the community would adopt the ship and its crew.

Photograph: Weekly Sentinel January 1942

On 17th January 1942, the *Sentinel* published an article about Alsager's Warship Week. A public appeal was to be distributed to every householder in Alsager with the target of raising £25,000. The cost of building *'His Majesty's Torpedo boat 55'* was allocated as the aim of the campaign. £25,000 was the cost of building the hull of a torpedo boat. The total cost of a complete torpedo boat was £28,500. The fundraising was led by Councillor R.H. Timmis with Sir Francis Joseph prominent in the promotion of the scheme. A dance had been held the previous Friday at St Mary's Schools organised by Agnes Edwards on behalf of the Girl Guides to raise funds for the scheme. One lady remembers as a child sitting in a makeshift boat at the event, waving a flag and singing *Rule Britannia*. The model boat was on display in St Mary's Schoolroom surrounded by Warship Week posters and slogans. Dancing was to the Sutherland Dance Band and novelty dances introduced for competitions. Prizes were won by Mr G. Band and Miss Cureton, Mr D. Peake, Miss E. Dunn and Private Moss, and Mrs Bowen. Prizes of eggs and silk stockings were won by Miss Cureton and Miss Holmes respectively. Prizes were presented by Mrs H. Steventon.

In February, Warship Week fundraising extended to the Alsager schools where National Savings Schemes were encouraged. Part of the fundraising was a paper salvage scheme whereby children were encouraged to recycle paper. Large amounts of paper were salvaged, and children rewarded with Savings Certificates and Stamps. The Sentinel reported the winners.

Mr Hughes, Headmaster Senior School (by Christ Church,) collects National Savings contributions in 1942 from his pupils for 'Warship Week'. Doug Bennett is standing (4th from right), his friend, Peter Dawson (standing 5th from right) and holding his savings book was an evacuee from Bradford. He came to live with his grandmother in Alsager. Peter Barker is 4th from the left. The Junior School was situated off Sandbach Road north by Alsager Institute. Photo: Staffordshire Weekly Sentinel 7th February 1942. The school's roll at the senior school in 1942 was one hundred and twelve.

According to certified results in the *Birmingham Daily Post* (BirmPost), 9th February 1942, Alsager raised £77,048, equivalent to £9 per each head of population for *Warship Week*. Of the appeals nationally, the most money collected in a local appeal was in Halifax Yorkshire. The First Lord of the Admiralty, Mr A.V Alexander started that appeal for the adoption of the cruiser *Ajax* for £1, 5000,000. Seventy-Five *Warship Weeks* appeals were launched in January 1942. The Executors of the late Joel Settle invested £9,000 in the Alsager fund.

By May 1942 Alsager adopted *Torpedo Boat 55*. Sub Lieutenant Granville-Smith, second in command of the boat, visited Alsager to thank the town. He called at the Church of England Schools with Chairman William Holland, and Alsager councillors Timmis and Moulton, and spoke to children about the work of his boat and congratulated them on their efforts during *Warship Week*. A large photograph of the boat was presented to the Alsager Urban District Council.

Motor Torpedo Boat 55, a photograph from the Weekly Sentinel 1942

Fundraising efforts were not just for *Warship Week*. In March 1942 at the 'Brunds' concert hall a concert was held to raise money for the Radway Green Spitfire Fund. This would have been when the hostel was still being used for Radway Green workers. Amongst the artists were Ernest Hampton and his band, and accompanist, Arthur Arden. Mr Jack East was the compere.

Prosecutions for infringements of lighting restrictions from houses were enforced in January 1942 in Alsager. There were ten prosecutions in January giving fines of between one pound and three pounds. Most fines were awarded to people in Wesley Place and Longview Avenue.

The number of road accidents in Alsager, as in most of south Cheshire, was high. The *Crewe Chronicle* published grim death statistics of the number of people killed. The reasons for so many deaths were due to the restrictions on street lights and vehicles. Occasionally cyclists were victims. In 1942 Jos Yearsley, aged thirty-nine, was hit by a bus whilst cycling in Alsager. The driver did not see him, and the bike was not displaying a red light.

In April Mr Frank Salter, postman from the Alsager post office, was awarded the Imperial Service Medal (Civil Service) for his work. The award was announced in the London Gazette. Frank, born in 1885, was conscientious and hard working. The medal was presented on completion of 25 years' service on his retirement.

In July 1942, the Alsager Royal British Legion held their annual fair on the cricket ground (Parsonage Field) to raise money for their benevolent fund. The event was opened by Mrs W. Foden and Foden's Motor Works Band under the direction of Mr F. Mortimer played for guests. There was a gymnastic display by Saltersford (Holmes Chapel) cadets, and an Ambulance competition won by Rode Heath team. St John's Ambulance Brigade manned a tent for the occasion. There were lots of stalls and sideshows including *'hand of fortune'*, hoopla, darts, and fishing pond.

In July 1942, the basic civilian petrol ration was abolished, making fuel unavailable to private car owners. Private cars were virtually unusable after this date.

In the same month, there was a widescale campaign to provide Red Cross parcels for British prisoners of war in Germany. A *'penny a week fund'* started and collection points for parcels was set up in Sandbach and Crewe. Alsager parcels were taken to one of the collection points where an army of volunteers dealt with them. Then began a tortuous route for the parcels before they arrived in Germany. Firstly, they were shipped to

Lisbon, and then on to Marseilles. From Marseilles, they were driven to Geneva in neutral Switzerland before being transported into Germany.

Memories of 1942- Mr Doug Bennett

Doug Bennett (Bennett, 2017) was a schoolboy in Alsager during the Second World War. He particularly remembers one of the events of 1942; the crashing of a Spitfire pilot in Alsager.

Doug was born on 2nd September 1930 and lived at 102 Station Road in the war years. Close to his house at the top of Well Lane they built a brick air raid shelter for residents. Doug recalls the sirens going off for an air raid on the Council Offices and having to go into the shelter. There was another underground shelter opposite the Police Station by Huntly Goss's home. Ernest Proudlove helped dig this shelter in 1939. Doug says of the Well Lane shelter,

'A couple of times a week we had to go in there. You could identify the German planes, they made a different sound, so we knew it was no false alarm. We used to play football against it. At some stage in the war the shelter was deemed unsafe and it was pulled down.'

Doug's father, Ernest, was an ARP Warden during the war. Doug recalls the Wardens were poorly equipped,

'They had a sand bucket and a water bucket and a stirrup pump. The idea was to put out incendiary fires. The team would meet at Hopwood's Cobbler's shop in Station Road but would have little to do.'

Doug remembers one night when a bomb dropped at the top end of Fanny's Croft in Alsager causing a bomb crater near to the stream. It was by the footbridge where the stream turned West below Alsager Hall. *'We went to have a look at it …it was just a crater and did no damage as such.'*

A resident of Audley Road recalled playing in the crater weeks after the incident when she was a child.

Doug also remembers the day the Spitfire crashed in fields; the site of Alsager Cricket Club today. *'We weren't allowed to go near it and we weren't sure if it was a British of German plane. I believe somebody managed to get some of the parachute silk for themselves before the ARP turned up.'*

Doug (2017) outside Alsager Cricket Club. The plaque commemorates the life of Sgt McNamara, RAFVR who crashed on the site on 25th September 1942. Mr Derek Fernyhough from Alsager was instrumental in trying to solve the puzzle of who the pilot was and eventually having the plaque to him erected at Alsager Cricket Club.

Sergeant John Frederick "Jack" McNamara 1314971, Royal Air Force, Volunteer Reserve. Born 1921. Death: 25th September 1942

Jack was the son of John and Maud Beatrice McNamara, of Barton Hill, Bristol.

As a trainee Spitfire pilot McNamara avoided buildings, including possibly a school, before crashing in Alsager. People in Alsager had always wondered what happened when a plane, rumoured to be a Spitfire, came down in a field on an old farm, which is now Alsager's cricket pitch. Derek Fernyhough was a 10-year-old schoolboy when he heard an explosion in class - and his obsession to find what had happened stayed with him over the years. Derek said, *'My mother told me that she'd seen a wing fall off an aeroplane and it crashed into the field behind our house and we came up here and there were bits of plane in the trees.'* That field proved to be the *'top field'* of donkeys owned by the family of Sheila Bailey.

Worcester aviation historian Andrew Long eventually cracked the mystery of who the pilot was after extensive work by BBC reporter Ben Godfrey and famous Birmingham historian Carl Chinn. (Bristol)

Mr Long started his search with just *'1942, autumn, Alsager and Spitfire'.*

He knew Spitfire pilots were trained at Hawarden, Cheshire, and it proved to be an important clue. A second trip to the National Archives at Kew in Surrey ultimately uncovered the accident report and consequently the full story of 25th September 1942.

McNamara was flying a Spitfire in training and he didn't estimate how close he was to the ground when he came through the clouds. As he tried to change course to avoid buildings, he pulled up, trying to gain altitude quickly. But the port wing snapped, and he crashed into trees on the farmland. If he'd hit the buildings, there might have been considerable loss of life on the ground. In 2007 a plaque in memory of Jack was unveiled on the side of the pavilion of Alsager Cricket Club, just metres from where the plane crashed. Madeleine Summerill was only 11 years old when she discovered the older brother she adored had perished in a plane crash. Sixty-five years later she was part of the ceremony to unveil the plaque in Alsager.

Jack's sister was eventually tracked down after an appeal on BBC Radio Bristol - and was astonished. She remembered when the telegram advising the family of Jack's death arrived in Bristol. *'My brother just blurted out "our Jack's been killed". I remember his face so clearly, it's just burned into your mind.'*

Madeleine Summerill and Derek Fernyhough, right, at the plaque unveiling at Alsager Cricket Club in 2007. The plaque in memory of Jack was unveiled on the side of the pavilion of Alsager Cricket Club, just metres from where the plane landed - and Madeleine was the guest of honour

Mrs Summerill said of her brother. *'We had been told it was a flying accident, the plane crashed, and he was killed. Anything else is total and complete surprise. Jack was full of fun. He was a great lad and sometimes I suffered because of it, being his young sister. He'd thought up all sorts of pranks to play on us all. Mum was a lovely cheerful person, always ready for a laugh, but it hit her terribly and she wore black for ages.'*

Jack McNamara is commemorated at Bristol Greenbank Cemetery, Bristol, on the Screen Wall S.17. Some of the individual graves, including Jack McNamara's in the cemetery, are no longer identifiable.

Other wartime memories of Doug Bennett

Doug Bennett also used the Air Raid Shelter outside his school by Christ Church. There were actually two shelters near to the school by Christ Church. Schoolchildren would have to carry their cardboard boxes containing gasmasks to school and take them into the shelters. Another pupil as a schoolgirl remembers using this shelter on the day war was declared when the sirens went off. Doug well remembers the National Savings scheme at school to raise money for the war effort. Certificates were fifteen shillings and every week pupils came with their small contributions to be entered in the National Savings book.

Doug remembers the public being given access to concerts and film shows at the *Heathside Hostel*. 'There were two concert groups in Alsager, one led by Harold Crampton and the other by Dennis Wilshaw. *We would sit alongside the women munition workers from Radway Green who lodged in the adjacent accommodation huts. The show was mainly made up of sketches and songs. There was once a Chinese Group that came to perform an opera. We also watched film shows there. The Alsager public were always encouraged to go to performances.*

Alsager became much busier in the war years. Before the war everyone knew one another but soon the village was full of strangers. Hundreds of women were redeployed from Woolwich Arsenal and were housed at Heathside Hostel. When they built Longview Avenue on the new Lynam estate these women and their families were given priority for rehousing. Milton House was requisitioned as an apprentice's hostel for Radway Green. There were also Americans billeted in Alsager. They were in a house in Sandbach Road or Station Road. I remember having to go for a scarlet fever treatment with Dr Bates. He was wearing his RAF uniform I remember.'

Dr George Bates, RAF, standing left. Freetown Sierra Leone, 1st May 1945

'Alsager got off very lightly in the war. Radway Green was not bombed, nor were the railways in Alsager, unlike at Crewe. I worked after the war at Rolls Royce, Crewe and remember seeing where the factory had been hit during bombing. Yes, in Alsager, we were lucky … we continued to play and watch the football down Cedar Avenue and the Parsonage Field. Alsager Cricket Club also played on the Parsonage Field (Alsager School playing fields (2017). There was a wooden bandstand on the field where Foden's Band played.'

Doug has continued to live in Alsager all his life and raised his family in the town. He continued to work in the Paint Laboratory at Rolls Royce Crewe for many years.

Other 1942 Alsager News

There was a proposal in 1942 for a Remand Home to be built near Alsager. In the end the idea was opposed by the Home Office, despite Cheshire County Councillors from Neston in the north of the county criticising the decision not to build it.

In July 1942 Douglas Harry Lynam, nephew of the Alsager Council Surveyor H.V Lynam, and son of Douglas Forrester Lynam of 180 Crewe Road, Alsager, was married to Winifred Holroyd in Shelf, Bradford.

Douglas was a Sergeant in the army. Douglas was born in 1915. He died in 1994.

In June 1942 Sir Francis Joseph K.B.E was created a Baronet. Apart from being Chairman of Settle Speakman Ltd he was a Director of the L.M.S Railway and President of Stoke City Football Club. The award came a few weeks after his daughter, Rosalind's wedding in St Mary's Church, Alsager. She was serving in the WRENs, but both the Joseph sisters had previously served as VAD nurses at the North Staffs Infirmary.

Photo: Tatler magazine 1942

The Joseph sisters ran the Girl Guides from Sir Francis's house before they enlisted. One former girl guide remembered troops used to camp at the back of that property at *Bankhouse Farm*. On the way home from Guides they would call and see the soldiers and get something to eat to supplement their rations.

New School

With the sudden growth of population Alsager was short of schools and 1942 saw the planning for a new school, the Alsager Junior Council School. The *Cheshire Observer*, in July, wrote the capital cost of the school was to be funded not by Cheshire County Council but by The Ministry of Supply, presumably because most of the additional demand for places was coming from Radway Green employees' children. The County Council would pay for running costs. Alderman Beard from the County Council said there was *'no accommodation for feeding school children in Alsager'*, and the town was *'deficient in available buildings for nursery schools, classes, or feeding'*. The new school was to be built on the new *'Radway Estate'* and work would start *'at once'*.

On 15th November 1942 church bells were rung at Christ Church for the first time since May 1940, in celebration of victory at the Second Battle of El Alamein.

Serviceman in the news in 1942

Major Walter Coomer, was the eldest son of Thomas Coomer, Hay and Straw dealer, of *Shady Villa*, Lawton Road, Alsager. He was born in 1894 in Madeley, Staffordshire, and in 1939 was on the RAF Officers Emergency Reserve List and living in Alsager. He served in the Royal Flying Corps then RAF in the Great War from 1917 as a mechanic then as a cadet pilot, service number M/27954'6. He qualified as a pilot and was sent to the Middle East in 1918 with a posting to Port Said, Egypt, in 1919. In 1920, on demobilisation he was granted an honorary commission as 2nd Lieutenant (*London Gazette* 15th June 1920) In the Second World War, instead of enlisting back with the RAF, probably because he could not fly owing to his age, he joined the Royal Engineers, serving as 2nd Lieutenant from 2nd May 1940, and was promoted Captain, and then he was made a Temporary Major in August 1940 and served in the Middle East. In 1942 his father Thomas died in Alsager but Walter, who preferred to be called *'Bill'* remained in the Middle East and missed the funeral. He is one of only a handful of Alsager and district men who served in both wars.

Major Walter Coomer (back row 1st left)

His brother Reginald, back row 4th from left, died in 1920 and was a prisoner of war in WW1.

Picture taken in 1914.

Walter worked as a house painter as a boy, and then a commercial traveller. He married Monica Walker in Epsom in 1926 and they had three sons. He died in Reading in 1982.

Captain Charles William Kennerley Potts - Alsager's *'Fighting Padre'*

Rev. Charles William Kennerley Potts

In the May 1937 edition of the *Alsager Parish News* the Rev Charles Churton Potts announced that his son, Charles Potts, who had been ordained an Anglican Priest had set sail from Southampton on 13th March to work under the South African Railway Mission, and having spent time with the Bishop of Capetown he ventured on a *'dreary'* three thousand mile journey to Northern Rhodesia. He found himself Priest in Charge of Lusaka and chaplain to the Governor. His duties included attending civic functions and leading divine worship every first Sunday of the month. In between these duties he ventured to Broken Hill and stations in North Rhodesia. This is the first indication we have of the pioneering spirit Charles Potts possessed but it gives no indication of his future military career when he became to be known as the *'Fighting Padre'*.

He was born in Skipworth, Selby, Yorkshire on 16th May 1910. His childhood was mainly spent in Coventry where his father was Vicar of Stoke parish (1918-25.) His father was then Vicar of Dunham Massey, Cheshire, before becoming Vicar of Alsager in 1933. His siblings were

Margaret, (born 1902) Florence (1904) John (1907), Grace and Theodore (1908) who were twins, and Robert.

Charles W.K. Potts was educated at Fettes College, Edinburgh where his grandfather had been the first headmaster. He went on to St Catherine's College Cambridge and Lincoln Theological College. He then held curacies in Latchford and Stockport. As Curate of Latchford in 1938 he was busily preparing 50 boys for confirmation.

By July 1938 Potts had returned from Africa and on 10th July 1938 the Vicar reported in the Parish News his son was assisting him in duties in Alsager parish. A tall man, Charles was over six feet in height. In the spring of 1939 he was in *'poor health'* according to his father writing in the Parish Magazine, but he was running the Linley Mission and organising a boys' club. By September 1939 Charles applied for a position as Vicar in the London Docklands and was appointed shortly afterwards.

On 2nd January 1940 Potts was granted a commission as an army chaplain which was recorded in the *London Gazette* and he was assigned to the Lancashire Fusiliers and the Sherwood Foresters. His brother 2nd Lt. Robert Potts joined him in the Lancashire Fusiliers in July 1940.

In his book, '*Soldier in the Sand*', (Potts) 1961, Charles wrote. *'I had been "base wallowing" in Cyprus and Cairo. I first went to the Middle East, leaving England February 1941. I was a Padre. I was posted to Cyprus.'* His regiment left for North Africa and Potts longed to go with them. His commanding officers wrote on his behalf, so he could join the North Africa campaign as Padre, but to no avail.

'I had started a Troops' Club in Cyprus and a Troops' Monthly Magazine. The Chaplains' Department of GHQ wanted to keep it going.'

On 6th April 1942 Charles resigned his commission as Chaplain to become a serving fighting soldier. He initially enrolled as a private soldier in the Sherwood Foresters and was sent to the Middle East. He was selected for the Officer Cadet Training Unit in Cairo and took up boxing as a hobby in his spare time. He was commissioned as Lieutenant in the *'Buffs'*, the West Kent Regiment. When he reached Infantry Base Depot at Suez he was distressed to hear that men over thirty were no longer being sent to fight in the desert. He appealed and won his appeal. He joined the 1st Battalion of the *Buffs* commanded by Lt. Col. Grenville Dorien-Smith.

He wrote, *'I was lucky in the North African Campaigns in that I joined on practically the same day that 'Monty', [General Montgomery] took command.'* The Allies had suffered setbacks after Rommel's *Afrika Corps* had made sweeping victories in the desert. Montgomery's tactics reversed the defeats.

Potts wrote, *'Dust made us permanently dirty.'* His water allowance for washing was one pint daily. He cleaned his teeth then washed in it, then shaved. *'I poured the water through a cloth into a half petrol tin.'* Collecting the water over days, *'we bathed in turn in the half petrol tin'*. They strained the water through a cloth and washed their clothes in it. In a letter home Potts wrote,

'We find one of the biggest snags in the desert is to find our way about on a dark night when there is no moon. One can lose one's way going to the latrine only 100 yards away. Scoop a trench in the sand and sleep in it, then wake in the morning and find the camp half a mile away. It's a great life. Here's another cyclone going by and a hellofabig one —wow! And another dust storm-again the camp is wrapped in a cloud of white dust.'

Potts' batman was a man called William Double. Giving orders to this man *'at the double'* soon became a tired joke.

Potts took part in the Second Battle of El Alemein (23rd October–11th November 1942), when Rommel attacked the British line near the Qattara Depression. The depression was considered impassable by tanks and most other military vehicles because of features such as salt lakes, high cliffs and/or escarpments, and very fine powdered sand. The cliffs acted as the border of the El Alamein battlefield, which meant the British position could not be outflanked. Both Axis and Allied forces built their defences in a line from the Mediterranean Sea to the Qattara Depression. These defences became known as the Devil's Gardens and are for the most part still there, especially the extensive minefields. No large army units entered the Depression, although German *Afrika Korps* patrols and the British Long Range Desert Group did operate in the area, as these small units had considerable experience in desert travel. Potts was part of the 8th Armoured Brigade. His 'A' Company was attached to the Sherwood Rangers Yeomanry. They were attacked by Stuka bombers while in trenches. All his platoon vehicles servicing three motor platoons were destroyed. His platoon was nicknamed, *'The Potteries'*, after his name and connections. He was next put in charge of a motor platoon, a carrier and an anti-tank section. Rommel's forces retreated after the second battle of El Alemein.

In the third Battle of El Alemein his unit was again attacked by Stukas. On the second day of the battle his unit was at Tank Headquarters. Lt Col Kellett called him over and said twenty to thirty knocked-out German tanks were being used by German snipers and they had to be flushed out.

Potts, who had been promoted to Captain shortly before the action, took a bag of sticky bombs and ventured towards the tanks. He said, *'It is a common experience of men in action for their mood to change considerably from horribly frightened to couldn't care a fig what happened to you. I was in that latter mood.'*

He walked out with his suitcase of bombs and then went on, carrying one primed bomb. He searched the tanks in turn and slapped the bomb on one tank he suspected. He walked with the bomb in his right hand and a revolver in his left.

Three of the German tanks were more remote. With covering fire, his men attacked these remote tanks with Bren guns. Potts moved forward alone. Suddenly there was German shooting and Potts' Bren carrier and its three men were left vulnerable to attack. Three Germans came running from one of the tanks Potts had *'searched'*. Potts was forced to retreat, machine gun bullets landing around his feet. He sounded the alarm so the men from the Bren carrier could be assisted and escaped into a deep trench. Later he discovered the derelict German tanks had been only a hundred yards from active German positions.

After the fourth day of the battle he took the funeral of a dead British soldier for the first time. It was the first of many. He read from the Army Prayer Book. He found these services a great strain and dangerous because they were still under attack from the enemy. He recalled that despite the danger he never hurried through a service. The British breakthrough came on 4th November after thirteen days of fighting when the tanks surged through. He called 5th November *'one of the most exciting days of my life'*, when his jeep was knocked out and then he went forward with two motor platoons and a three inch mortar to protect the infantry. On 15th November, he took a full Battalion Church Parade for his commanding officer.

In late 1942 Potts was informed he had been awarded the Military Cross. *'To my profound astonishment and not to mention considerable embarrassment I was informed three days before Christmas, I had been awarded a decoration. I had not the faintest idea of the reason for the award.'*

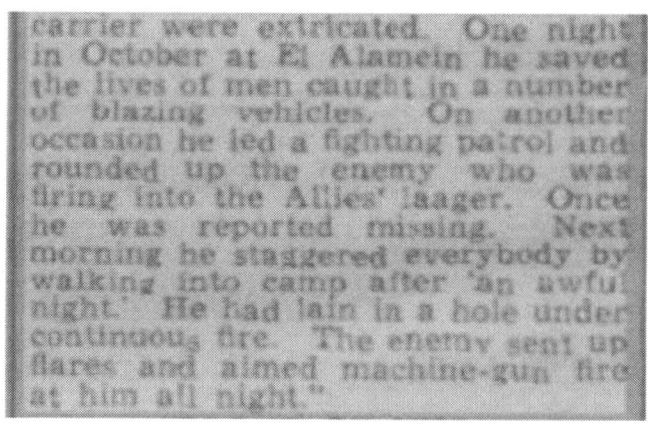

The Chester Observer, 2nd January 1943 gave a report on Potts' award for gallantry.

The story of the gallantry that won him the M.C. is cited in a message from Cairo this week and was the subject of a broadcast on Tuesday night. It is as follows: "Moving forward across 'no man's land' to deal with snipers operating from derelict tanks, Capt. Potts under steady small arms fire, had slapped a sticky bomb on one tank when he saw that the Bren-carrier covering his rear had been hit by a mortar shell. The occupants—an officer and two men—made for the cover of a derelict vehicle 200 yards from the enemy's main defended position. Capt. Potts, running a gauntlet of fire, doubled back 700 yards to get help, and the crew of the Bren-carrier were extricated. One night in October at El Alamein he saved

"PROUD OF HIM."

His father told "The Chronicle": "I was sorry when my son gave up his position as chaplain, but I am proud of him. I always knew he would make a jolly good soldier. From a small boy he has been full of adventure. I could not stop him. He was always climbing in dangerous places, always wanted to rove, and was always eager to see how others lived. He spent his holidays tramping and living like a tramp to see for himself what the life was like. But all the same he had a real gift for the job of parson."

The article goes on to report the Rev. Potts' reaction to his son's award demonstrating some of the qualities he saw in his son's character.

Potts wrote home to his fiancée. *'This is such a remote, strange, life in the desert, so cut off from life that all you sometimes feel is very far away and unreal'.* Pamela wrote to ask what colour wedding dress she should choose. He replied, *'Anything but Khaki!'* Potts married Audrey Pamela Stubbs in Wenlock, Shropshire, in 1944.

To the ethical question as to whether or not it is unchristian to kill a man *Potts wrote:*

'If I saw a lunatic at large and attacking a child I would do everything in my power to stop him even if I had to shoot and kill him. Hitler was a dangerous lunatic and his lunacy had infected a whole nation. It was our duty to protect the children, the weaker nations of Europe that were being scourged and enslaved by these dangerous lunatics.'

After the war Charles became a civil servant. He died in Lymington, Hampshire in 1986.

Deaths of Servicemen in 1942

Pilot Officer James Bernard Dunne: RAFVR

Date of death: 10th March 1942

Commemorated on Odd Rode War Memorial, All Saints Church

James Bernard Dunne was born in Miles Platting Manchester on 25th December 1915 the son of son of James and Emily Dunne (nee Heald) On 10th June 1936 James joined the police force. (Manchester Police Index 1812-1941.) By 1939, however, he is recorded in the 1939 Register as a *'Certificated School Teacher'*. He lived with his widowed mother at 11 Northolme Gardens, Burnage, Manchester.

In October 1941 James married Joan Arrowsmith in Crewe. (Date of Registration: Oct-Nov-Dec 1941 8a page 1142.) They took up residence at *Claphatch Cottage*, Scholar Green. James enrolled in the Royal Air Force Volunteer Reserve service number 106041 and joined 49 Squadron. He trained to be a Pilot Officer (Observer) and the London Gazette recorded he qualified on August 5th, 1941.

49 Squadron (Reports)
James served in Handley Page Hampdens aircraft. The Handley Page HP.52 Hampden was a British twin-engine medium bomber of the Royal Air Force. It was one of a trio of then large twin-engine bombers procured for the RAF, the other two being the Armstrong Whitworth Whitley and Vickers Wellington. The newest of the three medium bombers, the Hampden, was often referred to by aircrews as the *"Flying Suitcase"* because of its cramped crew conditions.

Crew of 49 Squadron

During the opening months of World War 49 squadron was employed mainly on reconnaissance, mine laying and leaflet dropping. On 11th May 1940 bombing attacks on Germany began; the oil refineries at München Gladbach being attacked. On 12th August, a most successful low-level attack on the Dortmund Ems canal was pressed home by Hampdens of 49 Squadron despite fierce opposition. Flt Lt R A. B. Learoyd received the Victoria Cross for his bravery during the attack, the first awarded in Bomber Command. Throughout 1941 many targets were attacked; ports, industrial centres, shipping, marshalling yards and airfields. In March 1942, the squadron took part in a successful attack on the Renault works at Billancourt, Paris.

Hampden I (AT174 EA-E) on its final mission, to Essen, on 10th March 1942.

On Tuesday, 10th March 1942, 49 squadron took off for a mission to Essen in Germany from RAF Scampton Airfield. The pilot was Pilot Officer W.H.T. Andrews. James Bernard Dunne was the Observer. They took off for their mission at 19:13 hours. The squadron contributed eleven Hampdens for an attack on 'Point B' in Essen Old Town. Four aircraft failed to return from the raid, including AT174 from 49 squadron. All the crew were killed when the plane was brought down over Germany. The crew were originally buried in Selm Cemetery and reburied alongside each other in the Reichswald Forest War Cemetery, near Kleve. The crew of Hampden AT174 (EA-E); were Pilot Officer W.H.T. Andrews; Pilot Sgt S.T. Drew; Pilot Officer J.B. Dunne; Observer Sergeant A.A. Gauld.

Reichswald Forest War Cemetery

The following year Joan Dunne was granted probate in James' will.

DUNNE James Bernard of Claphatch Cottage Scholar Green (Stoke-on-Trent) **Cheshire** who is presumed to have died on or since 10 March 1942 on war service Administration **Chester** 9 July to Joan Dunne widow. Effects £179 11s. 4d.

 **Sgt Observer Walter Frank Good: RAFVR**

Date of death: 8th April 1942

Commemorated on Church Lawton War Memorial

Walter Frank Good was born in Stoke-on-Trent on 7th May 1908 to Walter Wilberforce Good and Marion Good. His father moved to Biddulph where he was a mill manager. Walter had eight siblings. Walter, who was generally known as Frank, married Phyllis Lowndes in Conway in 1933. They had three children: Mary, Peter and Frank. Frank worked as a senior architect's draughtsman and by 1939 the family lived at *Conway*, Lawton Avenue, Church Lawton. He enrolled in the Royal Air Force Naval Reserve and trained as an Observer reaching the rank of Sergeant working at 15 Operational Training Unit. He was training under the direction of experienced pilots when his death occurred on 8th April 1942.

No. 15 Operational Training Unit RAF (15 OTU) was formed in August 1940 as part of No. 6 Group RAF Bomber Command at RAF Hampstead Norris to train night bomber crews on the Vickers Wellington. On 4th March 1941, a Wellington was attacked by a German fighter as it approached land at RAF Hampstead Norris. The airfield was then attacked on 12th May 1941 with ten high explosive bombs and one hundred incendiaries. One Wellington was destroyed, and the flare path and the southern taxiway were damaged.

The story of Frank's death on April 8th, 1942 is incorporated in *Just another Day* by Alan White, from the Severnside Aviation Society:

> 'This is a story whose end has to be told first. It happened in 1942, the third year of the war. In the Cotswold village of Cold Aston, it was just another day. The grim realities of war had not spoiled this tranquil place. Of course, local people were used to the sight of many aircraft in the skies, but these were mostly training aircraft from the nearby airfields of Little Rissington, Northleach, Windrush, Heyworth, South Cerney and Bibury.
>
> Wednesday the 8th of April 1942 was a typical day for Gerald Hathaway, a local lad of seventeen who worked on the land. Gerald came from a family who could trace their antecedents back to the Cotswold Yeomen and he had inherited a natural affinity with the land. Notwithstanding his love of the land, Gerald also had an interest in

aircraft and learned to recognise every detail of the many types of aircraft he saw daily. He would always take time to look out for an aircraft when he heard its approach.

The weather that Wednesday was typical for April—sunny, with squally rain showers. Gerald had to make many dashes for the shelter of the trees to avoid the rain. In the early afternoon Gerald made yet another dash for those trees and as he stood taking shelter from the squall he heard two aircraft.

It didn't take him long to spot and identify a swift Spitfire fighter flying out of the rain towards him into the direction of the sun. Gerald looked to his right. There in the distance he saw a Wellington Bomber, droning sedately and steadily on its course. It would soon pass in front of him. The Spitfire was also still speeding towards him. Gerald began to feel very disturbed. The aircraft appeared to be flying on a converging course.

Gerald felt sure that both pilots must have seen one another, but they were leaving it a bit late to take necessary avoiding action. Both aircraft came on, straight and steady. Gerald began to relax when he felt it was going to be a near miss. It seemed that the Spitfire was going to pass behind the Wellington by a whisker. But moments later an almighty bang filled the air and Gerald saw the right wing of the Spitfire strike the rear turret of the Wellington.

Everything happened very quickly. Pieces of metal flew off in all directions. A large object became detached from the back of the Wellington and fell at the top of the valley. The Spitfire wing came off and the fighter fell from the sky into the valley of the Broadwater stream.

The Wellington passed from Gerald's sight, falling behind a wood. Not knowing that the Wellington had crashed, Gerald's concern was for the pilot of the Spitfire and he ran for all he was worth to where he had seen it fall. With heart pounding and gasping for breath, he came upon the crashed and broken aircraft. He could see there was nothing he could do. The pilot had remained with the aircraft, having had insufficient height in which to successfully bale out. Gerald did not know it, but the Spitfire pilot, wearing the uniform of an RAF pilot officer, was American Pilot Officer James Robert Lee; an American who had fought and laid down his life for the last thing he saw before his death: the green and pleasant land of England.

The Wellington had staggered out of Gerald's sight behind a small wood. With its control cables severed at the tail, there was little the pilot could do to try and maintain height. It had fallen like a leaf, striking the top of the valley and sliding down the slope to stop short of the stream at the bottom.

Shortly afterwards a small number of villagers gathered on the opposite side of the valley. No-one approached. They stood in silence as officials from the Police, Rescue and the R.A.F. went about their business at the scene.

Because of wartime censorship, no-one was allowed near the aircraft and, of course, no detail of the accident was made public. The local press was not allowed to report on such incidents and none of those present would have known any of the airmen involved. They would have no inkling that there could not have been a more experienced pilot at the controls of the Wellington than Flying Instructor George Leeke. He must have made a desperate attempt to save his stricken aircraft, a fight that George could not have won even with the help of the other veteran in the crew, Stan Pook.

Both George Leeke and Stan Pook were flying instructors who had completed operational tours and were, in theory at least, being "rested" from their operational squadrons. Many pupils had already successfully passed through their hands. For them, and their pupils, Billy Wilson, Frank Good, Fred Fairclough and Eric Coleman, this would be just another day. Hours earlier, at 15 Operational Training Unit at Hartwell, Oxfordshire, George and Stan had briefed their pupils on the cross-country flight they were about to undertake. The pupils had been told that they were required to plot a course and put their theory into practice in the air under the watchful eyes of their experienced instructors. They had been flying that Wednesday in a Vickers Wellington IC, Serial No. L7818. For them, it would have been just another aircraft with no particular significance.'

The names of the airmen from Wellington L7818 are more accurately: Pilot: W/O 580297 George Ernest Leeke RAFVR killed. Obs: Sgt 1210053 Walter Frank Good RAFVR, killed. AG: Flt/Sgt 903242 Stanley William Pook RAFVR, killed. AG: Sgt 1065788 Eric Coleman RAFVR, killed. AG: Sgt 1311317 Frederick Keith Fairclough RAFVR, killed. AG: Sgt 1113163 William Wilson RAFVR, killed. The pilot of the Spitfire was 21-year old James Robert Lee of Comanche, Texas. He was flying a Battle of Britain veteran Spitfire Mk I (R6686) from 57 Operational Training Unit at RAF Hawarden.

Frank's Vickers Wellington Mk IC registration number **L7818** was a famous plane. In **L7818** Sergeant James Allen Ward of the Royal New Zealand Air Force won the Victoria Cross by climbing out onto the wing of his *Wellington* aircraft to put a fire on 7th July 1941. **L7818** was repaired and remained with No. 75 (New Zealand) Squadron but never flew on operations again, passing to 15 OTU on 27th October 1941 where Frank Good served in the plane.

L7818 after returning to RAF Feltham on 7th July 1941.

James Allen Ward RNZAF in cockpit of L7818 left and right wearing his Victoria Cross Ribbon. Ward was later killed in a mission over Hamburg two months after his famous exploit.

Frank Good is buried at Little Rissington in St Peter's churchyard. (Grave reference Plot South Row E Grave 6.) He was killed along with all the crew on 8th April 1942 during the cross-country exercise. Also buried near Frank is the American pilot of the Spitfire which crashed into Frank's Wellington L7818 and was written off (damaged beyond repair.) The location of the crash was at Broadwater, near Cold Ashton, which is nine miles East South East of Bristol, Gloucestershire. The plane had left RAF Harwell and had been due to land there. Frank's burial records indicate his RAF base as Hampstead Norris, Berkshire.

Frank Good's grave. A Commonwealth War Grave- Little Rissington (St Peter) churchyard, Berkshire.

Air Mechanic Alroy Jones: R.N

Date of death: 9th April 1942

Commemorated on Odd Rode War Memorial,

All Saints Church

Alroy Jones' birth was registered in Nantwich in 1923 though his naval record cites his birthday in Crewe as 22nd October 1922, which means he was only 17 at the outbreak of war. Nevertheless, he a qualified as an Air Mechanic (2nd class) when he served on *HMS Hermes* in 1942, service number FAA/FX. 83945.

HMS Hermes was an aircraft carrier, purpose-built for the Royal Navy. The ship began construction during World War I and finished after the war ended. She was the world's first ship to be designed as an aircraft carrier, although the Imperial Japanese Navy's *Hōshō* was the first to be commissioned and launched. The ship's construction was delayed by multiple changes in her design after she was laid down. After she was launched, her shipyard closed, and her construction was suspended. Most of the changes were made to optimise her performance following lessons learned from the construction of newer carriers.

Commissioned in 1924, *Hermes* served briefly with the Atlantic Fleet before spending the bulk of her career assigned to the Mediterranean Fleet and the China Station. In the Mediterranean, she worked with other carriers developing multi-carrier tactics. While showing the flag at the China Station, she helped to suppress pirates in Chinese waters. *Hermes* returned home in 1937 and was placed in reserve before becoming a training ship in 1938.

When World War II began in September 1939, the ship was briefly assigned to the Home Fleet and conducted anti-submarine patrols in the Western Approaches. She was transferred to Dakar, French West Africa, in October to cooperate with the French Navy in hunting down German ships trying to break blockades. Aside from a brief refit, *Hermes* remained there until Vichy France was established at the end of June 1940. Supported by several cruisers, the ship then blockaded Dakar and attempted to sink the French battleship *Richelieu* by exploding depth charges underneath her stern, as well as sending Fairey Swordfish torpedo bombers to attack her at night. While returning from this mission, *Hermes* rammed a British armed merchant cruiser in a storm and required several months of repairs in South Africa, then resumed patrolling for Axis shipping in the South Atlantic and the Indian Ocean.

In February 1941, the ship supported Commonwealth forces in Italian Somaliland during the East African Campaign and did much the same two months later in the Persian Gulf during the Anglo-Iraqi War. After that campaign, *Hermes* spent most of the rest of the year patrolling the Indian Ocean. She refitted in South Africa between November 1941 and February 1942 and then joined the Eastern Fleet at Ceylon.

Hermes was berthed in Trincomalee on 8th April when warning of an approaching Japanese fleet was received and she sailed that day for the Maldives with no aircraft on board. She was spotted on 9th April near Batticaloa by a Japanese scout plane and attacked by several dozen dive-bombers shortly afterwards. With no aircraft cover, the carrier and her escorting destroyer were quickly sunk by the Japanese aircraft. Most of the survivors were rescued by a nearby hospital ship. Three hundred and seven men from *Hermes* were lost in the sinking.

Hermes sinking 9th April 1942

Hermes movements 1941-1942

19th Nov 1941 *HMS Hermes* arrived at Simon's Town, South Africa for a refit.

31st Jan 1942   *HMS Hermes* completed her refit at Simon's Town, South Africa.

14th Feb 1942   *HMS Hermes* arrived at Colombo, Ceylon.

19th Feb 1942   *HMS Hermes* departed Colombo, Ceylon to receive Swordfish torpedo bombers of 814 Naval Air Squadron in the Indian Ocean.

25th Feb 1942   *HMS Hermes* arrived at Trincomalee, Ceylon and disembarked Swordfish torpedo bombers of 814 Naval Air Squadron.

9th Apr 1942   Japanese carrier aircraft attacked the harbour at Trincomalee, Ceylon at 07:00 hours. Two hours later, empty British aircraft carrier *HMS Hermes* and Australian destroyer *HMAS Vampire* were detected ninety miles further south. At 1035 hours, Japanese carrier aircraft attacked and sank *HMS Hermes* (three hundred and seven killed) and *HMAS Vampire* (nine killed); hospital ship *Vita* rescued survivors from both warships. At 12:07 hours, twenty Japanese carrier dive-bombers sank British ship *Athelstane* (all aboard survived) and British corvette *HMS Hollyhock* (Forty eight were killed, seventeen survived) in the Indian Ocean.

Alroy Jones is commemorated on the Lee-on-Solent war memorial Bay 3 panel 5. His body was never found.

Flying Officer Cranmer Kenneth Parkes: RAF
Date of death: 2nd June 1942
Commemorated on Alsager War Memorial

Cranmer Kenneth was the son of Cranmer Tom Parkes and his wife Winifred Maud Parkes, *nee* Blore who were married in Audley in 1915. His father served in the Army Service Corps 1914-1918 and was a founder Member of the B'hoys society of Alsager. His parents moved to Wainfleet, Lincolnshire to manage a brewery. His father was a company director, and formerly a *'Brewer's Assistant'*. He was brought up in the *Alsager Arms Hotel*. In the 1930s the family returned to live in Alsager and lived in Crewe Road.

Cranmer Kenneth was born in Spilsby Lincolnshire in 1920. He was educated at Newcastle-under-Lyme School and in May 1939 the *London Gazette* announced he had been granted a commission as a 2nd Lieutenant in the Royal Artillery. On 15th February 1941 2nd Lieutenant Cranmer Kenneth Parkes, Royal Artillery, was granted a Temporary Commission as Pilot Officer on being employed with the Royal Air Force. In 1941 Parkes joined No 1416 Flight, Service number 45236, and trained to fly Spitfires.

F.J Seward wrote of 140 Squadron,

> *'It reformed on 17th September 1941 at RAF Benson by re-numbering No 1416 Flight and now flew in the photo-reconnaissance role equipped with Spitfires and Blenheims. At first all the sorties were flown by the Spitfires, the target area being northern France. The Blenheims became operational in November, flying night sorties with flares. The Squadron built up its operations until in April 1942 it was flying over one hundred sorties a month, of which only four were on Blenheims Most of the targets were still in northern France but some included the Belgian and Dutch coast.'*

Significant dates of 140 Squadron

In March 1941 it was formed at Hendon to prepare for defence against a German invasion of England.

On 1st May 1941 the first flight from Hendon by 1416 Flight.

From 22nd June 1941 following the German attack on Russia the Squadron changed duties to reconnaissance at low level over the French coast.

On 5th September 1941, the Unit moved to R.A.F Benson.

On 14th September 1941 was the first operational sortie by Spitfire, on an oblique pathway down the coast south east of Cherbourg filming at 3,000ft.

140 Squadron, RAF Benson 1941

On 17th September 1941 the Unit transferred from 1416 Flight to 140 Squadron.

On 15th November 1941 140 Squadron had its first operational sortie by Blenheim aircraft over the Cherbourg Peninsula.

From 1st May 1942 there was a new establishment of twenty-three officers and two hundred and sixty one other ranks. The aircraft increased to six Spitfires Type G, two types F, two types 1A, six Blenheim IV and one Tiger Moth. In May 1942, the Squadron moved to Mount Farm.

Details of C.K. Parkes death

On the 2nd June 1942 Pilot Officer Parkes flying Spitfire AR234 was returning from reconnaissance duty over St Valery, France. His plane ditched near Beachy Head on the south coast of England on his return. His body was not recovered. He is commemorated on the Runnymede Memorial, Englefield Green, Runnymede Borough, Surrey, England. Panel 67.

Runnymede Memorial

Probate was granted on 2nd April 1943. £1,619.15s 6d was left to his father, Tom Parkes of *'Woodcroft'* Alsager.

Sergeant Samuel Cliff Wedgwood: RAF

Date of death: 17th September 1942

Commemorated on Alsager War Memorial

Samuel Cliff Wedgwood was born in 39 Queen's Street, Burslem, Staffordshire, on 10th June 1914 to Samuel and Georgina Wedgwood, *nee* Cliff. His father was a greengrocer. He had two brothers, Leslie, and John James Wedgwood, and a sister, May Wedgwood. His father died in March 1942. In the 1930s the family lived to Chancery Lane, Alsager. In 1939 Samuel Cliff Wedgwood was working as an audit clerk and living at home.

Samuel was a member of the RAFVR Royal Air Force Volunteer Reserve and trained as an Observer, service number 1204039.

The Observer was responsible for managing the detection and weapon systems - while the pilot did the flying. The Observer *'fought the aircraft'* and made the necessary tactical and navigational decisions.

Samuel was Observer in a plane which came down on 17th September 1942. He was a member of 12 OTU Squadron, 91 Group, and part of Bomber Command.

No. 12 Operational Training Unit RAF (12 OTU) was formed in April 1940 as part of No. 1 Group RAF Bomber Command at RAF Benson to train light bomber aircrew. During 1942 it operated night bombing missions. The unit moved to RAF Chipping Warden which was situated six miles North East of Banbury in Oxfordshire. The airfield opened in 1941 as a Bomber Command Operational Training Unit. The airfield closed in 1946.

Sergeant S.C. Wedgwood took off from Chipping Warden on 17th September 1942. The plane left at 20:24 hours. The mission was to bomb Essen in Germany. He flew with a Vickers Wellington (type III, serial BJ650)

Wellington Bomber

Sergeant Wedgwood's plane was hit by enemy fire. The RAF record of the mission is as follows *Date: 16-17 Sept: Unit: 12 OUT: Type: Wellington III; Serial No.:BJ730: Operation: Essen: Take Off: Chipping Warden. Crew: F/L M B Mallet 41939 Killed: Eindhoven General Cemetery: Sgt J H Evans 1048732 Killed: Eindhoven General Cemetery: Sgt S C Wedgwood Killed: Eindhoven General Cemetery: Sgt V F Lincicome 1188483 Killed: Groesbeck: Sgt J L La Bossiere RCAF Killed: Groesbeck*

Description: T/o Chipping Warden. Intercepted by a night-fighter and sent down to crash in a swimming pool at Veldhoven, Holland at 1.15 hours. Their 'eta' at Essen had been scheduled for 2220.

S.C. Wedgwood is buried in Eindhoven (Wiesel) General Cemetery, Noord-Baran Netherlands.

Samuel's probate was granted in 1943 to his mother Georgina Wedgwood - £478.14.4d- *Endon Villa*, Chancery Lane. Samuel's mother, Georgina, died in 1945.

The words on Sergeant S C Wedgwood's grave: 'Love Knows No End.'

Convoy Ordinary Signalman Leslie James Harris: R.N

Date of death: 25th September 1942

Commemorated on Alsager War Memorial

Leslie Harris was born in Brentford, London, in 1921, son of John and Rose Edwina Harris, nee Dorne. His parents were married in Hackney, London in 1911. Hs siblings were; Sidney Harris, born in 1911; Frank Harris, 1913; Robert, 1916; Kathleen, 1918; Donald, 1929. The family moved to Alsager during the Second World War to work at Radway Green munitions factory before returning to live in London. Leslie joined the Royal Navy, service number C/JX 234053, and in 1942 was posted to work on the *S.S New York*. Leslie was a trained signalman for which he would have had to pass tough examinations at Chatham Naval base. Leslie was a Morse code operator and had to be able to read at twenty-two words per minute and transmit at ten words per minute. He was also trained in semaphore and flag signalling. The Royal Navy introduced this role in 1939 particularly with convoys in mind. The life of Signalman was spent almost entirely at sea guiding convoys. Signalmen would not necessarily have been posted to the same ship after a convoy journey.

Leslie James Harris sailed in June 1942 on *SS Marylyn* to New York. It seems he did not enter the port of New York but was in transit. He could have been transferring to the *S.S New York* with his colleague, also a Signalman. The Immigration report (USA) gives Leslie's place of residence as *'Crewe'*, but several Alsager serviceman gave their address as Crewe because the town was bigger and more easily recognised. Page two of the immigration document gives his height as 5'8", blue eyes, fair complexion, and brown hair. His father's address was given as *'147 Crewe Road.'* Another family was occupying this address in 1939.

In September 1942 Leslie was serving on the *SS New York*. This ship was built in June 1924 as an American passenger ship for the Eastern Steamship Lines Inc. The ship was used in overnight journeys between Boston and New York via Cape Cod. In 1942 the ship was transferred to British ownership under the control of the Ministry of War Transport (MoWT). *S.S New York* was hit by U-Boat 96 on 25th September 1942.

The *SS New York* was part of convoy Rb1. This convoy consisted of old coastal ships and it formed a decoy for the troop-carrying convoys crossing the Atlantic. In his book 'The Decoys', Bernard Edwards the author stated that convoys Rb1, Sc107, and SL125 were all used as decoys during Operation Torch; the operation to bring troops from the USA to Britain after September 1942.

He writes, *'the sacrifice these convoys made in ships and men was appalling'*. Edwards states that *SS New York* had a *'shallow draught and high unprotected sides, which made it unsuitable for ocean going travel.'*

Eight ships were chosen to cross the Atlantic in the *'decoy'* convoy. Convoy RB1, code Operation Maniac, sailed from St Johns, Newfoundland on 21st September 1942. The convoy formed up in four columns. The convoy was protected by two destroyers *HMS Vanoc*, and *HMS Veteran*. From a distance, the convoy looked like troop-carrying ships and the German Commander Admiral Donitz ordered U-Boats to target the convoy. On the 23rd September, the warning of U-Boats was communicated to *HMS Vanoc* by the United States Navy. A total of seventeen U-boats were in contact with the convoy. The British destroyers forced several of the U-boats away. By the 25th September convoy RB1 was steaming in single file but when U-boats attacked it forced the convoy to scatter.

The *S.S New York*

At 23:57 hours on 25th September 1942, U-96 (commanded by Jurgen Hellriegel) fired a spread of two G7e torpedoes at the convoy RB-1 about six hundred and seventy miles west of Achill Head and reported two hits on a passenger ship of the '*Reina del Pacifico*' type. In fact, it was *the S.S New York* which had been hit. The Master of the torpedoed ship was Chilion Mayers. The *SS New York* was damaged by two torpedoes and caught fire but was not sunk by the U-Boat. The Vice Commodore of the convoy was aboard the *New York* at the time. It was immediately abandoned by the master, fifty-four crew members, three convoy signalmen and ten gunners after being torpedoed on the port side.

HMS Veteran (D 72) (commanded by Lt. Cmdr. T.H. Gardwood, RN) and *HMS Vanoc* (H 33) commanded by Cmdr. C.F.H. Churchill, RN) began to rescue survivors, but the latter ship soon re-joined the convoy after just picking up the carpenter and one gunner from a raft. These survivors were later landed at Londonderry, Ireland, on 27th September. About one hour after she was torpedoed, the *New York* was spotted by U-91 which did not realize that she had been abandoned. It fired three G7e torpedoes at 01:22 hours on 26th September at the empty ship but the torpedoes missed her. However, the ship eventually sunk after being hit by one G7a torpedo fired by U-91 at 01:35 hours. Twenty-eight survivors, including the master, had been picked up by *HMS Veteran* from the *S.S New York* and the *HMS Boston*, which had also been hit. The *Veteran* was sunk later that day with all hands by U-Boat U-404, commanded by von Bülow.

There were sixty-eight crew on the *S.S New York* and thirty-eight were killed including Leslie James Harris. Leslie's death was officially reported as *'missing at sea'*.

Bernard Edwards writes: *'Convoy RB1 is an enigma which to this day remains unsolved. The reason given for bringing these eight ageing flat-bottomed lake steamers across the ocean crawling with U-boats in the approach to winter was that they were needed for accommodation ships for the projected invasion of France.'* The truth is that D Day was yet two years away. With the other two convoys Edwards argues were used as *'decoy'* convoys 792 men were killed by U-boat attacks. *'All these twelve ships were sitting ducks for U-boats.'*

Leslie is commemorated at Chatham Naval Memorial, Kent. 59.1

The Commonwealth War Grave record states:

HARRIS, LESLIE JAMES

Rank: Convoy Ordinary Signalman   Service No:C/JX 234053

Date of Death:25/09/1942

Age:21   Regiment/Service: Royal Navy S.S. New York

Son of John and Rose Edwina Harris, of Alsager, Cheshire.

The Chatham Memorial to sailors lost at sea.

Leading Aircraftsman Bertram Rawlinson:

Royal Air Force Volunteer Reserve

Date of death: 27th September 1942

A Second World War serviceman not on Alsager, Church Lawton or Barthomley War Memorials but who had strong family connections with Alsager.

Born in 1920 in Talke, Staffordshire, Bertram was the son of Joseph and Laura Rawlinson. Joseph was a coal hewer of 107 Coalpit Hill Talke, Staffordshire.

Before he enlisted in the RAFVR Bertram was employed with the North Staffs Cooperative Dairy. He was a Methodist and a member of the Prosperous Hancock Memorial Church Choir, Kidsgrove. Other members of the Rawlinson family lived in Talke Road, Alsager and were associated with the mining industry.

Bert enlisted as a Leading Aircraftsman, RAFVR service number 955199. He married Winifred Smith of *Sunnyside*, Alsager, the daughter of Enoch Smith, a Colliery Ropeman, in September 1941. Winifred was born on 12th July 1920. Winifred was a garment machinist. Bert and Winifred lived after their marriage at the in-laws' house in *Sunnyside*, Alsager.

Bert's service was based at RAF West Kirby, Cheshire. in 1942. At this base, the men were given their initial training on their first entry into RAF. This included learning RAF parade ground drill with rifles, intensive physical fitness training, and training in ground combat and defence. They were supervised by Non-Commissioned Officers of the RAF Regiment. Men undergoing their basic training at West Kirby were accommodated in wooden barrack huts, each one housing about twenty men. Because West Kirby was a basic training camp with no airfield there, discipline was very much stricter than in any normal RAF operational or trade training camp. Recruits normally spent a period of eight weeks on their training at West Kirby before being posted on to their *'trade training'* camp elsewhere in the United Kingdom.

Bert's *'sudden death and funeral'* was reported in the *Staffordshire Weekly Sentinel* in October 1942. The squadron sent a floral tribute and were represented at the funeral along with the family and former colleagues of the Cooperative Dairy. His death was registered in Wirral. According to RAF records Bertram died *'on active service'*.

Bert died in the RAF Station Hospital on 27th September 1942 of meningitis.

West Kirby Isolation hospital

Bertram Rawlinson's grave, a Commonwealth War Grave in St Martin's Churchyard Talke

West of church. Row 12. Grave 4

Bertram is not commemorated on a designated war memorial.

The wording on the grave as submitted to the Commonwealth War Graves Commission. 'Till we meet again.'

Alsager in 1943

Timeline of the war (history)

February saw German surrender at Stalingrad: the first major defeat of Hitler's armies. Battle continued to rage in the Atlantic, and one four-day period in March saw twenty-seven merchant vessels sunk by German U-boats.

A combination of long-range aircraft and the codebreakers at Bletchley, however, were inflicting enormous losses on the U-boats. Towards the end of May Admiral Dönitz withdrew the German fleet from the contended areas - the Battle of the Atlantic was effectively over.

In mid-May German and Italian forces in North Africa surrendered to the Allies, who used Tunisia as a springboard to invade Sicily in July. By the end of the month Mussolini had been deposed, and in September the Italians surrendered to the Allies, prompting a German invasion into northern Italy.

Mussolini was audaciously rescued by a German task force, led by Otto Skorzeny, and established a fascist republic in the north. German troops also engaged the Allies in the south - the fight through Italy was to prove slow and costly.

In the Pacific, US forces overcame the Japanese at Guadalcanal, and British and Indian troops began their guerrilla campaign in Burma. American progress continued in the Aleutian Islands, New Guinea and the Solomon Islands.

As the Russian advance on the Eastern Front gathered pace, recapturing Kharkov and Kiev from Germany, Allied bombers began to attack German cities in enormous daylight air raids. The opening of the Second Front in Europe, long discussed and always postponed, was being prepared for the following year.

In Alsager

The lighting restrictions were being tightly enforced in Alsager. In January 1943, Teresa Fawcett, aged 25, of Bankside Court, was convicted at Sandbach Sessions, for displaying a light from her house during the black-out. The Wardens were sometimes overzealous in their work.

Penalties for offences committed by juveniles were harsh in the Second World War. In March 1943, an Alsager boy aged thirteen broke into a gas meter with a hammer and chisel at his own home and with the proceeds went to Hanley. He was already on probation. There was a discussion whether the boy should be taken into a foster home, but the authorities opposed this on the grounds he needed greater supervision. The boy's father pleaded the boy should be given another chance, but the Sandbach Children's Court decided his son should be sent to a Home Office School. The father was reminded he could be asked to pay the £5 surety he had promised when his son was first put on probation. The boy was to be sent to a Remand Home when a suitable vacancy arose.

A Nativity Play called *The Three Roses* was performed at The Linley Mission raising £4 for the Red Cross Aid to Russia fund. It starred Trevor Bowen and Mrs Lowndes. (Mrs Lowndes taught at Alsager School and was still there in the early 1960s.) Fundraising events took place virtually every month. They were patriotic and brought the community together.

On 6th February 1943, the *Sentinel* reported a successful British Legion concert for branch funds. It was held at St Mary's Schoolroom (church hall) with a large audience. The highlight of the show was the *'Laughter Revue Company'*, produced by Dennis Wilshaw and compered by Mr Edward Goff. Mr Frank Rigby organized the lighting. Wilshaw's own son, Dennis James Wilshaw (11 March 1926 – 10 May 2004) later became an English international footballer. A forward, he scored one hundred and seventy-three goals in three hundred and eighty appearances in the Football League. Members of the Revue Company were Billy McMahon, (a Great War Alsager veteran who worked at Hancock's store), Dennis and Dorothy Wilshaw, Marjorie Elsby, and Harold Crompton. The show also included instrumental items, monologues, sketches, and cameos. In the same month, a dance was held at St Mary's by the Heathside Dance Band, on behalf of the Heathside Fire Brigade Widows and Orphans Fund.

In April Mrs Dorothy Harpur (nee Goss) was elected the first woman Chairman of Alsager Urban District Council. This is a significant date in Alsager history. The Council had come a long way since its all-male composition in the 1920s.

In May 1943 Mr Wilfred John Braddock (1894-1960) was elected as a Labour member of Alsager U.D.C. He was a schoolteacher and lived in Talke Road. He came from a family deeply involved in politics. His brother John was leader of Liverpool City Council. His sister in law Elizabeth Margaret 'Bessie' Braddock, *nee* Bamber, was MP for Liverpool Exchange 1945-70. In 1946 Winston Churchill encountered Bessie Braddock, a plump Labour MP and Tory-hater, who told him: *"Winston, you are drunk." "Madam,"* he replied, *"you are ugly, but I will be sober in the morning and you will still be ugly."* The story was confirmed by Churchill's bodyguard Ron Golding, who heard his boss say it.

Picture: Bessie and Jack Braddock. Wilfred was a witness at John and Bessie's wedding in 1922 in Liverpool.

Dr Harpur gave his annual Health Report at the end of the year for 1943. There were thirty-four boys and thirty-two girls born and thirty-nine deaths in the town. There was one Civil Defence ambulance in the town which could be used for emergencies with the permission of the Medical Officer or an officer of the A.R.P.; Ambulances could also be obtained from neighbouring local authorities. The report reiterated there was no maternity hospital facility in the area. A school clinic and treatment centre was available at the 'Lawton Road building estate' (Radway estate) and an Infant Welfare Clinic was held every two weeks in Alsager and was well attended. There was a diminution in water supply in Alsager and new supplies were needed but the organic purity of the existing supply was found to be satisfactory. Two hundred and seventy-six sanitary inspections took place in Alsager during the year.

There were nineteen cases of Scarlet Fever in Alsager in 1943, five of diphtheria, five of dysentery, seven of tuberculosis, one of pyrexia, and one of *'Malta Fever'*. One hundred and seventy-five children were immunised in 1943 and no child had contracted diphtheria as a result. There had been four deaths from cancer in 1943, not an abnormal figure.

A wedding was held in Alsager in June 1943 at Wesley Place between Leading Aircraftsman Ernest Norman Griffiths and Winifred Evans, a member of the Women's Land Army which was recorded in the *Sentinel*.

This is one of the few references where we have a member of the Land Army coming from Alsager. There were Land Army girls working at Home Farm and Alsager Hall Farm. Occasionally, there were ceremonies at Reaseheath Agricultural College to award badges to the Women's Land Army personnel for having completed two years' service.

Such was the shortage of agricultural workers that Prisoners of War were used on local farms. Before his farm was annexed by the government Mr Bennion of *Heath Farm* employed an Italian and a German POW. Some POWs came from the POW camp at Sandbach Heath. Farmers were not encouraged to pay the POWs except to give them food. John Walker of *Higher Smallwood Farm* did pay POWs for working for him and even supplied a flat for a German POW to live in who had come from the POW camp at *Crewe Hall*. The authorities tolerated this arrangement. Farmers were given £1 for every acre ploughed, £2 to grow corn and £3 for an acre of potatoes. These amounts increased up to £10 as the war went on. Schoolchildren were also used to pick the potato harvest in both Alsager and Rode Heath. Children, mainly boys, were paid 4/- a day and women 6/- a day. John Walker had up to six horses working on his land. (Westwood, 2009) Throughout the war a double summer time operated to allow for work to go on late into the evening.

'Wings for Victory Week'

The major event of June 1943 was *'Wings for Victory Week'*, the campaign to raise money for the building of planes for the war effort. It was hoped to raise £50,000 towards the campaign in Alsager and district with the aim of purchasing one Wellington bomber and six Spitfires for the RAF. Leading the campaign were Mrs Dorothy Harpur, Chairman of the Council, and Sir Francis Joseph. Promises of support in local parishes were as follows: Scholar Green £3,000, Rode Heath £2,500 and Mow Cop £1,500. The fund raising was launched by a march-past of servicemen through Alsager with the salute taken by Air Commodore C.A Stevens M.C. RAF. The programme of events in *Wings Week* included: a knock out cricket match-Monday; exhibition in St Mary's Schoolroom-Tuesday; a cinema show in St Mary's Schoolroom on Wednesday evening; a concert in the same venue on Thursday evening. On Friday there was a fundraising dance. There was also a baseball game on the cricket pitch on the Saturday evening played by a black American team from Barthomley. On Whit Monday, a cricket match followed by a fun fair and dancing was held. In July, the *Sentinel* reported the result of *Wings Week* in Alsager. An immense £93,259 was raised from the following sources: National Savings Certificates £27,865. 10s; Post Office Trustee Savings Bank £4,689. 10s; Defence Bonds £24,305.10; gifts £752. 14.3d of which money came from the Radway Spitfire Fund and from the *Heathside Hostel*. Other parishes contributed significantly and above target: Rode Heath (over £5,000); Scholar Green, £3.000; Lawton, target £1,000 -achieved £6,000; Mow Cop, £3,000. The schools' drive was successful: Alsager C of E Juniors (£1,646) Alsager C of E infants (£1,081); Odd Rode C of E (£415); Lawton Park (£120); Lawton Gate (£1,570); Odd Rode Scholar Green C. of E. (£615).

On 29th July 1943 Labour Minister Ernest Bevin announced that women from nineteen to fifty would be called up for work in plane and munitions plants. Men eligible for military service could choose to work in the coal mines. The shortage of miners was solved from December 1943 by conscripts being chosen by ballot to be '*Bevin Boys*' to work in the mines.

In August 1943, after a silence of three and a half years, the bells were rung at Christ Church by the then Chester Guild of Bell Ringers with Rev. J.H.B. Andrews, Chaplain RNVR present.

In September 1943, there was a ceremony in Alsager to celebrate *Wings Week*. A ceremony was held at St Mary's Schoolroom where a plaque was presented by Wing Commander Read AFC, and certificates were presented to neighbouring parishes and schools. Sir Francis Joseph said there had been a change in the battle against the Nazis with the opening of the Sicilian campaign, the bombing of Germany. There was '*a clamour*', he said, to open a second front but Russia needed assistance. The Army had lost considerable amounts of equipment after the fall of France and Dunkirk. We had stood alone and needed to re-equip with planes, ships, and guns. The final figure for *Wings for Victory Week* in Alsager and district was £95,259. 14s. 0d. Certificates were also presented to local organisations who had assisted in raising the money.

Despite rationing Alsager celebrated its annual vegetable and flower show in September 1943 with a great exhibition of produce. It was organised on behalf of Red Cross funds and by the Radway Green Sports and Social Association at the Parsonage Field. It was held in conjunction with the Alsager Allotment Association. Other attractions included sports for children and a football match between Radway Green and a team called Green Meadow which resulted in a victory for Radway by twelve goals to one. There were three hundred and fifty entries to the show in fifty classes. Interest was high in the bottled fruit section which was encouraged to conserve and preserve food during rationing. There was an exhibition of how to bottle fruit from Miss B. Clegg from the Ministry of

Agriculture. One of the judges was the head gardener of *Rode Hall,* Mr G. Simpson, and the head gardener at *Boden Hall,* Mr T. Booth. The exhibits were shown in a large marquee and the event attracted large numbers of visitors. The show was important for several reasons: to raise the profile of increasing food production, increasing community participation, and to stimulate the activities of the Radway Sports and Social Association which held their own categories of competition. Sales of fruit increased funding for the Red Cross.

In October 1943 a Rode Heath man, Jim Fox, was taken as a prisoner of war when the Germans invaded the Greek island of Kos. Jim was in the RAF. He had avoided capture and with other servicemen lived rough in Kos. They caught a goat but were scared to light a fire to cook it in case they were seen. With them were high ranking officers who were rescued but who left Fox and his squaddies behind. After the war, the story was given to the *Sunday Pictorial* but never printed to protect the officers who had put themselves before their men. (Westwood, 2009) Fox was later taken prisoner but survived and worked as a heating engineer in Wheelock.

A less happy episode: In November 1943 two Alsager women were convicted of shoplifting in Hanley. Alice Morris of Lawton Road, and Ivy Kesteven, both thirty-eight, stole three jumpers, a baby suit and a boy's suit from Marks & Spencer's, and were fined £4 and £6 respectively. The goods were worth £1. 13s 4d. The store detective said one of the defendants made one genuine purchase while the other was stealing goods. There was an outstanding charge against the women for stealing gloves at a value of 16s from another store on the same day. The defendants pleaded guilty to the offences. It was stated both women had children and the fines would have been heavier but for this. *'There was no doubt that they went out with the deliberate intent on stealing'*, said the Chairman of the Court.

In November 1943 Alsager Urban District Council, realising that with an increased population, improvements were needed, put forward possible public works to the town. Mrs Harpur, Lady Chairman, said funds were now available to provide the following amenities: a play area for children, purchase of some land around the Mere, provision of bus shelters, street improvements, and provision of public seats. Councillor Holland said the public should have *'reasonable access'* to the Mere. A committee was set up to consider these improvements.

In the same month Mrs Harpur requested Cheshire Police provide one or more policewomen for Alsager. This was presumably because of the large number of single women living in the Alsager hostels who were thought young and vulnerable and needed a female police officer to protect them. Several months later, when nothing had been done to fulfil this request, the council made new representations to the Home Office. One Alsager chauvinist, and possibly racist, councillor was overheard asking sarcastically whether police replacement was for a *'black lady constable'*.

Armistice Day took place with the traditionally held afternoon commemoration at the Alsager War Memorial and afterwards in a service in St Mary's Church. The Home Guard were in attendance. Rev. Potts oversaw the service. It was to be one of his last services as he died early in 1944.

Photo: *Alsager Home Guard on parade*

Service personnel in the news in 1943

Commander William Hazlett Sayers RN, DSC. *The highest ranked Alsager born man who served in World War II.*

William Hazlett Sayers was born on 2nd February 1909 in Alsager. He was the son of Dr Matthew Sayers, Alsager G.P and Marion Sayers, *nee* Dewar. He had four siblings: Bill, John, Enid, and Nora. John died in 1929. Malcolm attended Stamford School, Lincolnshire.

He joined the Royal Navy and from 1931 to 1932 studied Engineering in Keyham Devon Naval College. He was commissioned as Sub-Lieutenant in 1932 and joined *HMS Shropshire* in 1933.

In 1936, he transferred to *HMS Pembroke*, Chatham, a land based barracks, training new-entry stokers, then in 1937 on *HMS Hostile*.

With the declaration of war, he served on *HMS Legion* which remained in repairs until 1941. Sayers married Maud Mary Smith in Meavy, Devon on 26th January 1940. He was made Lieutenant Commander (Navy List) 1st January 1941 and joined *HMS Legion* which had just finished repairs in Greenock. She was involved in convoy duties and she joined the 14th Escort Group. On 13th April, she rescued survivors from the armed merchant cruiser *Rajputana* which had been torpedoed in the North-Western Approaches by the German submarine U-108. *Legion* rescued 177 men, although another 40 went down with *Rajputana*. The rest of April was spent escorting convoys. In May she joined ships of the Home Fleet, searching for the German battleship *Bismarck*; but she had to refuel at Iceland, and so was not present at the sinking of the German battleship. *Legion* then returned to convoy escort duties. On 22nd June *Legion* and her sister *Lance*, escorted the aircraft carrier *Furious* to Gibraltar, on an operation to deliver aircraft to Malta. A few days later, (on 26th June), she and other destroyers screened the aircraft carrier *Ark Royal*, the battlecruiser *Renown* and the cruiser *Hermione* as they delivered aircraft from Gibraltar to Malta. This operation was repeated later in the month with *Furious*. In July *Legion* returned to Greenock to resume escort duties through the Western Approaches. On 20th August, she was deployed to reinforce the escort of Convoy OG-71 which was on passage to the UK and had come under attack from the U-boats U-559, U-201 and U-564. The escorts were eventually successful in driving off the attackers; the convoy arrived at Liverpool on 25th August.

In September, the ship and her flotilla returned to Gibraltar and resumed escorting capital ships supplying aircraft to Malta. She provided cover on 24th September for the convoys of Operation Halberd. During the operation, the ships came under heavy air attack but continued onward. On her return to Gibraltar after Halberd, *Legion* and *Gurkha* attacked and sank the Italian submarine *Adua* with depth charges. October was spent escorting convoys to Malta. She made an unsuccessful attack on U-205 on 23rd October and then rescued survivors from *Cossack* which had been torpedoed by U-563 west of Cape Spartel. She then rescued sailors from the stricken *Ark Royal*, torpedoed on 13th November, and tried to tow the aircraft carrier for repairs but it sank.

Legion moves alongside the Ark Royal to take off survivors

In 1942 *Legion* was involved in duties in the Mediterranean but on 23rd March she was bombed while in Malta and put out of action, eventually being scrapped. It is unclear what happened to Sayers but when he was in territory controlled by the Vichy French he was arrested and placed in a prison of war camp between May and December 1942 in North Africa. While he was a prisoner of war he was awarded the Distinguished Service Cross on 2nd October 1942 for *'bravery, endurance, and sustained devotion to duty at Malta and at sea during and after the passage of an important a convoy.'*

The London Gazette announcing the award of the DSC to Malcolm Sayers.

The DSC is awarded for meritorious or distinguished service before the enemy 'by men of His Majesty's Fleet.' N.B Personnel must have been Mentioned in Despatches before recommendation for the award.

On his release as a Prisoner of War, Sayers came back to Alsager on leave and then was appointed to serve on *HMS Indefatigable* in 1944 where the carrier was involved in attacks on the German ship *Tirpitz* and the protection of Russian convoys. On 5th January 1945 Sayers was promoted to Commander which was announced in the *London Gazette,* and assumed command of *HMS Ceylon.*

In November 1944, she had joined the British Pacific Fleet and sailed from Trincomalee on 16th January 1945, taking part in a raid on Pankalan Bradan en-route. By May 1945, however, she was back in the Indian Ocean, shelling the Nicobar Islands, and remained in that theatre until the end of the war. Sayers was mentioned in despatches again in June 1945. In October 1945 *Ceylon* returned to England for refit and lay-up. After the war Sayers remained in the navy and was appointed Commander of *HMS Sussex* in May 1947, and *HMS Resource* in 1949. Between 1952 and 1957 he worked at the Admiralty in Bath and at Chatham before retiring from the navy. He later worked for Perkins Diesel Ltd in Peterborough.

Malcolm, with his sisters, Enid, and Nora, and his brother Bill. Photograph 1974. Bill lived in Station Road Alsager and was a Trooper in the cavalry.

(photo family archive)

William Hazlitt Sayers died on 28th March 1986 in Manaton, Devon.

Private Roy Palfreyman: 4th Armoured Division Legion

Roy was born on 19th February 1920 in *Birch House*, 194 Crewe Road, Alsager, to Percy John and Olive Palfreyman (nee Long.) Roy explained in an interview that he came from a comfortably-off family and before the Second World War his family could employ two servants. During his youth, he became friends with Craig Wheaton-Smith of *Milton House*. Following in the family tradition he attended Wellingborough School, Northamptonshire before returning to live in Alsager. He entered the firm of Messrs Lawton's of Crewe, a furniture retailer in Mill Street where he worked until he was called up in April 1940. (Palfreyman) He wanted to join the Royal Army Medical Corps or the Transport Corps but was astonished to find he was enlisted to join the Tank Regiment

Following enlistment, he undertook basic training at Bovington, Dorset. In 1937 the Central Schools had become the Armoured Fighting Vehicles School, with driving and maintenance training at Bovington and gunnery at Lulworth. The Tank Corps was based at Bovington. Roy applied for a commission and was interviewed but his application was put on hold while he finished his basic training. In November 1940, he was assigned to the 2nd Armoured Division H.Q. based in Cambridgeshire. Roy decided not to pursue the commission.

In early 1941, the 2nd Armoured Division was sent to the Western Desert in North Africa to reinforce troops under General Archibald Wavell.

Roy Palfreyman landed at Port Said, Egypt, on Christmas Day 1940 having undertaken a long journey round the Cape of Good Hope, South Africa. Once in North Africa Roy's 2nd Armoured Division relieved the 4th Army Division (The Desert Rats).

He spent his 21st birthday in a bar in Alexandria. In January 1941, the British force named *'Western Desert Force'* under command of General Richard O'Connor (after taking Tobruk on 22nd January), executed a daring outflanking movement and took Mechili from Italian forces on 27th January.

On 7th April 1941, the Italian armoured division, Ariete, captured the British garrison at Mechili as a part of German Lieutenant-General Erwin Rommel's first offensive through Cyrenaica, the eastern coastal region of Libya, with the goal of encircling the British forces.

Roy describes what he saw of the event:

'I was driving an armoured car having to take a Liaison Officer to Corps H.Q When I returned to base all the British vehicles were spread out. (We usually spread vehicles out in the daytime to prevent attack.) A British officer stopped me and said there were Germans in the British compound and the British had been captured.'

Roy stopped his vehicle and under cover watched what was happening. He saw Michael Gambier-Parry, General Officer Commanding 2nd Armoured Division, come out with a white flag and surrender. The enemy had attacked under cover of a dust storm on 8th April and the British were captured.

Roy carefully put his armoured car into reverse trying not to create too much dust and he backed away. He was aware he might be fired upon, but he drove away unscathed and later saw a column of British vehicles and joined them. They were making their way to Derna but were informed by radio to instead head for Tobruk as Derna was under attack.

By nightfall on 7th April, the 9th Australian Division (less the 24th Australian Infantry Brigade) with the 2nd Support Group had blocked the Via Balbia at Acroma, about fifteen miles west of Tobruk, where the 18th and 24th Australian Infantry brigades were preparing the defences. A small force held El Adem, south of Tobruk, to observe the approaches from the south and south-west and at Mechili.

Roy says, *'On the way to Tobruk I stopped my armoured car and it would not restart so a sergeant with us fired bullets into the petrol tank to blow it up. Unfortunately, I had not retrieved my kit bag from my vehicle! I climbed into a lorry and had a free ride to Tobruk, but the Australian wouldn't let us in at first thinking we were Germans. Later we managed to get into Tobruk. Three days later I was able to take a boat to Alexandria.'*

On 10th May after the disaster of the surrender of the 2nd Armoured Division the Division was disbanded and units reformed.

Roy Palfreyman joined the 4th Armoured Division, *The Black Rats*, and was recruited by Major Craycroft as his personal driver and batman. Roy was happy to work as the Major's driver but less happy to be his batman. *'I had two servants at home before the war Sir!'* he explained, but Craycroft said there would be little cleaning duties involved. Later that year Craycroft was called back to England and Roy went back to driving a lorry. His function was to drive the fifteen miles to the front line taking supplies to the 5th and 3rd Tank Regiment.

One strange coincidence: He once picked a biscuit wrapper up off the sand and to his surprise it read, *'Hancock's Alsager Gingerbread'.* Someone from his home town must have been serving close to him.

After the Allies' victory at El Alamein and Tunis in North Africa, Roy joined the Italian campaign landing in Sicily, then moving up the Adriatic coast within Italy where he took part in the battle of Monte Casino before being given home leave in September 1943.

Montgomery recalled his 8th Army back from Italy and Roy returned to England. He enjoyed two weeks' leave. He had not seen his family for three years. He found Alsager very different, much busier. His mother no longer had servants and his father was in the Home Guard. His mother was a Transport Officer for the ARP.

> **Two Alsager men** are home on leave this week after serving in the Middle East. They are Roy Palfreyman, "Dulverton," Station-rd., and Ernest Wood, son of Mr. and Mrs. George Wood, Cross-street, who has been serving overseas for about three years. Also on leave are Joan Ebsworth, ATS, 23, Orchard-court, and Frank Kerry, of Sandbach-road.

Alsager Times 1943

Returning to his unit he moved to Worthing and later to Portsmouth. They were secretly shown plans of the invasion in Normandy, *'Operation Overlord'*, and underwent training in the spring of 1944. Roy's role in transport was straightforward with no special training.

He landed on *'Gold Beach'*, in Normandy on 8th June 1944 at 7.30 p.m. (D Day plus 2) as part of the 7th Armoured Division just after the beach head had been secured. He landed on a small landing craft where Military Police were directing operations. He saw a great deal of debris, but bodies had been removed from the beach.

'The German aircraft were dropping scatter bombs onto the beach, so we had to lie flat on the sand. If we stood up they went off like grenades.' Roy moved inland driving his lorry acting in a supply capacity.

Landings of supplies on Gold Beach 7th 8th June 1944. http://www.dday-overlord.com

'We were held up at Caen, the Germans put up severe resistance there, before we eventually managed to get into the town. It was a strategic place to capture.' The battle did not go as planned for the Allies, instead dragging on for two months, because German forces devoted most of their reserves to holding Caen, particularly their armoured divisions.

Roy's unit was sent south to Falaise. The road to Falaise is an everlasting memory to Roy. It was covered in burnt out vehicles and livestock; buildings were on fire; and folk had been shot by the retreating Germans. The stench was something Roy would never forget. The aim was to surround and trap the German 7th Army. By late summer 1944, the bulk of two German armies had become surrounded by the Allies near the town of Falaise. The Mont Ormel ridge, with its commanding view of the area, sat astride the Germans' only escape route. On August 20th, the Falaise Gap was finally closed. No one is quite sure how many Germans escaped from the Gap. However, a great deal of equipment was left behind; one German officer who escaped said: *'Even the number of rescued machine-guns was insignificant.'* The victory resulted in the destruction of most of German Army Group B west of the River Seine, which opened the way to Paris and the German border for the Allied armies. Roy recalls: *'We gradually followed the army northwards through Holland and Belgium. I was nearly killed in Arnhem in a cinema. There was an air raid and the ceiling cracked above us. When we went outside the front entrance just collapsed. We entered Germany and I was north of Hamburg on V.E Day. Unfortunately, I was on guard duty that night and a bumptious officer told me to make sure all lights were extinguished despite me saying, "the war's over Sir!" All the officers were having a whale of a time and displaying light from their building. I told them to honour the blackout but was told to forget it.'*

Roy says: *'After VE Day I managed to get a job as a groom for Brigadier Mike Carver's horses in Germany. I could ride and enjoyed looking after horses. Years later I saw Mike Carver on television and wrote to him with congratulations on being appointed as Field Marshall. He wrote back by return of post and thanked me for those "great days in Germany".'*

Roy being presented with his Medal from the French Consul

Roy was not finally demobbed until a year after D Day. He returned to Alsager to work in the family firm.

*Roy Palfreyman shortly after his presentation of the **Légion d'Honneur** in 2017.*

Sergeant Gordon Hedley Blaney: Royal Engineers 1918-2001

In 1943 Gordon Blaney was posted to North Africa as part of a Royal Engineers' team to plan for the El Alemein and Desert Campaign. (Mem)

When the Second World War started Gordon was 20, and he was medically examined on 19th June 1939 in Hanley and given a grade 1 for his health. The record also states that he was 5' 9" with brown hair and hazel eyes. He joined the Duke of Cornwall Light Infantry on the 15th September 1939. His basic training was spent on Bodmin Moor in Cornwall. His number in the army was 5439155.

On basic training, the regime was tough. For example, after a hard route march, the whole regiment was sent out on a cross-country run. Although he was exhausted, he latched on to a good runner and came home in the top twenty.

Gordon was then posted to Nottingham before being transferred to the Royal Engineers on 7th March 1940. He was issued with rifle number 143381. His army pay was one shilling a day. He arrived in Egypt on 8th September 1940 after a long journey including a stop-off in Cape Town, South Africa. To avoid enemy submarines at one stage the ship nearly reached the coast of South America.

In Cairo, he was responsible for organising troop and vehicle movements for the Royal Engineers under the command of Colonel Carlson at GHQ in the Transportation and Movement Control Branch of the Royal Engineers. He organised supplies and transport and coordinated movements for the Desert Rats. With the North Africa campaign won he was part of the liberation of Italy force at Headquarters Movements Sub

Area, Naples. Gordon was part of a special Royal Engineers force in Albania in 1944. He was demobbed in 1946 after serving seven years. After the war, he worked for British Railways and lived in Station Road, Alsager until his death in 2001.

Operations Room Cairo 1943

Gordon Blaney right.

Station Road, Alsager, on Remembrance Day 1998.

Deaths of Service Men and Women in 1943

Private Freda Statham :ATS
Date of death: 28th January 1943
Commemorated on Odd Rode War Memorial, All Saints Church

Freda was born in 1922 (birth registered October to December 1922) the daughter of Horace Frederic, and Margaret Maud Statham (*nee* Beresford), of Scholar Green. They married in April 1912 at Odd Rode Parish Church. Horace was a schoolteacher from Cinder Hill, Scholar Green and served in the Great War in France as a Gunner in the Royal Garrison Artillery. Freda had two sisters, Hilda, born 1913, and Marjorie, born 1914.

Freda joined the ATS (Auxiliary Territorial Service), service number W/230060. It is thought Freda was killed in an accident on 28th January 1943 in Cheshire. She is buried in Odd Rode churchyard, grave 977, a designated Commonwealth War Grave.

Freda's grave, Odd Rode churchyard

 **Captain Richard John Victor Goss: Grenadier Guards.**

Date of death: 17th March 1943

A serviceman not on a local war memorial but with strong local connections.

Richard Goss had a strong Alsager connection. He was killed in action 17th March 1943 near Medenine, Tunisia. His parents were Clarence Richard 'Dick' Goss and Martha Letiere Goss of Hartley Wintney Hampshire. He was the grandson of Adolphus Goss of Alsager. He lost two uncles, Raymond and Hubert Goss, who are named on the Alsager War Memorial, both being killed the Great War. His father, who was also in the Grenadier Guards, always kept up his close associations with Alsager despite being based in London with his regiment. (In the Second World War, Richard 'Dick' Goss became 'Air Raids Precautions Officer for Devon,' in charge of eighteen offices. He was awarded the MBE for his work. Richard Goss is buried in Christ Church graveyard, Alsager.) Richard John Victor Goss, his son, was born in Grimsby on 26th March 1918.

Richard John Victor Goss, sitting front (aged four) at his aunt Dolly's wedding in Alsager in 1922. His father Clarence 'Dick' Goss, Grenadier Guards, was born in Alsager and two of his brothers were killed in the Great War.

R.J.V Goss was gazetted 2nd Lieutenant into the Grenadier Guards on 12th August 1938 from the Cambridge University OTC, service number 76754.

He later served in the 6th Motor Battalion, Grenadier Guards, in North Africa with the 8th Army. The War Diary Record of the Grenadier Guards 6th Motor Battalion gives details of the action in which Richard Goss was killed on 17th March 1943.

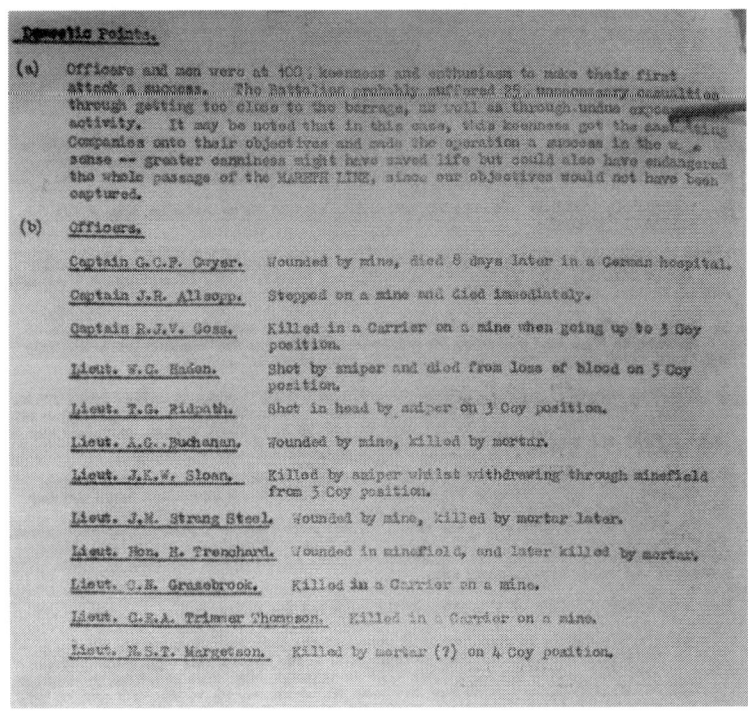

Details of how Goss was killed in the war diary.

The War Diary later reported the mistakes made at the battle, particularly the weakness of using a motor battalion for an infantry assault. The Motor Brigade was considered not to have the armour required for an assault.

Memorial to Richard Goss and his father, Clarence Goss in the Guard's Chapel in London

NORTH WALL GUARDS CHAPEL Birdcage Walk Westminster
IN HONOURED MEMORY OF/ CAPTAIN C. RICHARD GOSS, M.B.E./ GRENADIER GUARDS 1918 - 1930/ BORN 19 JULY 1889 DIED 14 SEPTEMBER 1966 / AND OF HIS SON/ CAPTAIN RICHARD JOHN VICTOR GOSS/ GRENADIER GUARDS 1938 - 1943/ BORN 26 MARCH 1918/ KILLED IN ACTION IN TUNISIA 17 MARCH 1943/ NOTHING IS HERE FOR TEARS. NOTHING TO WAIL/ OR KNOCK THE BREAST. NO WEAKNESS. NO CONTEMPT/ DISPRAISE OR BLAME. NOTHING BUT WELL AND FAIR/ AND WHAT MAY QUEST US IN A DEATH SO NOBLE

Richard Goss is buried in Sfax War Cemetery, Tunisia.

 **Private Fred Maddock: Pioneer Corps**

Date of death: 11th May 1943

Commemorated on Odd Rode War Memorial, All Saints Church

Fred Maddock and photo of original grave.   Family archive.

Fred was born 1st August 1902 to John, a farm labourer, and Ellen Maddock in Rode Heath. He had five siblings. His older brother, John, served in the Royal Defence Corps in the Great War. Fred worked as a labourer for Cheshire County Council on road repairs

He married Alice Jeffries in Congleton in 1920. They lived at 10 Spring Terrace, Rode Heath, with daughters Eunice and Eva. In 1939 the couple and their children moved to 81 Sandbach Road, Thurlwood. In the Second World War Fred enlisted with the Pioneer Corps, service number 7397977 and served in the North Africa campaign. The Royal Pioneer

Corps was a British Army combatant corps used for light engineering tasks. It was formed in 1939 and was shipped to North Africa to build runways.

Fred was killed in action on 11th May 1943 in Tunisia during the battle for Tunisia which ended two days later with the defeat of the Axis Forces. Fred is buried in grave 7. D. 15 in the Commonwealth War Graves cemetery at Medjez-el-Bab. (His body was reburied in this cemetery in 1944 -the original burial site is not recorded in Commonwealth War Grave records. (CWGC))

Medjez-el-Bab was at the limit of the Allied advance in December 1942 and remained on the front line until the decisive Allied advances of April and May 1943. Medjez-El Bab War Cemetery is approximately sixty kilometres west of Tunis.

Fred's wife Alice Ann Maddock died in 2002 aged 101. She remained at 81 Sandbach Road all her life.

 **Sgt Harry Pierpoint: Air Gunner, RAFVR**

Date of death: 24th May 1943

Commemorated on Alsager War Memorial

Harry Pierpoint photographed in Canada in 1940

Son of Harry Pierpoint and Hannah Elizabeth Pierpoint (*nee* Dean) Harry was born in 1921 in Wolstanton, Staffordshire. His father was a bus conductor and ARP Warden during the war, and in 1939 the family were living in Walley Drive, Stoke-on-Trent. Harry had two brothers Reginald and Norman. During the war Harry's family moved to Alsager and Harry joined the Royal Air Force Reserve, service number 1181213. In 1940, he trained in Canada.

Harry Pierpoint 3rd from right in Canada

Harry Pierpoint front row, 2nd from right, Canada 1940

In May 1943, he was with 35 Squadron on a bombing mission to Berlin that left from Graveley base in the UK.

The Lancaster Bomber serial W4861 was hit over Holland by a night fighter and crashed near Markelo, killing five of the crew on board including Harry. There were two survivors.

This aircraft was one of a batch of 200 Lancasters ordered from Metropolitan Vickers in 1940 and built as 70 Mk.1 (W761-4982) with

Merlin 20 engines and 30 Mk.111 (W4983-5012) with Merlin 28 engines from September 1942 to May 1943.

The aircraft were delivered to Woodford for assembly and flight-testing. They were delivered to No.12 Squadron in January 1943.

W4861 had previously taken part in the following Key Operations: Lorient 13th/14th Feb 194343; Nuremburg 25th/26th February 1943; St. Nazaire 28th February/1st March 1943; St. Nazaire 22nd/23rd March 1943 – (This flight was flown by W/C R.S.C.Wood.) CO No.12 Sqdn;

The plane also completed a mission over Berlin on the 27th/28th March 1943.

When lost W4861 had flown a total of 190 hours. It took off at 23:19 hrs on 23rd May 1943 from Wickenby. It exploded and crashed near Markelo (Overijssel), south west of Hengelo, Holland. Those who died are buried in Markelo General Cemetery.

The following report is published in the book *Huzaren van de nacht* (Hussars of the night) part 1 by the Dutch author Coen Cornelissen, ISBN 90-6693-100-0. (Cornellissen):

Dortmund again:
After a pause of nine days the Allied Supreme Command planned an attack on Dortmund. On 24th May 1943 Dortmund was instructed as target for eight hundred and twenty six bombers. Such a large air force had not been organised since the "1000 Bomber raids", of summer 1942. Commander Sir Arthur (Bomber) Harris had only one target: Dortmund had to be destroyed. The bombardment was claimed by the British to be successful: almost two thousand buildings were destroyed, and various factories were hit directly, especially Hoesch Stahlwerke.

Harry Pierpoint, with No. 12 RAF Squadron, was based at Wickenby, Lincolnshire. R.A.F. Wickenby was a purpose-built bomber base constructed in late 1942 and early 1943. It had two T2 type hangars and one B1 type. The B1 and one of the T2 hangars can still be seen on the airfield site. The T2 near the threshold of runway 21 was recently acquired by the airfield owners and after many years of industrial use is now, once more, an aircraft hangar. The airfield covered about six hundred acres, and had the usual three runway configuration with peripheral tracks, hard standings, a brick watchtower and numerous brick and metal buildings for the aircrews and ground staff. A number of the buildings were to the east (Communal Site, Living Quarters, WAAF Quarters) and stretched to and beyond the Lissington road - a road travelled on many an evening by the airmen and women who visited their favourite pub, *The White Hart* at Lissington. The Sick Quarters were to the south of the airfield together with a Communal Site and Living Quarters. Wickenby was occupied in September of 1942 by No. 12 Squadron (a/c code PH) who brought with them Wellington II/III's, but during the winter of 1942/43 they converted to the AVRO Lancaster. The Squadron flew the Lancaster throughout the rest of the war. On 7th November 1943, C Flight was expanded to become 626 Squadron (a/c code UM), also flying the Lancaster. Wickenby played a large part in the bomber offensive, taking part in many of the major raids including: Berlin, Munich, Nuremberg, Essen, Maillie-Le-Camp, and Caen. Aircraft from Wickenby were also involved in mine-laying. Outside the hangars Lancasters were ready for action, just like at dozens of other airfields in England. One of them was the Avro Lancaster Mark I W4861 PH-M. The bomber was a real *'veteran'*, because it had already ninety flight missions and it *'survived'* nothing less than three crews. The Lancaster now had its fourth crew, but nevertheless the massive aircraft was in good condition.

The crew:

Pilot F/O William N. Mounsey, age 27
Navigator P/O William B. Whitaker, age 22
Air Bomber Sgt. Albert Dews, (survived) age 22
Wire Operator Sgt. Robert S. Miller, age 19
Flight Engineer Sgt. Walter B. Jowett, (survived) age 23
Upper Gunner Sgt. Kenneth G. Legg, age 23
Tail Gunner Sgt. Harry Pierpoint, age 22 from Alsager in Cheshire.

Engineer Walter Jowett described what happened on the mission: (script paraphrased)

'All crew members had to report themselves for the briefing and for instructions about the target: our target was Dortmund. After the briefing nobody was allowed to leave the camp, for reasons of security. At the outside the provisioning was hurried: bombs were rigged, and fuel was replenished till we had more than two thousand gallons. The engines were checked. The pilot and the flight engineer flew with the plane a few trial rounds and gave all information to the ground staff. In our case the fuel supply appeared not to act adequately.

In the evening, the crew members were brought to the different planes. They boarded with parachutes, and with coffeepots, as they were told to drink something before flying. The engines were ready to start, and the meters showed RPM's (revs per minute). The green warning lamp showed us permission to go to the runway, to start and to take off.

Pilot and flight engineer were working together, and they did a little prayer, that the enormous weight of the heavy load would be controlled.........
We hoped for the best.... If the engines should fail now it should be end of the exercise. Thank God - we were climbing.
We made course for Lincoln and climbed continually, till we reached the desired flight level of 20.000 feet for Germany. Our navigator kept us informed about our position. Above the sea in the direction of Holland, we had a good visibility towards Dortmund! As we continued we could see burning Lancasters going down, fortunately it was not our plane!
As we approached our target we set our compass direction to avoid a collision with our colleagues. Our Air Bomber prepared to drop the bombs. The pilot gave his permission and off they went to the poor, old Dortmund. We were thinking of London and our other cities which had suffered so much. After a certain period, the air bomber used a camera to shoot pictures before the plane began our return to our base.'

Petrified with fright:

It seems the Lancaster crew finished their job and were going homewards. Walter Jowett continues his story:

'Suddenly we were surrounded by a dazzling light. A German floodlight on the ground succeeded in catching us. We knew that anti-aircraft shells would follow within some seconds! Our pilot pushed the steering stick downwards and we were going down in a dangerous nosedive, through which we lost the floodlight.
After a few minutes we could breathe again, I waited for instructions to climb again, but nothing was happening and increasingly we were falling! I watched the pilot, who sat petrified in his chair. There was no time to lose. We lost about 4000 feet, so I pulled the steering stick towards me with my arms over the pilot's shoulder. When after a minute or so the plane was climbing again, the pilot showed interest and asked for full speed. Of course, I did so, but this resulted in five feet long engine exhaust flames and the enemy could observe the miles away. We were lucky: no contact was made. The pilot did not say a word about this incident.
One hour passed without problems, I controlled the fuel. I leaned forward to the dashboard, looked downwards and unbelievable but true, I saw a German Messerschmitt Bf.110 under our plane flying from port-side to starboard. I cried through intercom to everyone and hoped the pilot would intervene and would instruct the front Gunner.'

Walter Jowett had seen correctly. Flying Officer August Geiger, brand-new decorated with the Ritterkreuz (the Knights Cross) had approached unseen. Combat leader Lt. Richard Harig guided him to the home flyer and just before half past two at a height of six thousand feet Geiger pushed the fire-buttons:
Jowett continues his story:

'I was disappointed. Within a few seconds a shower of 20 mm shells perforated the 550 Gallon fuel tank. I knew we had only a few seconds to abandon the plane, to go downstairs and to pull the escape-hatch away. To my surprise air bomber (Albert Dews) was disabled. I thought he was wounded or dead, pulled him to the other side and at that same moment he got up. The iron bottom plate had to be removed and thrown outside, so we could jump. I pointed downwards and when I went upstairs, navigator (P/O Whitaker) ordered the other crew members to jump and to show the escape route. I put on my parachute.

The air was very hot, so I jumped through the escape hatch. When I was falling outside, I felt a strong jerk and I fainted....... The fresh air woke me up again and at first I thought of the bike, which I had borrowed the previous evening and which I had not brought back! My next problem was to find out if I would land in Holland or in Germany. A little bit later I made a perfect landing between cows. The bullets of the burning wreckage were flying everywhere. Nobody was to be seen, so I ran away and after about one and a half kilometres I decided could hide myself in the vegetation. Then I fell asleep.

In the morning I was woken by passing chattering children. They did not talk German, so everything was okay. I came to a house and the people who lived there let me in and gave me some food. Unfortunately, we could not talk to each other.'

The air bomber, Albert Dews (aged twenty-two) also succeeded in escaping from the burning plane. The plane landed near the farm of Berend Jan Vosman, nowadays the parking place for the *AC-Restaurant* on the A1- highway. Jowett's parachute was hidden in a ditch. Vosman took the Englishman into his house so he could recuperate, and was given eggs and coffee. The Lancaster had crashed a few hundred metres from the hamlet of Groenland near Markelo. The remaining five crew members did not survive. They were found lifeless at the crash location (and were buried in Markelo). A little bit later the first Germans and the police arrived. Exactly to the standard procedure the following message arrived in Almelo next morning at 10.30 am.:

'At 10.30 a.m. the following alarm message was sent by M.P. Commander T. of Markelo:
On behalf of the Commander of Military Police in Markelo, the tracing and arrest of two English airmen is desired. They belong to an English plane, which crashed in the night of 23 to 24 May 1943 at about 1.30 a.m. in the community of Markelo. Signed by G.'

Jowett wrote:

'While I walked through a small village I asked myself who I could contact to get back to England. I walked up a hill with fields and after hardly one kilometre I heard a voice behind me: "For you my friend the war is over!" When I was looking backwards I saw a Dutch policeman, who pointed a pistol at me. I was totally surprised. He took me with him to his house and called the Luftwaffe……. After different stopovers I came into a prisoner of war camp in Eastern-Prussia.'

Albert Dews stayed quietly in the comfortable living room of the Vosman family but soon the police arrived to arrest the airman. Dews left so hastily, that his mica *'Escapebox'* was left behind. The box was saved for many years by Mr Vosman's daughter Marie; a remarkable souvenir of a memorable night. Dews was eventually caught and taken to Hedera Prisoner of War Camp, while Jowett was taken to a camp at Kopernikus.

In March 1992 Jowett and Dews visited the crash location and Berend Vosman's farm. The farmer was eighty-eight years old, but he could remember the events well. In 1998 Jowett came back to lay flowers at the graves of his fellow crewmen.

Narrative on loss of W4861, by Sgt A. Dews.

'We arrived over the target on time, dropped our bombs and were immediately coned. By the time we got free we were down to about 8,000'. We set course for home and decided to regain height. In retrospect, we may have been better staying at 8,000' and getting out quicker. We reached about 20,000' again over Holland and then we were shot down by August Geiger. He was working with a decoy. I was watching the decoy in front when Geiger came in from below and behind and set us on fire. The Flight Engineer thought I was dead and lifted me off the escape hatch. He bailed out quickly and I followed him. We had no intercom working, but at least the Navigator and Wireless Operator could see the position we were in, as the whole of the port wing was ablaze. I do not know why they did not follow us out.' **Note.** August Geiger shot down fifty-three of our bombers was promoted to Hauptman and

awarded two Iron Crosses. Geiger was shot down on 29th September 1943 and drowned because he was not wearing a lifejacket.

Markelo General Cemetery, Overijssel, Netherlands. Markelo is a village and commune 23 kilometres south-west of Hengelo, on the Hengelo-Deventer road. The cemetery lies about one kilometre east of Markelo, on the southern side of the town. The British plot is in a prominent position north-east of the entrance. Sgt Pierpoint is buried in Plot 4. Row B. Grave 6

Local resident Mrs Rowden tending Harry's grave in 1949

Harry Pierpoint's grave today

Lance Corporal Alfred Eric Moseley: RAMC

Date of death: 2nd June 1943

Commemorated on Alsager War Memorial

Alfred Eric Moseley was born on 21st June 1915 in Alsager. He was son of Robert and Elizabeth Ann Moseley (*nee* Bebbington) His father was a collier. The family lived at 103 Crewe Road.

Alfred Eric Moseley.

His brothers and sisters were: Sydney Robert Moseley, 1905-1997; Frederick James, 1906-1972; John William, 1908-died in infancy; Harry, 1909 -1988; George,1911-1991; Florence 1913-1914; Freda, 1917-2005; Gladys, 1919-1919; Ernest, 1922- 1992.

Alfred Eric Moseley attended Christ Church, Alsager, and as a young man was a bell ringer at the church and was a member of the Central Council of Bell Ringers, Cheshire Diocese. He enlisted for the army in Stoke-on-Trent. He joined the Royal Army Medical Corps, as Private 7383142, in 197 Field Ambulance. He married Mary Penelope Preston in Whitchurch, Hampshire, in 1941. In 1942 his unit was stationed in Singapore. After the surrender to the Japanese they were placed in Changi Prison, Singapore, in cramped conditions. As medical staff they were forced to look after the one hundred and five thousand prisoners there.

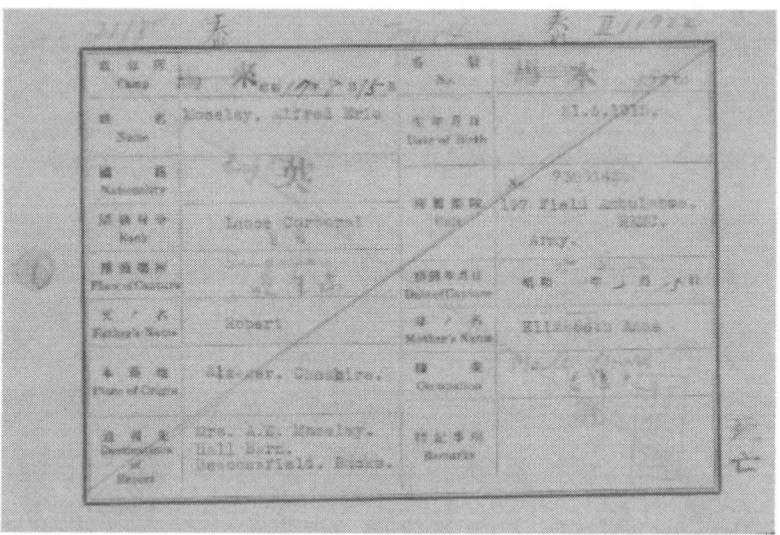

A.E. Moseley's Japanese Prisoner Card. It shows he was captured on 15th February 1942 and gives his occupation as 'male nurse'. Alfred's mother was residing in Buckinghamshire at the time of his capture.

The only food available was rice. The men started to contract diseases such as dysentery and Beriberi, due to a lack of vitamins. On 31st October 1942 a group of six hundred and fifty prisoners, including A.E. Moseley, and 197 Ambulance, was transferred overland from Changi Prison, Singapore, to work on the Burma railway setting up primitive hospitals at the forced labour camps.

Another record card shows his name crossed out because he had died. It gives his regimental number as 7383142 and his date of birth as 18th June 1922.

Alfred Eric Moseley died at Takaneen on 22nd June 1943. He was originally buried at Takaneen (Takanum) forced labour camp, grave number 16. He was reburied in 1946 at Kanchanaburi Commonwealth War Graves Cemetery, one hundred and twenty-nine kilometres northwest of Bangkok.

Takanum was a forced labour camp on the Burma Railway. It was two hundred and eighteen kilometres from the start of the railway between Non-Padauk and *'Three Pagoda Camp'* on the border with Thailand. There was a *'Coolie Camp'* hospital run by Dr Hardy. In his diary Dr Hardy described the sanitation and disease problems at Takanum camp. (Pri)

> Of all the diarrhoeal diseases, cholera was the worst and most feared. Hardie recorded a cholera outbreak at Takanum Camp in the monsoon season of 1943: ' this is cholera all right. There have been 10 deaths already, death supervening within 36 hours of the onset of serious symptoms'.[18] Three days later there were 56 cases and 35 deaths. To prevent spread of the disease the bodies were burnt in hideous funeral pyres. In probably the worst affected camp (the remote Sonkrai Camp on the Thai-Burma border) there were 219 cholera deaths from 315 cases (70% mortality) in 37 days.[19]

A. E. Moseley died of acute enteritis in Takanum Camp on 22nd June 1942.

The Burma railway

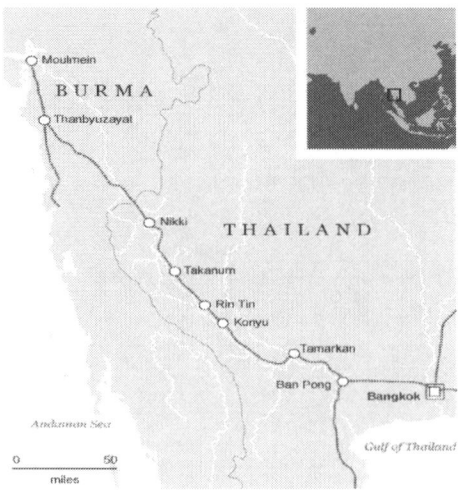

Alfred's grave

On 17th October 1945 probate was granted for Alfred Eric Moseley. *'Alfred Eric Moseley of St Saviour's Nursery, Sutton Road, Shrewsbury, who died on War Service.'* His effects were left to 'Nancy' Penelope Moseley, £371. 9s 2d. In 1947 Elizabeth Ann Moseley, Alfred's mother, was still living at 103 Crewe Road, Alsager, at the time of her death.

 **Sergeant Vincent George Louvaine Smith: RAFVR**

Date of Death: 15th June 1943

Commemorated on Church Lawton War Memorial

Vincent was born in Kidsgrove on 18th April 1915 to George and Ethel Smith (*nee* Corners) who lived at the Rookery. George was a pottery worker who had served in the Royal Field Artillery in the Great War. Vincent had a sister, Ethel Marjorie born 16th July 1916.

In 1939, according to the 1939 Register, Vincent was living with his parents at a property in Church Lawton called *'Marv Elaine'* and was employed as a Potteries Design Manager. His father was an Air Raid Warden.

In 1941 Vincent married Mary Hollinshead (marriage registered in Crewe January-April 1941.)

Vincent joined the Royal Air Force Volunteer Reserve and trained to be a Flight Engineer, service number 1178195, and was assigned to work with 9 Squadron.

In the night of 14th - 15th June 1943, RAF bombers carried out a major bombing at Oberhausen. Of the one hundred and sixty-five aircraft that dropped their bombs, seventeen did not return. Two of them were taken over North Brabant and arrived in Schijndel and Tijen respectively. This last plane was an Avro Lancaster III of the 9 Squadron that crashed at the Maas bank at 01:55. The pilot was P/O John Evans (20), and all the seven crew perished. The Lancaster LM329 (*call sign* WS-Q) had taken off at 22:56 hours from Bardney Airport and was shot down by German fighter pilot Wilhelm Herget who was born in Stuttgart in 1910 and died in April 1974 in Stuttgart.

The seven crew members of the LM-329 are all buried at Uden War Cemetery, Netherlands; Grave 5 G 5-11: John Evans, Pilot; Sgt Vincent George Louvaine Smith, Plane Mechanic, (28); Sgt Robert Borthwick, Navigator (31); Sgt Vincent John Tarr, Navigator; Sgt Alan Wilson Waite, Bomber Director (22); F/Sgt Walter James Chapple, Radio Telegraphist

(32) sharing his grave with Sgt Herbert Ivor Ashdown, (19); and Sgt Derek Walter Brough, (20).

Uden, Netherlands, was occupied by the Germans until its liberation in September 1944. In the earlier years of the war Commonwealth and Allied servicemen were buried in the garden of the parish priest which adjoined the Roman Catholic Cemetery. Later it became necessary to provide another burial ground for them and in 1943 the municipality acquired the Roman Catholic Cemetery, unused since about 1918, for this purpose. After the war, more than one hundred graves from the garden of the parish priest, and several isolated graves from various parts of the commune, were moved into this cemetery. Vincent's body was transferred to this cemetery on 17th March, 1954.

Vincent's grave

Wording on the grave chosen by his family:

'At the going down of the sun and in the morning, we will remember him.'

Alsager in 1944

Timeline of the war (history)

With advances in Burma, New Guinea and Guam, Japan began its last offensive in China, capturing further territory in the south to add to the acquisitions made in central and northern areas following the invasion of 1938. However, its control was limited to the major cities and lines of communication, and resistance - often led by the Communists - was widespread.

The Allied advance in Italy continued with landings at Anzio, in central Italy, in January. It was a static campaign. The Germans counter-attacked in February and the fighting saw the destruction of the medieval monastery at Monte Cassino after Allied bombing. Only at the end of May did the Germans retreat from Anzio. Rome was liberated in June, the day before the Allies' 'Operation Overlord', now known as the D-Day landings.

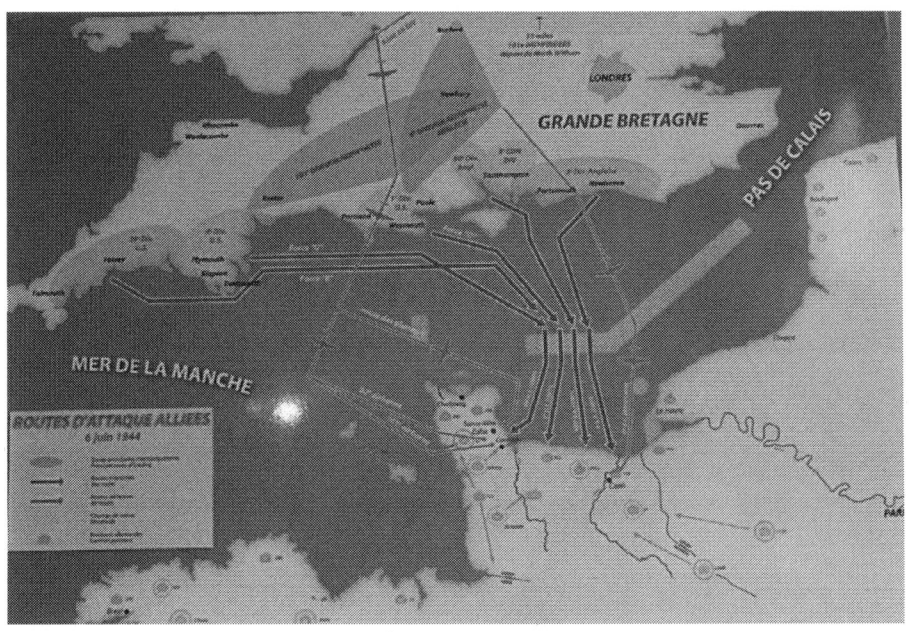

On 6th June - as Operation Overlord got underway - some six thousand five hundred vessels landed over one hundred and thirty thousand Allied forces on five Normandy beaches: codenamed Utah, Omaha, Gold, Juno and Sword. Some twelve thousand aircraft ensured air superiority for the Allies; bombing German defences, and providing cover. The pessimistic predictions that had been made of massive Allied casualties were

not borne out. On 'Utah' beach twenty-three thousand troops were landed, with one hundred and ninety seven casualties, and most of the four thousand six hundred and ninety four American casualties that day occurred at 'Omaha' beach, where the landing was significantly more difficult to achieve, meeting with fierce German resistance. British regiments came ashore between Hermanville and Colleville at 'Sword' beach. Overall, however, the landings caught the Germans by surprise, and they were unable to counter-attack with the necessary speed and strength. Anything that was moving and German was liable to be attacked from the air. Despite this, in the weeks following the landings Allied progress was slowed considerably, by the narrow lanes and thick hedgerows of the French countryside. Nevertheless, Cherbourg was liberated by the end of June. Paris followed two months later.

Hitler's troubles were compounded by a Russian counterattack in June. This drove three hundred miles west to Warsaw, and killed, wounded or captured three hundred and fifty thousand German soldiers. By the end of August, the Russians had taken Bucharest. Estonia was taken within months, and Budapest was under siege by the end of the year.

*In the Ardennes, in France, in December a German counteroffensive - the Battle of the Bulge - killed **nineteen thousand** Americans and delayed the Allies' march into Germany.*

In Alsager

In January 1944, the Cheshire War Agriculture Committee advertised in the *Cheshire Observer* to let the tenancy of *Manor Farm*, Alsager. The farm was made up of ninety-eight acres. (*Manor Farm* is situated close Dunnockfold Road.) When the Second World War began in September 1939, Britain was faced with an urgent need to increase food production, as imports of food and fertilisers were drastically cut. The area of land under cultivation had to be increased significantly and quickly. The Ministry of Agriculture and Fisheries set up War Agricultural Executive Committees in each county *('County War Ags')* to carry out a farm survey between 1940 and 1941, and to use the information collected to bring uncultivated land under the plough and to improve poor farms. Each Committee was given the power to serve orders to farmers *'requiring work to be done, or, in cases of default, to take possession of the land'*. It is not known if *Manor Farm* was in default.

In January 1944, a recruitment drive for the Women's Land Army met with a big response in South Cheshire. *'Applications have poured in'*, the Cheshire Secretary of the WLA told the *Crewe Chronicle*. Recruitment was limited to single girls of between seventeen and thirty-five. Recruits would be taken on for tractor driving, milking, pest destruction, and general farm labouring. Applicants were interviewed and received a medical examination. Women already in farming were not accepted into the scheme. In November 1943, one thousand five hundred women were employed in the WLA in Cheshire. The peak number employed had been one thousand six hundred. The numbers had declined because of illness, and because a large proportion of the girls married. Unlike the Services, Women could leave the WLA to marry. Some married farmers or farmer's sons. These women could not remain in the Land Army as they might be then classified as being their own employers! There were fourteen hostels in Cheshire each catering for between eighteen to twenty-seven girls. WLA Clubs had been formed for lectures, and demonstrations on dressmaking, glove making, and toy making took place. The clubs met fortnightly or monthly. The WLA had forty representative officers in Cheshire.

The death occurred in January 1944 of the Reverend Charles Churton Potts aged 73, Vicar of Alsager. He had been ordained in 1895, had served in Alsager for ten years, and had previously worked, amongst other places, in South Africa, Coventry, and Dunham Massey. He had four soldier sons and three daughters. Two of his sons, Sergeant J. C. Potts and Mt T Potts, attended the funeral at St Mary's church which was conducted by the Bishop of Chester.

One of the district's smallest communities at Hassall Green held their own Red Cross fundraising event in February 1944 raising £88 through a bring and buy sale and a whist drive.

1944 saw the launch of the *Alsager Times* newspaper (AlsagerTimes) which gives many examples of events in the town. In February, a memorial service was held in Lawton Parish Church conducted by the Rev Martyn-Jones for Joseph Brookes who had died of wounds in Italy. The service was joined by members of Joseph's family including his wife who lived in Butt Lane. The paper also reported where servicemen and women had returned to the area on leave. In February, the paper reported L/AC

Sidney J. Tudor was home on leave after serving two years training with the RAF in Canada. He was the son of Mr & Mrs F Tudor of Audley Road, Alsager. He had been in the RAF from early 1940. His brother Frank Tudor was a Warrant Officer in the RAF having served twelve years. A third brother, Harold, also a Warrant Officer in the RAF, had served seven years in the Middle East having worked a total of eleven years. Harold and Frank were home on leave in October 1944.

As the *Alsager Times* was unable to write about censored matters, (for example ROF Radway Green was never mentioned), it often published on subjects such as the future of Alsager. In January 1944 Driver Norman Spite RASC service number T 10465884, serving in North Africa wrote to the Council suggesting improvements to Alsager when the war was over. Spite had suggested Alsager needed a development plan to include new industry, and a new town hall, better schools, public access to the Mere, provision of a cinema and more public open spaces. Spite suggested Alsager had a pottery factory, but the council should develop the town to have *a 'semi-refined nature'*. Spite anticipated Alsager would grow to fifteen thousand people in the ten years after the war rising ultimately to twenty thousand. The Council responded to Driver Spite in February 1944 publishing the letter in the *Alsager Times*. The Council must have been shocked to receive such correspondence from a serviceman and its answers were vague. It did anticipate Alsager would become *'one of the new post war towns safeguarded from the sprawl of neighbouring towns and cities by a rural zone around it'*. The council agreed the town would need new schools including a nursery school, and a new fire station (This was only achieved in 2016!). Spite had also recommended Alsager should join administratively with neighbouring parishes such as Church Lawton and Odd Rode. Local government change in Alsager did not come until 1974 when Alsager became part of Congleton Borough Council. In 1944 Alsager Urban District Council was unwilling to make any comments about local government administration. It did wish to see the building of a new library and a public hall for Alsager. Letters from the public were critical of Spite's recommendations saying he *'may be a good soldier but a poor financier'*, and he did not understand money and how far it would go. Many thought his ideas were *'too ambitious'*, and would not be achieved in *'our time'*. Norman Spite was keen to open the debate about the future of the town.

Norman Spite continued to write to the *Alsager Times* when he was in Italy with the Central Mediterranean Forces to recommend Alsager reintroduce its annual carnival after the war. Spite even managed to get his ideas printed in the *Daily Mirror* on August 24th.

HIS 'OFFICE' A PETROL CAN, HE PLANNED THE HOME HE'S FIGHTING FOR

OUR soldiers are fighting for their future homes. One of them combined his fighting with planning the changes he'd like to see in his home town.

From the African desert, where his "office" was an upturned petrol can, he sent his blue-print to his local council, and by the time he reached Rome with the Eighth Army he received their startled thanks—and a plea for constructive proposals from other soldiers.

Planning soldier is 21-year-old Driver Norman Spite. His home town is Alsager, Cheshire.

There's no narrow parochialism about the Alsager Driver Spite wants to see.

That local lake, lost now in the tangled weeds—he would build a concrete promenade round it, with a floating bandstand in the centre—boating and bathing in summer, ice skating in winter.

He wants to extend the town's boundaries, attract new industries.

"It is said that it's up to us soldiers to build a new Britain," he wrote.

Norman Leslie Spite F.R.G.S. was a Fellow of the Royal Geographical Society. After the war, he attended Chester College and trained as a teacher. He was born in Rode Heath in 1923. His father, Norman Lacy Spite, formerly of the Kings Liverpool Regiment in the Great War, was a poultry farmer. In 1939, they lived in *'Hill View'* Rode Heath. Norman died in Chester in 1984. Spite foresaw many of the changes which would come to Alsager but many of the facilities he desired, such as a purpose-built cinema, never transpired. In 1944 people were not aware how tough post-war austerity would be and how debt-ridden the country would become.

On 24th March, 1944 another local serviceman LAC Gilbert Band, (Band) RAF, of 13 Crewe Road, wrote to the *Alsager Times* to back up Norman Spite's remarks*: 'As we lads in the forces realise, Alsager is growing in size and becoming of importance. Ever since the first few days of the war Alsager awoke from her pre-war peacefulness. Since then many things have changed which everybody is aware of, and after the war Alsager cannot go back to its old standard ...Many of the things could be done which Dvr. Spite so bravely forecast. So, with the help of the people and the careful handling of the financial side Alsager could become a well-developed prosperous township.'*

Gilbert Band's letter to the Alsager Times in March 1944

Gilbert Band

Gilbert Band was born in Alsager in 1925. He did his basic training in Padgate Warrington after being called up in 1944, service number 2220697. He went on to be part of the D Day Normandy landings in July 1944 arriving by ship. He fought all the way to Belgium and as a 19-year-old wirelesss operator was serving in Antwerp when there was a bombing raid. On 19th December 1944, the Germans launched a V2 rocket at Antwerp and five hundred and twenty-nine people including two hundred and ninety-six servicemen were killed at the Rex cinema.

The off-duty servicemen, who included Jack Higgins aged twenty-nine of the Royal Artillery (from Audley), and who was killed, had been enjoying a screening of *The Plainsman* with Gary Cooper.

Gilbert Band saw the V2 Rocket hit the cinema and was amongst the men who went to the aid of survivors. He had wanted to go to see the film but had been persuaded by a friend to go for a drink instead. Jack Higgin's son, who was a baby at the time of his father's death, went on to teach at Alsager Secondary School in the 1960s.

Gilbert Band was part of No. 151 Repair Unit (Aircraft), which was based at Wevelgem, Belgium, 1944/45. He was demobilised in 1947.

Gilbert Band with 151 Repair Unit 1944

Other Alsager News from 1944

In May, Alsager Army cadets were formed. No. 3 Company ACF, Cheshire Regiment opened at its temporary HQ at Christ Church School. In addition to military training the corps provided practical hobbies, film shows, and discussion groups. A syllabus was designed for cadet forces, so the instruction went beyond military work. The educational, religious, physical and recreational side of being in the ACF was promoted.

In June 1944, Alsager U.D.C. debated the poor library facilities in the town. Only thirty new books were acquired every two months. By comparison Councillor Harpur said the library at *Heathside Hostel* was better and had more modern books. Following a meeting with the County Librarian the following month more books were promised for Alsager Library along with new bookcases and a new noticeboard. Despite the apparent paucity of books in the local library there was a campaign in Cheshire to collect books to send to servicemen. Alsager collected nine thousand books for servicemen and women. Alec Shaw remembers helping in the door to door collection of books. If children collected book they were promoted; *'Corporal'; 'Major,' 'Field Marshall,'* and so on, depending on the number of books they collected. Plans were also made at this time to transfer the library from Alsager Institute into spare rooms at the National Westminster Bank.

In June, Odd Rode and Lawton Royal British Legion held their first annual dinner since 1939. It was held at the Rode Heath Institute and was attended by fifty ex-servicemen and Sir P. Baker Wilbraham. There was much discussion about the difficulty in members gaining war pensions. Mr A. Ogden of the local branch said they had tried to advise and help forty ex-servicemen in the last twelve months.

The wireless or radio was important to local people during the war and sometimes local servicemen managed to be part of recorded shows. Corporal F.R. Morris, organist at Christ Church for five years until 1942, took part in a show called *'Greetings from West Africa'*, which was broadcast on a Sunday morning.

There were complaints because a meeting of the Communist Party was held in Alsager Working Men's Club. Some members said the WMC should not have any political affiliation. The Secretary, F.E. Condliffe said there would be no further meetings of a political or sectarian nature at the club. The WMC was an important place in Alsager for social occasions, and often the concerts contained classical music. Two serving musicians, Mus. Charles Tobias, violin, and O/S J. Pechek, piano, entertained the club members with music by Tartan, Schubert, Kreisler, and Chopin. Perchek also sang Purcell and Handel.

The Reverend Dan Nicholas was appointed the first vicar of a separate Christ Church parish in June 1944 but he was still a chaplain in the RAF which delayed his induction. He was ordained in May 1932 having attended Wells Theological College. His first appointment was to Madeley in the Diocese of Lichfield. On 9th June 1942 he was appointed Squadron Leader in the Chaplaincy Section of the RAF. (London Gazette 9th May 1942.)

Rev. Dan Nicholas with Christ Church Choir members on an outing to Blackpool. Early post war photograph. Until the end of the war he continued to wear his RAF uniform during services. (Barker, 2017)

In June 1944 Flight Sergeant B.M. Hall was gazetted Pilot Officer in the RAF. His promotion was announced in the *Staffordshire Weekly Sentinel*. He was the son of the late T.W Hall of *Wood Villa,* Talke Road, Alsager and was previously a pupil of Sandbach School and a clerical worker for the General Post Office. He had joined the RAF in 1941.

In the same month the national campaign, *'Salute the Soldier'*, was well underway. It had commenced in April 2017 with a special week of activities. £50,000 was the target for the appeal. In addition to the gunnery (anti-aircraft) demonstration, the parade included a contingent of the Royal Navy, American Army, WRNS, Staffordshire Battalion Home Guard Band, Scouts, Guides, and civil defence units. Most of the United States troops came from Sandbach where they were billeted at the property which became the Leonard Cheshire Home. From Radway Green paraded an Anti-Aircraft detachment and a women's fire brigade team. A charity cricket match was held between the Home Guard and *HMS Excalibur*.

It was a fundraising effort to invest in the services. One Alsager girl, thirteen-year-old June Clarke, was mentioned in the *Biggleswade Chronicle* on June 2nd. June, a newspaper delivery girl, raised £600 for the campaign by canvassing her customers. Why the article was used in a Bedfordshire-based newspaper is unknown, but it was common for regional newspapers to share each other's stories. Many children took part in fundraising efforts such as this, including scrap metal collection and participation in savings schemes. By October plaques were presented to Alsager people in St Mary's Schoolroom to celebrate *'Salute the Soldier'* collections. Included amongst the dignitaries on the podium were Sir Francis and Lady Joseph, Mr L.S Flatman (ROF Radway Green), Councillor James Clowes and Councillor R.H Timmis (Alsager War Savings Committee). Representing the army Colonel Hayes-Newington thanked the people of Alsager, and responding Councillor Clowes said, *'When the Salute the Soldier campaign was*

in progress we were just embarking on the stupendous task of invading the continent. No one expected at that time, within a few months the British Army would have crossed the borders of Germany'. The total money raised in the Alsager campaign had been £212,214. £163,802 had been raised in National Savings over the previous four years in the Alsager District. Certificates were presented to schools and other groups of people involved in promoting National Savings. Peter Barker remembers Councillor James Clowes because he suffered greatly from his First World War wounds. The skin on his face used to become enflamed and he would often have to wear a bandage around his face. The Lawton *'Salute the Soldier'* campaign had the target of raising £3,000. Promotion of the campaign included a free film show of the siege of Tobruk and Malta, whist drives, and dances.

The *Alsager Times* did manage to inform its readers about local service personnel. In March 1944 it reported Corporal A. Mansfield of 11 Poolside Court, Alsager had been wounded on active service. Joseph Orpe of Talke Road was reported as wounded but was recovering. In the same edition Private Leonard James Yorke, born in 1918 of 89 Crewe Road, and of the North Staffordshire Regiment, and son of Mr John and Elaine Yorke of *Lyndhurst* Lawton Road Alsager, had been made a prisoner of war and was taken to Germany. He had been serving in Italy and following his capture and sent a post card saying he was in *'perfect health'*. Yorke was 25 and joined the army in September 1939 and was evacuated from Dunkirk in 1940 before being transferred overseas in 1943. (North Africa). Educated at Lawton Gate School, Yorke worked for Messrs W.H.Grindley before the war. He was a member and chorister of Wesley Place Church. He had a brother, W.E. Yorke who joined the army in 1943 and was serving in Italy. Leonard survived and died in 2002.

On 18th March the *Crewe Chronicle* reported seventy Wardens attended the Alsager Wardens' Dinner at the *Alsager Arms*. It shows how large the civil defence system had become in the town. Mr C.P Twemlow, Chief Warden, presented prizes. Tributes were paid to local wardens and that they were *'ready for any emergency'*. Constituent parts of the Warden service included the Rescue Service and ARP, and the event was attended by representatives of the Home Guard, 233 Sqn. Air Training Corps, and the Council.

The paper also reported that Trooper Arthur Turner of West Street, Mount Pleasant, had been wounded in both legs in Normandy and had been transferred to an English hospital. He had previously served in the Mediterranean theatre. Marine Eric Abell of *Navigation House*, Lawton, seriously wounded in the Normandy fighting was reported as off the *'danger list'*.

New wave of Evacuees

In 1944 another group of evacuees arrived in Alsager, the first to come since the failed evacuation scheme of 1939. This was part of a final wave of evacuation (codenamed *"Rivulet"*) of children from London. The *Alsager Times* of 15th July said one hundred and fifty-six evacuees had arrived from London, more than the one hundred expected. Only fifty of them, all children, were in the official evacuation scheme. Alsager's final quota was supposed to be one hundred evacuees. Twenty-seven evacuees were billeted in Odd Rode and fifty-seven more mothers and children were expected to arrive. Billeting Officers in Odd Rode put out an appeal for more accommodation and several large houses had been identified.

The council were asked to consider the financial plight of evacuees in Alsager at their July meeting. One female evacuee, who had moved from London with her family, could not afford any furniture for her new home. The councillors thought it was their duty to assist the woman. The amount of the grant was undisclosed. A Billeting Tribunal was set up to consider appeals against billeting decisions made by Alsager U.D.C. Forty evacuee children arrived from London in July 1944 and were settling into the community. Two boy evacuees joined the local cadets as soon as they arrived. Preparations had been made for a hundred children and the WVS had arranged billets. *Creswellshawe House* acted as the headquarters where the children stayed their first night. The children seemed very pleased with the facilities and the locals took to the children. One of the children on seeing the Mere asked if they were looking at the sea. Another of the children said, *'Cor that's a big bomb crater!'*

Pilot Officer A. M. McKie DFM

The Staffordshire Weekly Sentinel reported that Pilot Officer A. M. McKie DFM. of 37 Crewe Road, was home on leave after taking part in bombing raids on the German battleship *Tirpitz*, and involvement in *'other adventures'*.

He was the son of Norman and Mary Isabella McKie of *Milverton*, Haslington. His father was a merchant seaman. He lived with his uncle Wilfred at 37 Crewe Road following the death of his parents. His uncle Lieutenant R. McKie was commander of Alsager Cadet Force. Alexander Millar McKie, service number 55810, previously 573076, was awarded the Distinguished Flying Medal in August 1944.

Alexander Millar McKie was born 17th July 1922 in Crewe. He joined the RAF in 1938 at RAF Halton as part of the groundcrew. He did his pilot training in 1942 but failed his examinations. He went to Florida to train but again failed pilot training, so he went to Canada to train as a navigator. He passed out as Navigator and was made a sergeant, service number 573076.

Returning to England he joined Operation Training Unit, 106 Squadron. He re-took his pilots examinations and was commissioned Pilot Officer on 15th July 1944. He was award the DFM in August 1944 after thirty operations. Transferring to 617 Squadron, he was part of the *'Dambusters'*. McKie joined after the famous bombing raids on the Dortmund dams but took part in the bombing of the *Tirpitz* with the following crew of his Lancaster bomber Mark I (NF920) KC-E, Operation Tirpitz 29-10-44. · F/O D W Carey DFC RAAF (Survived) · F/S L W Franks (Survived) · P/O A M McKie (Survived) · P/O D H McLennan RCAF (Survived) · F/S A E Young (Survived) · F/O G A Witherick DFM.

Alexander Millar McKie of 37 Crewe Road Alsager

The German battleship *Tirpitz*, launched in 1941 was the sister ship to the now infamous *'Bismarck'*. The *Tirpitz* fully loaded weighed approximately fifty thousand tons and had a crew of two thousand three hundred and forty men. Her overall length was two hundred and fifty-one metres with a beam of thirty-six metres and a draught of nine metres. Her armament consisted of four 15-inch twin mounted turrets, six 5.9- inch twin mounted turrets, eight 4.1- inch twin mounted anti-aircraft guns and twelve single mounted anti-aircraft cannons. The *Tirpitz* was a threat to Allied and British convoys while she was operational. It was feared that she would break out from her port to open sea where substantial British Naval forces would be needed to prevent her sinking large amounts of convoy traffic. Whilst she was operational these Allied naval resources had to be kept on hand. In January 1942, she was moved to the Trondheim fjord in Norway. A great deal of Allied resources were expended on the destruction of the ship including many air raids, mini-submarine attacks and even the land attack on St Nazaire in France to destroy the only dry dock she could use. After many attempts by the Allied forces to sink her she was moved again in early 1943. She was further damaged by the Allies on the 3rd April 1944 after a surprise attack by fighters and bombers from *HMS Victorious* and *Formidable*. During these efforts, the *Tirpitz* took a heavy battering, her own smoke defences having failed. The damage was so great the German command decided she was no longer seaworthy and she was towed to a more secure hide away at Tromso Fjord in Norway. Under the command of Wing Commander Willie Tait, 617 and 9 Squadrons flew out of Scotland. The *Tirpitz* was at their absolute limit of range. It was a clear day and the *Tirpitz* did not make a smoke screen to defend itself. The attacking planes dropped twenty-eight 12,000lb *Tallboy* bombs on her. At least two hit her square on and this time the attack was more than she could take. With direct hits to the hull she started to rapidly flood and list. She then suffered a large internal explosion and capsized.

This was the end for the *Tirpitz*. She now lay keel up with one thousand to one thousand two hundred of her one thousand nine hundred-man crew dead or injured. McKie then joined 9 Squadron in 1945 and was demobilised in May 1946 (Flight Lt.) In January 1949 when he relinquished his commission but retained his rank he was appointed to R. Aux A.F. (Royal Auxiliary Air Force.) After the war, he was a salesman in a pharmaceutical company. He married Kathleen Jones in 1945. They had two sons. The marriage was dissolved, and he married Rene. He died on 1st August 2008.

> **DIED IN CANADA**
>
> **Crew Pall-Bearers For City Ship's Captain**
>
> Officers and men of the 7,000-tons freighter Rhondeau Park were pall-bearers when their captain, Mr. John C. McKie, of 38, Lime Tree-road, Peverell, Plymouth, was buried in Mount Royal Cemetery yesterday.
>
> Capt. McKie, taken ill suddenly, died on Tuesday at Sorel, Quebec, where his ship was being reconditioned for another trade. Funeral service was held in Montreal Sailors' Institute.
>
> Capt. McKie had been master of the Rhondeau Park for three years. Aged 53, he had spent the greater part of the last war on convoy work, serving, among other ships, in the Aquitania and Britannica.
>
> Born at Alsager, in Cheshire, he went to sea as a Merchant Navy apprentice at the age of 15. A commander in the Royal Naval Reserve, he served in the 1914-18 war and received the Reserve Decoration.
>
> He married Miss Lillian Lamb, of Plymouth. His two daughters are overseas, one in Cairo and the other in Rome. In addition to the Rhondeau Park, he also had command of the Liberty ship Sambre.

Another uncle of Alexander Millar McKie was Commander John C. McKie, born in Alsager 28th November 1891, and captain of convoy ships, *Aquitania,* and *Britannica* in the Second World War and who also served in the Great War. He died in Canada in 1946 and his obituary appeared in the *Western Morning News* in May 1946 (Wes)

Other news from Alsager in 1944.

In 1944 Sapper Morrow of the Royal Engineers sent his parents a surprise present, one which they did not display openly. *'A German flag – black swastika in a white circle against a red background – captured by Sapper R. Morrow R.E has been received by Mr & Mrs R. Morrow of 27 Crewe Road. Sapper Morrow has been serving in North West Europe since D Day plus five, and is now in Holland after taking part in the campaign in France and Belgium. He speaks highly of the warm welcome extended to the troops by the Belgian and Dutch people. Before enlisting some eleven months ago Spr. Morrow was training at Manchester University.'*

Mellor Family

Archie Mellor was born on 8th January 1916 and by 1939 was already a Sergeant Pilot in the RAF. His home was at 48 Fields Road, Alsager. His father Harold was a colliery agent. The *Alsager Times* reported in January 1944 that Flight Lieutenant Archie Mellor, once reported as a prisoner of war, was free and had returned to Alsager on leave. He married Hazel Dean in Saskatchewan Canada in 1943 where he was training. In 1946, his profession a motor engineer, he moved back to Canada with his wife Hazel and son William. His brother, Howard Mellor, born in 1908, was also in the RAF and became a Flying Officer serving in the Administrative and Special Duties Branch. He was a solicitor before the war with Norris & Mellor, Burslem, and worked in partnership with Robert Wilberforce Fisher DCM, who served in the Royal Armoured Corps in the war. Howard also served in the Auxiliary Fire Service in Alsager in 1939. He married Isobel Forsyth in Cannock in 1945.

In March 1944, the *Alsager Times* reported the accidental death of Owen Wilding, aged sixty- six of 82 Station Road Alsager. Owen was the driver of a locomotive which was travelling through the Harecastle Tunnel when he thought there was a problem with the injector mounted on the outside of the engine. Owen must have looked out of the cab with his torch when his head hit a steel girder in the tunnel. As the train emerged from the tunnel seventeen-year-old acting fireman Arthur S Hinks saw Wilding hanging out of the cab so he stopped the train. Hinks called the guard and seeing Wilding was badly injured they sent for a doctor who pronounced him dead. Apparently, the steel which killed Wilding had been put there to hold up the brickwork in the tunnel which had been showing signs of weakness. Wilding's torch and cap were found in the tunnel. The Coroner said Wilding had died from severe head injuries. Hinks was praised for his prompt action in stopping the train. The railway was a significant employer for Alsager people during the war.

An important part of the work in the Home Front was the making of small items to help the war effort. In August 1944 Alsager WVS based in *Prospect House* organised the making of camouflage nets for the Ministry of Supply. Nine hundred and eighty-six nets were manufactured by members of Alsager WVS in morning and afternoon shifts. The WVS also sent £4 to the Red Cross Prisoner of War fund saved from cleaning expenses. Mrs L.W. Johnson sent a letter of thanks to members of Alsager WVS and asked for their support in future projects.

On 7th September 1944, the compulsory blackout was replaced by a partial *'dim-out'*. Restrictions were eased and Alsager Council announced street lighting would begin on 1st October. The Government thought the threat posed by bombing raids had significantly reduced. The Surveyor, Mr Lynam, told the *Alsager Times* he realised it was difficult for householders to find lighter materials to replace black-out curtains. The Wardens were asked to advise the public in how to maximise light in their homes without infringing the remaining regulations.

There were opportunities to study at evening classes in Alsager at the Alsager Evening Institute. In 1944 several students, including Dorothy Rigby, Constance Parks, and Annie Heler passed shorthand qualifications. Several children won scholarships to Crewe Secondary School and Sandbach Grammar School. Derek Fernyhough won The Sandbach Foundation Scholarship.

July saw the inaugural meeting of the Alsager Tenants Association. New Alsager residents, unlike native born Alsager people, were more ambitious and expected more in terms of facilities. Mr John Richardson, first Association President, complained about high wartime rents, the difficulties in transport, and the need for a children's playground. Membership of the Association was one hundred and forty-one and they were concerned because their area, Longview Avenue, was not yet represented in a Council Ward. They wished to assert their electoral rights. They were also opening a social centre in Longview Avenue to be managed by the Association. They also demanded access to the Mere. The council agreed to acquire land for public access to the Mere but pointed out that rights of access to the water were held in covenants by house owners adjacent to the water.

Housing was a major issue in Alsager in 1944. The Council put out an appeal to the public to let them know if they had any rooms to let. The council was using the Citizen's Advice Bureau to compile a register of houses to let in Alsager. Local born people were jealous that ROF families from London were given preference to the new housing in Longview Avenue. But the Alsager Tenants Association complained the Council were using *'back door methods'*, to choose applicants for housing. At a Council meeting in November 1944 the Members refuted the allegations and offered people the choice of applying for housing through a register and they outlined plans for the design and lay-out of the Wilbraham Estate. The Council Surveyor, Mr V Lynam insisted most of the houses on the Wilbraham estate should be semi-detached and not in blocks of four as preferred by the County Planner. The Council also proposed the use of prefabricated houses to deal with the housing shortages. Some of the prefabs were eventually built in Hassall Road close to where Alsager School is today.

Alsager prefab in Hassall Road

Meanwhile the traditional events in Alsager continued. The *'village fair'* organised by the British Legion took place in July. *The Staffordshire Weekly Sentinel* said the atmosphere at the show *'represented a peacetime occasion'*, where people could forget their *'wartime worries'*. Little Susan Hammersley presented Mrs Flatman, wife of the controller of ROF, with a bouquet for opening the event. Foden's Motor Works Band in their smart black, scarlet and gold uniforms, conducted by Fred Mortimer played, and there were donkey rides and a Punch and Judy show for the children. There were only two entries for the physical training competition, but there were more entries for the *'30 Guineas Challenge Cup'*, which was won by a team from St Joseph's College, Trent Vale. This seems an expensive prize for a wartime event. The crowds were also entertained by Talk' o' the Hill Male Voice Choir.

Mrs Flatman leaving the stage at the July 1944 show. Mr Leslie Hammersley (wearing buttonhole) stands second to her right.

In August 1944, the Radway Green Sports and Social Club held a Gala on the Parsonage Field in aid of the Red Cross and St John's Ambulance. It was opened by Mrs J. MacLeod wife of the BBC announcer. Perhaps he was supposed to have appeared in person but had to substitute his wife instead! Longton Town Silver Band played for the crowds, there were sports events, and a vegetable show put on by Alsager Allotments Society. In the evening, the produce was auctioned off for the charities. Despite rationing there was flexibility when it came to raising money for the war effort. There was also a *'fur and feather'* show of hens, pigeons, and caged birds. The Home Guard and sailors from *HMS Excalibur* also put on a display

Public Houses were popular in Alsager and often became very crowded. Alec Shaw (Shaw) recalls that his father, licensee of the *Lodge Inn* throughout the war had to contend with *'hordes of workers, servicemen, and munitions workers'*, wanting to frequent his father's pub. *The Lodge* became so crowded that customers sat on the stairs to find room to have a drink. Alec says that *The Lodge* had very primitive toilet facilities during the war before the Brewery modernised them, a urinal for men and a toilet in a shed for women.

The pub became very noisy, smoky, and crowded. Women munition workers mingled with Royal Marines and black American soldiers and sometimes a fight would ensue between the servicemen. He remembers a Royal Marine breaking his leg during a brawl in the back yard at *The Lodge*. The American troops were usually keen to buy larger than usual quantities of liquor to take back to *Barthomley Rectory* where they were based in an annexe, but Mr Shaw had to restrict the quantity of alcohol he gave them. There were beer shortages and often the pub would only open for three days a week and a sign was put up on the pub door, *'Closed no beer'*. Normal opening times were 10.30 am to 3 pm, then 5.30 to 10pm on weekdays; 11am to 2pm and 7 to 10pm on Sundays. Once, a rumour spread in Kidsgrove that a consignment of beer had been delivered to *The Lodge* and Mr Shaw found rows of men sitting outside the pub on the pavement. The American troops would often drive around Alsager in Bren Gun carriers and Jeeps until one day they disappeared. Presumably the contingent had been moved to the south of England in preparation for D Day. Despite their leaving, Alsager and its pubs remained very busy. Long convoys of buses and coaches continued to come through Alsager to bring the workers to Radway Green. *The Lodge* with its coke stove in the bar continued to be very smoky and busy.

According to Alec Shaw, who was just a boy during the war, they were *'wild times'*, in Alsager with the coming together of people from every part of the country and further afield looking for fun in their spare time. It was a very different world from the polite society of the Alsager's leading families.

Ruby Esther Stainton

In November 1944 came the news an Alsager nurse had been awarded the M.B.E for her brave service in France on two occasions, and in the Middle East.

> **ALSAGER NURSE DECORATED**
>
> Sister Ruby Esther Stainton, daughter of Mr. and Mrs. J. Stainton, 55, Fields Road, Alsager, who is serving with the Queen Alexandra Imperial Military Nursing Service Reserve, attached to the British Army of Liberation, has been awarded the M.B.E. (Military Division) in recognition of gallant conduct "in carrying out hazardous work in a very brave manner." Sister Stainton, who received her training at the Staffordshire General Infirmary, Stafford, and volunteered for service before the outbreak of war, served with the British troops in France and Belgium in 1940, then for three years in the Middle East, before going to France a second time.

Ruby Esther Stainton was born on 29th February 1914 in Hastings. She trained as a midwife in Burnley and joined the QAINS, service number 209238, and was first mentioned in the *London Gazette* in December 1941 where she was promoted Sister from 30th May 1941. In 1943, she was living at 55 Fields Road, Alsager. When she returned to France in 1944 she wrote to her parents, *'Everything is fine and dandy. We received the greatest welcome from the boys. It was like the desert all over again.'* Her MBE came in late 1944.

> **EXTRACTS FROM THE "LONDON GAZETTE."**
>
> *November* 10, 1944.—The KING has been graciously pleased to give orders for the following appointments to the Most Excellent Order of the British Empire, in recognition of gallant conduct in carrying out hazardous work in a very brave manner :—
>
> *To be Additional Members of the Military Division of the said Most Excellent Order :—*
>
> Sister Miss Ruby Esther Stainton (209238), Queen Alexandra's Imperial Military Nursing Service Reserve (Alsager, Stoke-on-Trent).

Ruby married Harry Mason in December 1952. In 1962, she was recorded as working in a nursing capacity at ROF Alsager. She died in Stoke-on-Trent in 2006.

Pilot Officer Nelson Arthur Bevans DFC

In 1944, it was announced Nelson Arthur Bevans had been awarded the Distinguished Flying Cross for *'the utmost fortitude; courage and devotion to duty.'*

Born 30th July 1908 in Alsager, he was the youngest child of John and Sarah Bevans of Alsager Road, (which later became Audley Road in Alsager.) His father was employed as a goods railway guard. Nelson went to the National School, Alsager.

In 1927 he became a Postman and in 1939 he was recorded as a *'Supervising Postman.'* In the 1930s he had moved to Newcastle-under-Lyme and lived at 197 Basford Park Road with his wife Gwendoline, whom he had married in 1932.

He enlisted in the 7th Squadron, RAFVR service number 178641. In 1943 he initially served in Stirling aircraft. Lancasters then began to replace Stirlings, and with the approach of the Allied invasion, France became the main target area for bombing in Lancasters. During the early stages of the liberation campaign many daylight attacks were made on German troop positions. Bevans was based at RAF Oakington during 1944. On 30th June 1944, he was gazetted Pilot Officer. On 17th November 1944, he was awarded the Distinguished Flying Cross. The Distinguished Flying Cross or DFC was in the main awarded to officers of the Royal Air Force, and many members of Bomber Command were awarded this decoration with its distinctive diagonal blue stripe, one of three flying awards having this style of ribbon. The DFC could be awarded for a tour of operations, or an immediate award for one operation. Made from silver, the medal did not carry the recipient's number, rank and name but was only dated with the year that it was awarded. Nelson Bevans died in Stoke-on-Trent in 1991.

Award of DFC to F/Lt. Tom Scott: Royal Air Force Volunteer Reserve, Mosquito Navigator

(Tom Scott, bottom left with Flying Officer Ted Lacy top left, Flying Officer Cobbledick front right)

Tom Cecil Scott lived the latter part of his life in Lodge Road, Alsager. (Finlow) He was born on 1st March 1921 in Newcastle-upon-Tyne. In

1939, he was living in *Maple Cottage,* Lyndhurst Drive, Gateshead with his widowed mother, Elizabeth and his sister Blanche. He worked as a clerk in the War Department. He married Betty Pollock, a hairdresser, in Newcastle-upon-Tyne in 1943. He joined the RAFVR (service number 135621) and crossed the Atlantic in 1940 to Canada where he completed his training as a RAF navigator. He was commissioned Pilot Officer in the *London Gazette* of 2nd April 1943, the award backdated to 4th December 1942.

After returning to Britain after training he took part in *'Fog Investigation and Dispersal Operations',* a secret experiment to rid airfields of fog. Calcium chloride sprays had shown some promise for absorbing fog in the 1930s but by 1940 the only proven dispersal method was heating on a massive scale. Churchill instructed the *'Petroleum Warfare Department',* an organisation originally tasked with creating burning obstacles against invasion, to develop a tool for the job. *'Fido'* was a system of fuel tanks, pipes and rows of burners running the length of a runway. Once lit, it created a fiery scene burning a hundred thousand gallons of fuel an hour with a great roaring sound. The flames were visible for sixty miles and the heat could disperse the thickest fog in a matter of minutes. The system did clear fog but the cost in terms of fuel and pollution was high.

Scott went on to work as a member of 248 Squadron part of 18 Group Coastal Command flying Mosquito planes from Banff airfield, Aberdeenshire. The DH98 de Havilland Mosquito was the successor to the de Havilland DH.88 Comet, a twin-engine British aircraft designed for and winner of the 1934 MacRobertson Air Race between London and Melbourne. The DH 98 served in many roles during and after the Second World War. Mosquito-equipped squadrons were asked to perform medium bomber, reconnaissance, tactical strike, anti-submarine warfare and shipping attack and night fighter duties, both defensive and offensive, until the end of the war. Mosquitos were widely used by the RAF Pathfinder Force, which marked targets for night-time strategic bombing. Despite an initially high loss rate, the Mosquito ended the war with the lowest losses of any aircraft in RAF Bomber Command service. The Mosquito had a two-man crew. The plane continued to serve during and after the Second World War. It was one of few operational front-line aircraft of the era constructed almost entirely of wood and was nicknamed *The Wooden Wonder.*

Picture: RAF Mosquito

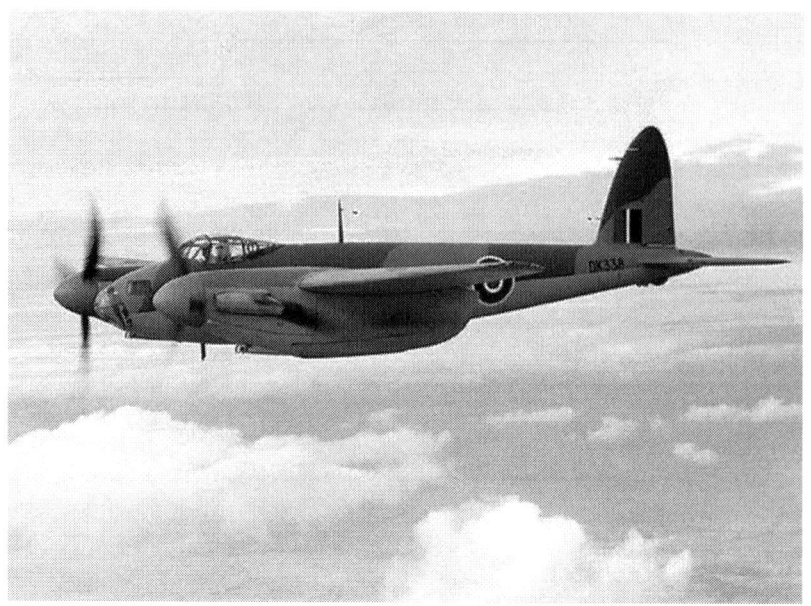

In *A Separate Little War: The Banff Coastal Command Strike Wing Versus the Kriegsmarine and Luftwaffe 1944-1945* by Andrew D. Bird. (Bird) he describes the missions undertaken from RAF Banff. He summarises the role of the Strike Force as,

'*Every day for nine months from September 1944 to the end of the war, young British, Commonwealth and Norwegian airmen flew from Banff aerodrome in northern Scotland in their Mosquitoes and Beaufighters to target the German U-Boats, merchantmen and freighters plying along the coast and in the fjords and leads of southwest Norway, encountering the Luftwaffe and flak ships every step of the way. This Scottish strike wing fought in some of the bitterest and bloodiest attacks of the war, all at very low level and at close quarters. Their contribution to winning the war was crucial and while the cost in precious lives and equipment was in the same proportion as Bomber Command, they inflicted far greater damage to the enemy in relation to their losses.*'

248 Squadron 1943-45

Tom Scott as Navigator flying with Ft/Lt. Yeates was responsible for navigation and photographic reconnaissance, taking photographs from his cockpit of bombing raids. He and Yeates took part in numerous bombing missions over the North Sea against enemy craft.

Yeates was first to be awarded the Distinguished Flying Cross, the citation as follows:

In April 1944, this Officer piloted one of a formation of aircraft which attacked a U-Boat, strongly escorted by 3 armed ships, 2 minesweepers and 12 Junkers 88s. In the fight, Flying Officer Yeates attacked the most powerfully armed of the escorting vessels and silenced its guns at the critical moment. He then engaged one of the enemy aircraft which he shot down. His determined gallantry and efforts contributed materially to the success of the operation. This Officer has completed many sorties and invariably displayed unfailing devotion to duty.

Yeates was awarded a BAR to the DFC in the London Gazette 29th September 1944:

Within recent months this Officer has completed many reconnaissance and participated in numerous successful attacks on enemy shipping. He is a gallant and tenacious fighter and has set a fine example in pressing home his attacks in the face of heavy opposing fire. In August 1944, Flying Officer Yeates attacked a medium sized merchantman inflicting much damage. Afterwards, he attacked 2 anti-aircraft guns on the mainland.

Tom Scott as part of the unit was also awarded the Distinguished Flying Cross in 1944 with the following citation of 3rd October 1944

> Flying Officer Thomas Cecil SCOTT (135621), R.A.F.V.R., 248 Sqn.
> This officer has participated in very many sorties, including numerous successful attacks on enemy shipping. He is a highly efficient and resolute navigator whose ability has contributed in good measure to the successes obtained. By his appreciation of the responsibilities entrusted to him and his unfailing devotion to the task on hand, this officer has set a very fine example.

In the book *Coastal Command* by John Campbell, (Campbell) one of Scott's missions is remembered. On 10th June 1944 four Mosquitoes were patrolling thirty feet apart between Ushant and Isle de la Seine to discover U-Boats leaving Brest. In Scott's Mosquito with him was Flying Officer Yeates. A U-Boat conning tower was seen to break the surface and the Mosquito section climbed to five hundred feet to observe the now surfaced U-Boat, the U-821 commanded by Oberleutnant Knackfuß. Its conning tower caught fire and the submarine seemed abandoned. Depth charges from a Liberator plane sank the submarine.

One of the memorable missions undertaken by Scott took place on 4th May 1945 shortly before the end of the war. The official record is as follows:

'Banff Strike Wing's final attack on shipping in the Kiel and Kattegat areas, finishing over Denmark: The squadrons involved were 143, 235, 248, 333 and 404, led by Wing Commander Pierce, consisting of forty one Mosquitoes, eighteen Mustangs for fighter cover; three Air Sea Rescue Warwicks were on hand to drop lifeboats to any ditched crews. A convoy was spotted consisting of an N—class Minesweeper, Three Merchant Vessels, one ex-Dutch gunboat and two smaller enemy vessels. The German Merchant Vessel WOLFGANG L.M. RUSS of 3750 tons was sunk and another German Merchant Vessel, the GUNTHER RUSS of 998 tons was damaged. The Danish Merchant Vessel ANGAMOS of 3540 tons was also damaged. The flak barrage was intense which resulted in four Mustangs failing to return. Two Mosquitoes suffered battle damage and landed in neutral territory. During the attack on the shipping near Samso Island all the vessels were 'seen to be hit' by either by rocket

projectiles and/or 20mm cannon fire. One Mosquito landed back at Banff with the German ensign (Scott's plane) and part of the mast off a ship, embedded in the nose of the aircraft, after colliding with it at low level, while pulling up over the ship. Later reports state that all ships were left either smoking or on fire.'

Amazingly when the plane landed, the ship's pennant was snagged on the bottom of Yeates' and Scott's plane. Yeates and Scott agreed to retain the four-foot-long masthead and pennant, which nearly destroyed their plane, and keep it as a memento. Their Mosquito had to be scrapped due to damage to its starboard tailgate leading edge. The pennant trophy was saved and according to *Fly Past* magazine in 2005 it was offered by Tom Scott and its custodian Mrs Pitman as a tribute to Banff Wing at its museum. Tommy said he *'would not be here'* if it wasn't for Yeates' incredible flying to get the plane back to Scotland.

Bird's account of that mission comes from a personal description by F/Lt. G.N.E. Yeates, DFC. The Mosquitoes hit them with all their armament and many wet and dry hits were observed. The merchantman *Wolfgang L.M Russ* caught fire immediately, rockets penetrating the main hold and then it exploded, ten minutes after being hit, and sank. Eight members of her crew survived and one of the escort vessels went down. The crew were picked up alive. They left the second merchantman the Danish *Angamos* of 3,540 tons badly damaged and K3 suffered 16 fatalities. Crewmen tackled fires in the stern, ammunition store and crew accommodation. Flight Lieutenant Yeates said:

> 'Gunners aboard an escort ship kept firing back at us, so we had to keep going at them. When I pulled out I could see the masthead coming straight at us and ducked automatically. I misjudged the height and there was a huge bang as we passed over the escort ship. The aircraft was vibrating badly as we climbed away to assess the flak damage.'

Bird writes that, *'Yeates then rejoined the force. The wing turned north for home and immediately sighted a small cargo vessel, the German, Gunther Russ of 998 tons on a northerly course. This was attacked by those aircraft with ammunition remaining and they left it burning. As Yeates and his navigator, Flight Lieutenant Tommy Scott DFC broke away from its final strike the fuselage panels started vibrating in the slipstream. Not knowing what had caused the damage the 22 year old pilot just concentrated on keeping it flying. Mosquitoes jostled to photograph the damage they saw. RS504 (Scott's plane) had hit the top of K3's timber masthead, tearing the Mosquitoe's plywood construction from the nose cover to the bomb bay and gutting the aircraft. The nose cover housing the 0.303 Browning's machine guns and 20 mm cannon bays was ripped open as the cannon breeches in the forward part of the bomb bay; the port engine's inner cover had also been wiped off. Both hoped it would see them back safely.'*

Tom Scott's plane managed to land safely back in Banff.

After retiring from the RAF, Scott became an accountant in the Civil Service. He lived in retirement in Lodge Road, Alsager, and in later life was a member of the Probus organisation. In 1997, he collaborated with Tony Finlow from Alsager and many of his wartime photographs were used in publications. Tom Scott died on 22nd November 2007. Ft/Lt Yeates was unfortunately killed in a flying accident in 1947

...

> Mrs. Leadbeater.
> Here is a further list of those in the Home Forces who have sent letters of thanks to Councillor James Clowes, secretary of the Alsager branch British Legion parcels' fund, for 10s. gifts which they have received: Private D. Arkcoll; L/Sergeant T. Bruffell; Private R. B. Thomas; Cfmn. E. Oakes, R.E.M.E.; Sapper H. Heath; L.M. Basford; Sapper A. W. Beech, R.E.; Joan Ebsworth, A.T.S.; S./Sgt. W. Edmond, R.A.; L/AC. James Bloor, R.A.F.; Sapper R. P. Ledward; J. Webster, R.A.F.; Driver T. Fennington; L/Cpl. Douglas Allen; Sapper J. B. Berridge; L/ACW. K. Leech, M. E. Ebsworth; Lieut. Frank W. Kerry, R.E.; Gunner Bert Shortland; Gunner A. Dale; W. I. Wood; Sapper W. Barker, R.E.; Gunner J. Kennerley; AC2. Frank Cotton; Leonard F. Roberts; R. H. Bingham, A.T.A.; Lieut. E. Cartwright, R.E.; Lilian McKee.

Food Parcels

1944 The Alsager Times printed a list of service men and women serving in the British Isles who gave their thanks to the Alsager British Legion for food parcels.

Deaths of Servicemen in 1944

Private Joseph Ernest Brookes: Northamptonshire Regiment

Date of death: 24th January 1944

Commemorated on Church Lawton War Memorial, All Saints Church

Joseph was born on 12th August 1916 in Newcastle-under-Lyme to Harold and Emma Ann Brookes, of Butt Lane. His mother's maiden name was Newlinson. In 1939 Joseph was living at *'High Lea'*, Old Butt Lane, Congleton Rural District, with his parents and brother. He worked as a pottery mould maker. His father was a *'Motor Driver'*. His brother, Harold, born in 1921, was a pottery statistics clerk. Another brother Alfred and his wife lived in the neighbouring property. In 1940 Joseph married Adeline Holland (Marriage registered Jan – March 1940).

When war was declared Joseph joined the Northamptonshire Regiment service number 5122095, and was assigned to the 2nd Battalion. The Battalion saw active service as part of the British Expeditionary Force (BEF) in the battles of Belgium and France and had to be evacuated from Dunkirk. After being evacuated to England they spent two years on home defence, re-training and re-equipping. 2nd Battalion then joined the forces sent to invade Madagascar in May 1942 and then travelled to India and overland to Persia (now Iran) and Iraq in September of the same year. It travelled to Egypt and next fought in Sicily and Italy.

On 3rd September 1943, the Allies invaded the Italian mainland, the invasion coinciding with an armistice made with the Italians who then re-entered the war on the Allied side.

Troops from 2nd Battalion, Northamptonshire Regiment, part of the 17th Brigade of the 5th Division, wait to board landing craft at Catania, Sicily, for the invasion of Italy, 2 September 1943.

The Northamptonshire Regiment was part of 17 Brigade. Allied objectives were to draw German troops from the Russian Front and more particularly from France, where an offensive was planned for the following year. Progress through southern Italy was rapid despite stiff resistance, but by the end of October, the Allies were facing the German winter defensive position known as the Gustav Line, which stretched from the river Garigliano in the west to the Sangro in the east. Initial attempts to breach the western end of the line were unsuccessful and it was not until 17th January 1944 that the River Garigliano was crossed, and Minturno taken two days later. Rome was the ultimate target for the Allies, and there were only two routes by which it could be reached; Highways 6 and 7. The latter had been flooded by the Germans, so Highway 6 was the only one through which the mission could be accomplished.

The highway was dominated by the town of Cassino and the mountain behind it. The Germans had stationed their men on every peak, giving them a spectacular overview of the Allies in their preparations for battle. A total of four assaults required before Cassino and Monte Cassino were finally liberated.

The first assault was launched on 17th January 1944 and was spearheaded by the British X Corps, who forced a crossing of the Garigliano River. Up against them was the German 94th Infantry Division which not only failed to stop the crossing but then started incurring huge losses which caused panic among the German XIV Panzer Corps. Joseph was buried in Minturno War Cemetery on 19th December 1944, having been re-buried from an *'isolated site'*. In the Commonwealth War Grave records Joseph is described as a Lance Corporal not a Private. He is buried in Grave Reference: I, A,25. The site for the cemetery was chosen in January 1944, but the Allies then lost some ground and the site came under German small-arms fire. The cemetery could not be used again until May 1944 when the Allies launched their final advance on Rome and the US 85th and

88th Divisions were in this sector. Minturno is about eighty kilometres north of Naples, close to the coast. The cemetery lies several kilometres south of the town on the SS7 road to Naples and is situated in the locality of Marina di Minturno (Garigliano). Minturno War Cemetery contains two thousand and forty-nine Commonwealth burials of the Second World War. The burials are mainly those of the heavy casualties incurred in crossing the Garigliano in January 1944.

 **Serjeant George Bosson: Royal Artillery**

Date of death: 30th January 1944

Commemorated on Odd Rode War Memorial

George Bosson was born in Kidsgrove in July 1918, to Harold and Edith May Bosson (nee Wood) and the birth was registered in Wolstanton. His father, originally from Scholar Green, was born in 1892, and worked as a coal hewer. The family lived in 1939 at 17 Galley's Bank Kidsgrove. George had a sister, Hilda, born in 1920, who was a *'Silk Mill Overlooker'*, and Gordon, born in 1922, a *'Haulage Hand'* (a miner) working underground. George Bosson joined the army in 1938 as a career soldier aged twenty having worked in the mining industry. He was attested in the Royal Artillery, service number 884765.

In 1942 George married Doris Marjorie Hancock, who was born on 27th August 1917; the wedding was registered in Crewe (October to December 1942.) They lived in Mount Pleasant on the Cheshire side of Mow Cop. George was promoted through the ranks to Serjeant and was assigned to the 81st Anti-Tank Regiment of the Royal Artillery. The Regiment served in the North Africa campaign and then in the liberation of Italy in 1943. In Tunisia the 81st were part of the 1st Infantry Division

At the end of 1943, following the Allied invasion of Italy, Allied forces were bogged down at the Gustav Line, a defensive line across Italy south of the strategic objective of Rome. The terrain of central Italy had proved ideally suited to defence. *Operation Shingle* was originally conceived by Winston Churchill in December 1943, as he lay recovering from pneumonia in Marrakesh. His concept was to land two divisions at Anzio, bypassing German forces in central Italy, and take Rome, the strategic objective of the current Battle of Rome. Allied forces in this attack consisted of five cruisers, twenty-four destroyers, two hundred and thirty eight landing craft, other ships, forty thousand soldiers, and five thousand vehicles. Although resistance had been expected, as seen at Salerno during 1943, the initial landings were essentially unopposed, with the exception of the Luftwaffe's strafing runs. By midnight, thirty-six thousand soldiers and three thousand two hundred vehicles had landed on the beaches. The attack, including the 81st Anti-Tank regiment, on 22nd January 1944 consisted of three groups including the British force on *Peter Beach*, 6 miles (9.7 km) north of Anzio. However, some twenty-four gunners from the 81st were captured at Anzio when their position was overrun.

George Bosson died of wounds on 30th January 1943. It is unclear if the wounds were caused on the 22nd January or later. The casualty records do not clarify this.

George is buried in Anzio War Cemetery Grave Reference: IV, B, 7. The wording on his grave was chosen by his widow Doris, who died in Stafford in 2002. Greater love hath no man, who died that we might live. Where he lies, So does my heart also.

George's personal record card does not give us any further details.

 **Private John New: Duke of Wellington's (West Riding Regiment)**

Date of Death: 5th February 1944

Commemorated on Odd Rode War Memorial

John New was the son of Son of Emmanuel and Elizabeth New, *nee* Whitmarsh, of Rode Heath. He was born on 22nd February 1914 in Rode Heath. His sister May was his oldest sibling. His brother Edwin was born in 1916. John's father was a *'sewerage attendant'*. His brother Harold, who died in infancy, was born in 1921. His sister Hilda was born in 1925, Kathleen in 1928, and his brother Leslie in 1930. They lived at *'The Poplars'*, Rode Heath. After school John, known to his friends as *'Jack'*, became a bricklayer.

At the time he enlisted he was living in Chapel Lane.

He served in the 1st Battalion Duke of Wellington's (West Riding Regiment) service number 14339790. At the outbreak of the Second World War the 1st Battalion Duke of Wellingtons (West Riding Regiment) was sent to France as part of the British Expeditionary Force. During the retreat from Dunkirk they formed part of the rear guard. In 1942 the 1st Battalion landed in North Africa and took part in a number of key battles in 1943. They fought at the Battle of Medjez Plain and the Battle of Banana Ridge and in the Battle of Djebel bou Aoukaz. In 1944, they landed at Anzio and were in action in some of the most desperate fighting of the war. John New was killed in the battle of Monte Casino.

Landing craft at Anzio.

Originally buried in Campo Verano cemetery Rome, John New was reburied on 18th January 1945 in the current grave plot He is buried in plot 1.A.3 in Rome War Cemetery, Città Metropolitana di Roma Capitale, Lazio, Italy which was designed by Louis de Soissons. It contains four hundred and twenty-six Commonwealth burials of the Second World War.

In his will Jack left £450. 9s 9d to his father.

Wording on Jack New's grave;

'Memories of a smiling face. A broken link, we cannot replace. Love from all.'

Corporal James Victor Gibson:
Royal Tank Regiment, R.A.C. 51st (The Leeds Rifles)
Date of death: 23rd May 1944
Commemorated on Odd Rode Memorial, All Saints Church

Victor Gibson 4th from left back row (hatless) in Rode Park Cricket team 1930s

James Victor Gibson was born on 24th July 1912 to Henry and Eleanor Gibson (*nee* Burke). The birth was registered in Wolstanton in 1912 (3rd Quarter 6b page 216.) His parents lived in Yew Tree Terrace, Ravenscliff Road, Kidsgrove. James had five older brothers and sisters, Clara, Mark Arthur, William, and Evelyn. Although he was a native of Kidsgrove he spent most of his youth in Rode Heath. James went to Wolstanton Grammar School and studied for a languages degree at Sheffield University. His father was a coal miner. James served as a policeman in Stafford for two years. Clara, his sister, was a teacher with Cheshire County Council at Rode Heath School. James was to follow his sister into teaching and in 1939 was living with his married sister Clara Gibbs, and her husband Frank Gibbs, in *Wood View*, Rode Heath. In the 1939 Register James is recorded as *'Certificated Teacher'*. He was single and taught at Odd Rode Boys' School and was a member of Odd Rode cricket team. Two of his brothers were killed in the Great War and another was captured at Dunkirk and was in a German Prisoner of War camp.

At the beginning of the war, James was living in Chapel Street, Rode Heath. In 1940 James married Gwendoline Brookes in Newcastle under Lyme. James joined the Royal Tank Regiment 51st, (The Leeds Rifles) service number 7918851.

At the end of May 1940, with the British Expeditionary Force (BEF) being evacuated from Dunkirk and the imminent threat of German invasion of England, the 25th Army Tank Brigade was re-designated 2nd Motor Machine Gun Brigade and its regiments reorganised accordingly. Each of 51 RTR's three MMG squadrons consisted of three troops, each with six Humber Snipe or Hillman Utility (*Tilly*) two-seat cars, two carrying Vickers medium machine guns, two Bren light machine guns and two Boys anti-tank rifles. In July 1940, volunteers from the units of 25th Army Tank Brigade formed No 5 Troop of No. 5 Commando at Bridlington. In August 51 RTR and the rest of the brigade moved to Northumberland to guard the coastline with machine gun posts along the cliffs and sand dunes. The 25th Army Tank Brigade was reconstituted at the end of 1940, and its regiments began to receive a trickle of tanks on which to train. By the end of 1942, when James joined them, 51 RTR was fully trained and fully equipped with Churchill tanks. In January 1943, the regiment embarked, with the rest of the 25th Tank Brigade, for North Africa, where it came under the command of V Corps of the British First Army in the Tunisian Campaign.

Tunisia

The regiment took part in containing the German offensive of Operation Ochsenkopf in February - March 1943. At a place called *Steamroller Farm*, two Churchill tanks ambushed and shot up an entire German transport column before re-joining the rest of their squadron.

On 7th–8th April 51 RTR supported IX Corps at the Fondue Pass. The 128th (Hampshire) Brigade of 46th Infantry Division crossed the Wadi Marguellil during the night and at 5.30 am on 8th April began its main attack, supported by 'C' Sqn 51 RTR, and by noon was on its objective.

A carrier and a Churchill tank of 51st Royal Tank Regiment during 6th Armoured Division's attack on the town of Pichon, Tunisia, 8th April 1943. Photo Wikipedia.

The 25th Tank Brigade came under the command of Brigadier James Noel Tetley of the Leeds Rifles at the end of the Tunisia campaign. He was the only Territorial Army officer of the Royal Tank Regiment to command a brigade on active service. The brigade, including 51 RTR, remained training in North Africa for almost a year, before they were required for service on the Italian Front. The regiment celebrated Cambrai Day (20th November, commemorating the tank Battle of Cambrai) in Algeria. 51 RTR embarked on 16th April 1944 and landed at Naples, where it was equipped with Churchill tanks, with a few Shermans and Stuarts. Following the commencement of the liberation of Italy the brigade distinguished itself in support of the 1st Canadian Infantry Division in the assault on the *'Hitler Line'* in May 1944. The purpose of the *'Hitler Line'* was to prevent the Allies from entering Rome. It was the hardest part of the German line to conquer, a barricade of steel, concrete and barbed wire

20 feet thick. At the request of the Canadians, its regiments adopted the Maple leaf as an additional badge, later worn by 51 RTR's successors, the Leeds Detachment (Leeds Rifles), Imphal (PWO) Company, East and West Riding Regiment.

James Victor Gibson was killed on 23rd May 1944 in the battle to breach the *'Hitler Line'*. He was buried on the battlefield at and re-buried at Cassino Cemetery on 2nd February 1945 in plot II. K. 11. In 1945 probate was granted to his wife whose wartime address was in Kidsgrove.

James Gibson's grave Cassino.

Lance Serjeant Thomas Brough: Worcestershire Regiment

Date of death: 4th July 1944

Commemorated on Church Lawton War Memorial, All Saints Church

Thomas was born on 9th March 1910 in Kidsgrove Staffordshire to Joseph and Sarah Brough. Joseph was a store keeper from Kidsgrove born in 1881. Sarah was born in 1887. (Cen) In 1911 the family lived at 8 Liverpool Road Kidsgrove. Thomas had a brother, Joseph Brough, born in 1908. Thomas married Marion Dulson in 1932 in Congleton (marriage registered Jan –March: 8a 539). Marion was born on 29th November 1911. By 1939 Thomas and Marion were living at 1 Sandbach Road, Church Lawton. He was working as a general labourer. They had a son, Thomas, born on 21st March 1933.

It is likely Thomas enlisted in the 11th Battalion of the Worcestershire Regiment Service number 5258120 and later transferred to the 1st Battalion when the 11th was re-designated in 1943.

On 22nd June 1942, the original 1st Battalion Worcestershire (a war service battalion raised in 1940 still fighting in North Africa) had surrendered, along with thirty thousand other British Commonwealth troops, at Tobruk during the disastrous Battle of Gazala. Of the men of the original battalion, only sixty-eight officers and men remained. The 11th Battalion was therefore disbanded. On 1st January 1943, it was renumbered the 1st Battalion, during a parade which included the Colonel of the Regiment George Grogan VC and Field Marshal Claud Jacob.

The reformed 1st Battalion transferred, in September 1943, to the 214th Infantry Brigade, 43rd (Wessex) Infantry Division, alongside the 5th Battalion, Duke of Cornwall's Light Infantry and 7th Battalion, Somerset Light Infantry. The battalion continued training in preparation for operations in North-Western Europe for D Day. Together with the rest of the 214th Brigade, the battalion landed in Normandy, as part of Operation Overlord, on 24th June 1944, and soon fought in Operation Epsom.

It is likely Thomas Brough was killed in the village of Mouen, Normandy on 4th July 1944. His body was originally buried in the village and only later transferred to its final resting place in the Banneville-La Camapagne War Cemetery. In their book *'On the Bloody Road to Berlin'*, Duncan Rogers and Sarah Rhiannon Williams describe how the Worcestershire Regiment attacked the village of Mouen. Two weeks prior to the Worcesters' attack on Moen a terrible war crime took place in the village which was then held by the German 12th SS Engineering Battalion (which had elements of the Hitler Youth in its ranks.) On the 17th June seven Canadian prisoners were taken near the village and interrogated by the NCO of the 12th SS Engineering Battalion. Hours later the prisoners were taken to the outskirts of Mouen and shot in cold blood by the Nazis. Local French civilians were used to dig a pit for their grave. No one was ever convicted of this war crime.

Two weeks later the Worcesters attacked the village,

> *'The plan was that the Worcestershires should attack by daylight – but under the cover of an intense artillery smokescreen, mixed with high artillery explosive fire located on enemy forward positions in the hedgerows just west of the village. From the start line to our first objective we had to move 800 yards through a cornfield that afforded no cover from enemy small arms and machine guns.'*

The commanders decided to attack in diamond formation behind the artillery barrage. As they moved forward there was an enemy counter attack with artillery. It is likely Thomas Brough was killed in this attack.

A farmhouse in Mouen during the attack. Photo: On the Bloody Road to Belin *by Rogers and Williams.* (Williams)

Thomas was re-buried at Banneville-la-Campagne which is a village in Normandy 10 kilometres east of Caen. The cemetery lies 100 metres south of the Route de Rouen (the D675) between Caen and Pont l'Eveque. The Allied offensive in north-western Europe began with the Normandy landings of 6th June 1944. For the most part, the men buried at Banneville-la-Campagne War Cemetery were killed in the fighting from the second week of July 1944, when Caen was captured, to the last week in August, when the Falaise Gap had been closed and the Allied forces were preparing their advance beyond the Seine. The cemetery contains two thousand one hundred and seventy Commonwealth burials of the Second World War, one hundred and forty of them unidentified, and five Polish graves.

Thomas Brough's grave reference X1 E 14

Private William Hulse: The Highland Light Infantry

(City of Glasgow Regt 2nd Battalion-Glasgow Highlanders)

Date of death: 17th July 1944

Commemorated on Odd Rode War Memorial

William Hulse was the son of Frank and Alice Hulse, *nee* Bason, of Scholar Green, and was born in 1914. His birth was registered in July-September 1914; 8a 546. His parents lived at 8 Congleton Road, Scholar Green. His father was a '*Sand Pit Labourer*' and William had two brothers, Frank, born in 1912, and George born in 1916. He joined the 2nd Battalion, Highland Light Infantry (City of Glasgow Regiment) service number 996983. The Battalion prepared for D Day and left for Normandy arriving on 17th June 1944. The following War Diary shows Battalion movements

City of Glasgow Highlanders July 1944

Operation Greenline, 15th–17th July 1944 Esquay

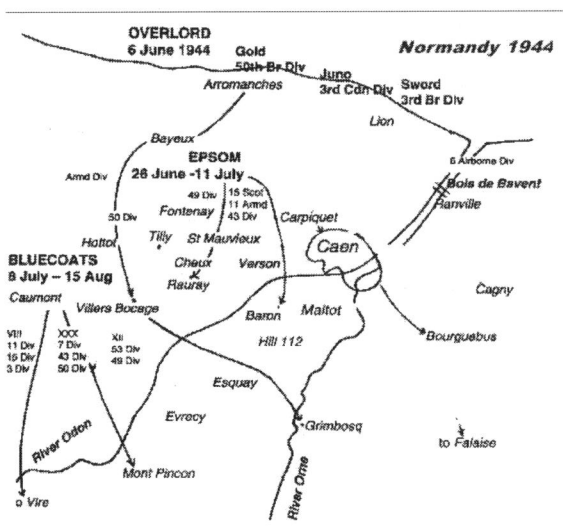

On the left flank of the 15th (Scottish) Division, the crossroads at le Bon Repos and the higher ground overlooking Esquay-Notre-Dame were attacked by the 2nd Glasgow Highlanders of the 227th (Highland) Infantry Brigade (227th Brigade), supported by Churchill tanks of the 107th Regiment Royal Armoured Corps (107th RAC) of the 34th Tank Brigade and the 141st Regiment Royal Armoured Corps (141st RAC) of the 79th Armoured Division, equipped with Churchill Armoured Vehicle Royal Engineers

(AVRE) and Churchill Crocodile flame thrower tanks. The Scottish advanced from the north-east, south-west over the northern slope of Hill 112, towards the defences of the III Battalion, 21st SS-Panzergrenadier Regiment. As the infantry emerged from dead ground they were met by massed mortar fire, which temporarily disorganised the battalion, as did a smoke screen placed on Hill 112, which had merged with fog and covered the area. The Scottish still managed to cross the start line on time at 9:30 p.m. and captured the S.S. survivors of a flame attack by the *'Crocodiles'* on the road running from Croix des Fila to le Bon Repos. The advance continued downhill under *Monty's Moonlight* and covering fire from the 107th RAC Churchills on higher ground just south of Baron. (The 344th Moonlight Battery, Royal Artillery was a searchlight unit of the British Army that provided artificial illumination, or *'Monty's Moonlight'*, for night operations.) Esquay was captured by 11:00 p.m. but not held, as its position below a saucer of higher ground made it a shell-trap. [20]

The two leading tank squadrons and two troops of *'Crocodiles'* from the 141st RAC were engaged, while the third squadron waited in reserve behind the crest, under frequent mortar fire during the evening and night. Four tanks were lost but many of the crews returned after dark. The troops dug in on the surrounding rises at positions determined earlier using reconnaissance photographs. The attack was interpreted by the Germans as a move on Hill 112 and Tiger tanks of 102nd Schwere SS-Panzer Abteilung were sent up the southern slope to repulse an attack that never came. Further west, the rest of the division had captured Point 113 but not Évrecy, which left the Glasgow Highlanders overlooked from both flanks, although German counter-attacks by infantry of the 21st SS-Panzergrenadier Regiment and tanks of the 10th SS-Panzer Regiment at first concentrated on Esquay, which had already been evacuated. The Germans counter-attack then fell on the positions around le Bon Repos, where two Panzer IV were knocked out by 6-pounder anti-tank guns. The Scottish were pushed back several times, only for the medium artillery of XII Corps to bombard the Germans back out.

Hulse was killed during the above action during the evening of 16th - 17th July during the mortar attacks on the 2nd Battalion by the Germans. His final resting place is unknown.

William Hulse is commemorated on the Bayeux Memorial, at Panel 17, Column 2. France. The town of Bayeux, in Normandy, lies 30 kilometres north-west of Caen. The Bayeux Memorial is situated in the south-western outskirts of the town. The Bayeux Memorial stands opposite the cemetery and bears the names of more than one thousand eight hundred men of the Commonwealth land forces who died in the early stages of the campaign and have no known grave. (Photo: Author)

Guardsman Edwin Buckley Jones : 3rd Battalion Grenadier Guards

Date of Death: 17th July 1944
Commemorated Odd Rode War Memorial

Edwin Buckley Jones was born on 23rd February 1922 to Eli and Fanny Jones, *nee* Billingham. His father was a *'Colliery Shunter'*. They lived at 14 South Street, Mow Cop, Cheshire. He was named after his uncle, also called Edwin Buckley Jones who served in the Royal Field Artillery in the Great War. After school, young Edwin worked as *'Chemical Worker in Exhaust House'*.

He enlisted with the Grenadier Guards service number 2622792. The Battalion was part of the British Expeditionary Force sent to France in 1939. The 3rd Battalion was in the 1st Guards Brigade attached to the 1st Infantry Division, commanded by Major General Harold Alexander. As the BEF was pushed back by the German *Blitzkrieg* during the battles of France and Dunkirk, the battalion played a considerable role in maintaining the British Army's reputation during the withdrawal phase of the campaign before being themselves evacuated from Dunkirk.

The 3rd Battalion, still part of the 1st Guards Brigade, was attached to the 78th *'Battleaxe'* Infantry Division for two months in Tunisia until it was exchanged for the 38th (Irish) Brigade and became part of the 6th Armoured Division, where it would remain for the rest of the war.

Entrance to Arrezo Cemetery

The Germans made a stand in front of Arezzo early in July 1944 and there was fierce fighting before the town was taken on 16th July by the 6th Armoured Division with the aid of the 2nd New Zealand Division. Jones was killed on 17th July 1944. He was buried near where he fell, then reburied on 26th March 1945 in plot VB9 in Arezzo War Cemetery, Tuscany. The site for this cemetery was selected in November 1944, and graves were brought into it from the surrounding area. Both the 4th and the 8th Indian Divisions were involved in the fighting in this region, and Plots VII-IX in the cemetery contain Indian graves. Arezzo War Cemetery contains one thousand two hundred and sixty-six Commonwealth burials of the Second World War.

 **Lance Corporal Richard Shiel Woodcock:**

Royal Armoured Corps, 13th/18th Royal Hussars

Date of death: 27th July 1944

Commemorated on Alsager War Memorial

Richard Shiel Woodcock was born in 1911 in Butley, near Chester-Le-Street, Durham, the only son of Andrew and Doris Woodcock (*nee* Cooper) His father was a butcher. He had a sister, D.M Woodcock.

He married Faith M. I. Willis in 1941 in Alsager. They lived at *'The Bungalow,'* Radway Green. Richard was employed before the war in *'matters of national importance'*. It is likely he was employed at Radway Green. He was a member of Alsager Working Men's Club.

In June 1943 Woodcock joined the 13/18th Hussars, a Tank Regiment. He took part in the D Day landings with the regiment.

The 13/18th Hussars were an armoured regiment as opposed to an assault regiment - meaning that they were lighter and faster in order to pursue the enemy through the holes in the enemy defences broken by the assault regiments. The unit had squadrons of three 75mm Sherman tanks and one *'firefly'* (a Sherman with the 17-pounder gun) whereas the Assault regiments had three squadrons of five troops of three tanks each - usually Churchills with the six pounders - and later with Churchill tanks with the 95mm howitzer. Each troop had a Lieutenant as Tank Commander as well as a sergeant and corporal - sometime two corporals - the commanding officer of the squadron was a Major and the regimental commanding officer would be a Lieutenant Colonel.

The War diary for the regiment reads:

On 18 July 1944, between SANNERVILLE and BANNNERVILLE. *'On the afternoon of the 17th [July 1944] the Sqn. moved to a preliminary forming up area south of DOUVRES la DELIVRANDE; in a Regtl. column we then moved by night back across the Orne river and canal to a concentration area east of HEROUVILLETTE. 1st Troop had previously re-joined us and had been replaced [at Monty HQ] by a composite Regtl Troop. The Squadron remained in this concentration area until next day, whilst plans and recces were carried out with 1st*

Battalion Suffolk Regt., with whom we had landed on 'D' Day. Early the next morning we moved out to the area north of the CHATEAU at ESCOVILLE prior to marrying up with the Suffolks for an attack on SANNERVILLE. This attack was not to be launched until 'A' and 'B' Squadrons had captured the ground south east of ESCOVILLE and the village of TOUFFREVILLE during which period 'C' Squadron was in reserve but were moved forward to the high ground north of SANNERVILLE to support the assaulting infantry [sic]. The Suffolks entered the village without difficulty and the remainder of the Squadron joined 2nd Troop on the high ground. At the request of the Infantry Colonel 4th Troop were sent into the village for mopping up and 3rd Troop to the orchards north east to deal with snipers. As soon as the situation was static the Suffolks consolidated the ground between SANNERVILLE and BANNERVILLE and asked for tanks to be sent forward. Whilst this was going on 4 Tanks were knocked out by unseen enemy S.P.'s (guns) from the south east, two of the Tanks were later recovered by the ARV. In this action Tpr. Spavin and L/c. Woodcock were killed. Lt. Uttley, PR. Ward (for the 2nd time) Tpr. Williams'72, L/Sgt Ellis Cpls Barnes, tar. Maggot, PR. Denyer and Tpr. Foster were wounded. The Squadron returned to the area and remained for the next 3 days until 22nd July in a counter attack role.'

Lance Corporal R.S. Woodcock did not die as the War Diary states but was evacuated from the battlefield and returned to England where he died on 27th July. He died at the Canadian Military Hospital, Basingstoke, Hampshire on 27th July 1944. He is buried in Christ Church Cemetery. (North ground) Alsager. *The Alsager Times* gave an account of his funeral. The coffin was draped in the Union Flag and members of the British Legion gave a guard of honour. His widow, Faith Woodcock of *Heath Farm* was present, along with her brother A.C.D. Willis, who was serving in the RAF. There were beautiful floral tributes.

Probate was granted to Faith Mary Isobel Woodcock (widow) £377. 9s 2d on 1st November 1945. In 1947 Faith Woodcock married Ernest Moseley, brother of Alfred Eric Moseley who is commemorated on Alsager War Memorial.

Ernest Moseley

Lance Corporal of Horse Lewys William Evans: 2nd Life Guards

Date of death: 3rd August 1944

Commemorated on Odd Rode War Memorial

Lewys Evans was born in December 1920 in Rode Heath to John Walter Evans and his wife Sarah (*nee* Follows). His birth was registered in January to March 1921. The family were associated with canal transport business. He had a sister, Florence, born in 1924, and a brother, John, born in 1927. In 1939 Lewys's family were living at 11 Low Street, Rode Heath, a canal side house. Lewys's grandmother, Myra Follows, a former canal boat woman, was living with them. When war broke out John Walter Evans became an Air Raid Warden in Rode Heath. Several people in Rode Heath remember Lewys walking around the village during the war in Scottish regimental uniform. At some stage he transferred to the Life Guards.

Lewys Evans joined the Life Guards of the Household Cavalry, service number 2982567, 2nd Battalion. British cavalry regiments mechanised for the Second World War, and the Life Guards and The Blues formed the 1st and 2nd composite Household Cavalry Regiments, the second of which is described by General Brian Horrocks as *'the finest armoured car regiment I have ever seen'*. They saw action in Palestine, North Africa and in North West Europe as reconnaissance units. It is unknown if Lewys trained with the Battalion in the traditional cavalry role as a horseman.

Traditional role of the Household Cavalry

The Irish Black is the horse of choice for the Household Cavalry, but other breeds are also incorporated. Shire and Clydesdale draft horses are used as drum horses.

The rank of sergeant does not exist in the Household Cavalry. The equivalent is Corporal of Horse, which also applies to any other ranks with the word sergeant in it, such as Regimental Sergeant Major, which is replaced by Regimental Corporal Major. King Edward VII also declared the rank of Private should be replaced by the rank of Trooper in the cavalry.

Lewys Evans reached the rank of Lance Corporal of Horse by 1944.

Prior to 1944 the regiment served at Baghdad 1941, Iraq 1941, Palmyra, Syria 1941, El Alamein, and North Africa 1942-43. In 1944 the 2nd Life Guards were part of the Guards Armoured Division. The division remained in the United Kingdom in training, until 13th June 1944. It then landed several armoured command vehicles at Arromanches after D Day. It was part of VIII Corps where its first major engagement was Operation Goodwood, the attack by three armoured divisions towards Bourguébus Ridge in an attempt to break out of the Normandy beachhead.

Lewys was killed on 3rd August and was originally buried in the village of St Jean des Essartiers, a tiny village in the Calvados region of Normandy. It is likely Lewys was killed near the village of Estry following German counterattacks as described by Patrick Deforce in his book *The Black Bull* (published by Pen & Sword) (Delaforce) about the 11th Armoured Division:

'August 3rd, 1944: Various German counter attacks were building up and the General anticipated 9th SS Panzer would exert strong pressure from Monchamp and Estry. If the Estry and Perier ridges fell, then the whole of V11 Corps would go rolling back the 7 miles to Bény-Bocage. Quite soon a small village between two ridges, was recaptured by the Germans. A glorious hot day now brought heavy attacks all along the thin red line.'

In September 1945 Lewys was reburied in the Bayeux War Cemetery, Calvados, grave reference: XXV. F. 17. Bayeux War Cemetery is the largest Commonwealth cemetery of the Second World War in France and contains burials brought in from the surrounding districts and from hospitals that were located nearby. It is situated in the south-western outskirts of the town of Bayeux, in Normandy, which lies 24 kilometres north-west of Caen.

Lewys Evans' grave:

'Son of John Walter and Sarah Evans; husband of Marion R. Evans, of Sauchie, Clackmannanshire.' (It has not been able to ascertain any information concerning Mrs Marion Evans)

Where no shadows fall

In perfect peace

He awaits us all'

Ordinary Seaman Cyril Dennis Longshaw: Royal Navy, H.M.S Quorn

Date of Death: 3rd August 1944

Commemorated on Odd Rode War Memorial

Cyril Dennis Longshaw was born on 19th May 1925 in Mow Cop to Arthur C. Longshaw, and Mabel A. Longshaw (nee Haycock). His father was a *'colliery rope splicer'* and they lived at *Meadow Cottage*, Church Street, Mow Cop. He had three siblings, Clifford born 1919, Eva born 1922, and Raymond born 1927. Cyril joined the Royal Navy, service number, P/JX 523500. He served aboard *H.M.S Quorn* and died at sea on 3rd August 1944. *H.M.S Quorn* was a destroyer built in 1939. It had four 4-inch guns

H.M.S Quorn

In June 1944 *HMS Quorn* was used as an escort for convoys during Operation Neptune, the D Day Landings. On 3rd August, she was hit and sunk during a heavy attack by a *'human torpedo'* and low flying aircraft in the region of Courseulles-sur-Mer, Normandy. She was operating in the British Assault Area off the Normandy beaches, at 8 knots, when a tremendous explosion occurred on the starboard side amidships. The whole of the starboard side of the midship section abreast the funnel was destroyed. The ship immediately took a 40 degrees list to starboard and within a minute was on her beam ends, but within 1 ¾ minutes of the explosion had righted herself to a 50-degree list and had broken in two amidships.

Both ends of the ship were observed to sink rapidly until about 30 feet of the stern and 15 feet of the bows were above water.

Those that survived the initial attack spent up to eight hours in the water before being rescued, and many of these perished. Four officers and one hundred and twenty-six ratings were lost.

HMS Quorn (Lt. Ivan Hall, RN) was sunk by a German *'Linsen'* explosive motorboat or a German *'Neger'* manned torpedo off the invasion area.

This is an eye witness account by Norman Ackroyd (a survivor) of the events of the night of 3rd August 1944: (Rec1)

'The ship had been part of the beachhead defence force for some nights before, on the night of August 3rd, we sailed as normal just before dusk and went to all night action stations (I was part of No 3 guns crew on the quarterdeck) again as normal, this time however we were accompanied by an American radar ship and we were informed over the tannoy that at dawn we were going in close to Le Havre in order to bombard submarine pens. The American ship was to control the shelling. Just before midnight however there was a massive explosion amidships and I understand we had been hit in the boiler rooms, the ship broke in two, and sank in a few minutes. I personally was blown overboard by the blast and found myself in the water fully dressed. A large number of my shipmates must have gone down with the ship but there were quite a lot of us in the water. The American ship left the scene at full speed which caused a lot of resentment at the time, but it was explained to us later that if she had stayed she would possibly have sustained the same fate as the Quorn. A lot of those with me in the water did not last the night but quietly slipped away. I was in the water for eight and a half hours before we were picked up by an armed trawler looking for us, by that time we were only a small band. We were informed after that the ship had been sunk by a German human torpedo on which the pilot sat on a type of torpedo which had an explosive torpedo slung underneath and that the German pilot had been picked up by another of our destroyers of the defence force. We were also told that we had run into a number of these torpedoes which were being carried into the beach head by the tide but as a result of the Quorn being sunk the alarm had been raised and the other torpedoes had been dealt with.'

There is another account of the sinking from the German perspective by Ferdinand Hoffman written in 2005. He was aboard a *'human torpedo'* or *'Neger'*.

The *'Neger'* was based on the G7e torpedo and sported a spartan cockpit covered by a Perspex dome where the warhead would have been. It had sufficient positive buoyancy to run awash while supporting a second G7e, with warhead, slung below. The vessel had a range of 48 nautical miles at 4 knots and displaced 2.7 tons. The pilot navigated via a wrist compass and air was provided through a Dräger self-contained breathing device. The pilot aimed his weapon by lining up an aiming spike on the nose with a graduated scale on the dome. Subsequently, a second aiming spike was added closer to the dome. It, however, made little difference as water washing over the dome made visibility extremely poor. A simple lever in the cockpit irreversibly started the torpedo and released it. Though not designed as a suicide weapon, the *'Neger'* would frequently become one when the torpedo started running but failed to release, and carried the craft and its pilot toward the target.

The 'Neger', human torpedo

About two hundred vessels of this type were manufactured in 1944. The first *'Neger'* vessels entered service in March 1944. However, the *'Neger'* turned out to be very hazardous for its crew, and up to 80% of the crews were killed.

3 Aug 1944

Sinking the Quorn (Employment of a human torpedo on the 02/03.08.1944) (Report of Ferdinand Hoffmann, written down by Alfons Steck) (Hoffman)

'At the beginning of the war I was an enthusiastic German and volunteer. After an examination as a miner I was sure to become a volunteer of war. If you hear all your life only the propaganda of the Nazis and no other opinion, you probably cannot act in another way. As youngsters, we had been drilled in the German Jungvolk for a war from the beginning, but we ourselves did not notice this. Maybe, there was no other decision possible as to become a volunteer. In the end, I decided to join the navy. After a first mission on the destroyer Z 25, a following a mission at the eastern front, where we

should reach the Caspian Sea, after the defeat of Stalingrad and the retreat from there and after a mission on the weather observation ship Kehdingen to Franz-Josef-Land, I falsified my leave pass because of a story with a woman. I was caught and had to apply as a volunteer to the human torpedoes, in order to escape from a court-martial. In Surendorf at the Baltic Sea I got my Examination. There we were trained and learned how to handle the emergency diving-dress. Already in the time of examination one of our comrades died, when he shot his torpedo, but the explosive torpedo did not depart from the human torpedo. After the invasion of France, we should have a mission there. By train we came to France close to Paris. We continued only slowly, because the partisans had blown up the railroads nearly everywhere und this firstly had to be repaired. Because I had a toothache, I was able to leave the place of our accommodation to Paris, where I was attended by a French doctor. In this way, I could visit the Eiffel Tower, too. The next day we drove to the coast, but we had to interrupt our ride again and again because of the lots of low-level flying aircraft. At last we arrived at the bay at the mouth of the river Seine, from where we had to attack the Allied fleet. We were not located in a village, but somewhere outside on the beach. In the evening our Marders (Tank destroyers) were tied into the water by pioneers and round about 10 p.m. we started our attack. We had been informed, where the Allied ships should have been. I did not know anything about the attack of explosive boats after our attack in the same night. We had been told too, that the German Air force would fly an attack on the ships to help us to orient ourselves. It had been expected, that the ships would fire on the aircraft and that we in this way could find the ships. But there was nothing to be seen of German aircraft and there was nothing to be seen of firing ships, it was rather dark, you could see next to nothing. The sight out of the cupola of a human torpedo is extremely bad. At last however I found the warships. I saw a destroyer, fired my torpedo and hit the destroyer. The time was about 03.00 a.m. I am sure, that the ship was a destroyer, because I had seen the high upstanding canon, and I am of the opinion, that the destroyer sank at once. An old cruiser, which had been hit in the same night and which was destined by the Allies to be sunk as a breakwater, would have given a much higher silhouette and could not have been changed by mistake despite the fact, that it had been an old ship. After my shot I turned at once and tried to reach the saving coast. I was terribly afraid. With my human torpedo I passed the middle of the Allied ships and I always thought, they truly must have seen me. The ships towered incredibly high out of the water, the situation was ghostly, but firstly I got away. Round about 05.00 a.m., when the dawn came, I was hit. An English gun boat took me over, went into the bank and returned. When the bullets of a machine gun tore the cupola of my torpedo into pieces, I made myself as small as possible and I pulled down my head as deep as possible, in order not be hit. In spite of that I was hit in my neck by splinters of the cupola and later on, when I was a prisoner of war, I was a treated in an English military hospital for a short time. When the gun boat approached, I sank down with my torpedo round about 20 m on the ground of the sea, but I kept sitting in it. I still had my emergency diving suit and so I could breathe for some time. Under water you can hear every noise and I noticed that the gun boat over me turned again and again. I supposed, they shoot me at once, because I had sunk their destroyer only a short time ago. So, I stayed waiting down on the bottom of the sea. When I heard, the gun boat was no longer there, I dived up and tried to reach the French coast by swimming. I still wore my life-jacket and swam about 1 hour. At some time or other I must have lost consciousness, because I cannot remember, how I got on board of the English gun boat, which saved my life. At once everything was taken away until I only wore my trousers. Before the beginning of my mission I had sewed a death's head on to my cap. This cap, my clock and my compass were taken at once as a trophy. From this gunboat I was carried to a greater warship. When I climbed up the ladder-rope and arrived at the deck, I saluted smart: 'Heil Hitler!' At that time, I still was extremely proud of myself. From this warship I was carried to the French Side of the Channel and separated at once from the other prisoners of war, because I had told the English soldiers before, that I had sunk one of their destroyers. From here I was brought into captivity to England, where I was kept about 4 weeks and in was interrogated by the British Secret Service. Because I had told them already on the destroyer, that I had sunk one of their destroyers.'

Cyril Longshaw is commemorated on Portsmouth Naval Memorial. Portsmouth Naval Memorial commemorates over nine thousand sailors of the First World War and almost fifteen thousand of the Second World War who have no known grave but the sea. It is situated on Southsea Common overlooking the promenade.

Portsmouth Naval Memorial

 ## Serjeant George Henry Beresford: 23rd Hussars Royal Armoured Corps

Date of death: 4th August 1944

Commemorated on Church Lawton War Memorial, All Saints Church

George Henry Beresford was born in Wolstanton in 1917 (birth registered Oct to Dec 1917) the son of George Henry Beresford and his wife Nelly Beresford *nee* Hallett. His father was a metal dealer. In 1939 the family lived in *Greenbank House,* Liverpool Road, Congleton Rural DC. The family had a domestic servant, Hilda Ashley. Serjeant George Henry Beresford joined the 23rd Hussars, Royal Armoured Corps, tank regiment, regimental number 7905407, 'C' Squadron.

The 23rd Hussars regiment was raised in December 1940 from a cadre of personnel taken from the 10th Royal Hussars (Prince of Wales's Own) and the 15th/19th The King's Royal Hussars. It was assigned to 29th Armoured Brigade of 11th Armoured Division. The 11th Armoured Division landed in France in June 1944, taking heavy casualties in the Battle of Normandy.

The regiment landed in France on 15th June, 1944 and by the 17th it had concentrated at Coulombs in Normandy. From 26th to 30th June, the 23rd was involved into the crossing of the Odon and in the Battle of Point 112. The 11th Armoured Division in Sherman tanks concentrated around Cully on 26th June. The plan was for the brigade to advance with the 2nd Fife and Forfar Yeomanry on the left, the 23rd Hussars on the right and the 3rd Royal Tank Regiment in reserve. The regiment had 'H' Company 8th Rifle Brigade and 'G' Battery 13th Royal Horse Artillery as part of its regimental group. The advance began on 26th June to Cheux and the attack ended on 30th June when it returned from Hill 112 to Putot-en-Bessin. It was then involved in the Battle of Caen from 1st to 22nd July. On 2nd July it moved to Rauray and then to Cully on the 15th for a day's rest, but it then was back in the line waiting for action. The attack on Caen began on 16th July with the division moving across the Orne and reaching its forming-up point the next day. It went into battle on the 18th and was heavily engaged (held up). On the 20th, the 7th Armoured Division took over and the regiment moved to Demouville. On the 22nd it was to refit at St. Germain. The 23rd was then involved at Le Bény-Bocage, Chenedolle, and Le Bas Perrier from 22nd July to 7th August.

It spearheaded Operation Epsom, reaching the Odon river between Mouen and Mondrainville. It was embroiled in Operation Goodwood, where its assault on Bourguébus Ridge on the first day was brought to a halt. Operation Goodwood was a British offensive, that took place between 18th and 20th July 1944 as part of the battle for Caen. The objective of the operation was a limited attack to the south, to capture the rest of Caen and the Bourguébus Ridge beyond, forcing the Germans to keep powerful formations opposite the British and Canadians on the eastern flank of the Normandy beachhead. Goodwood succeeded in this limited aim. At least one historian has called the operation the largest tank battle that the British Army has ever fought. After Goodwood, the losses of armour within the division were so high that the 24th Lancers were disbanded, and its remnants absorbed by the 23rd Hussars. The Regiment then took part in Operation Bluecoat, intended to secure the key road junction of Vire and the high ground of Mont Pinçon, which would allow the American exploitation of their breakout on the western flank of the Normandy beachhead. Operation Bluecoat was an offensive from 30th July until 7th August 1944. British forces advanced to about 5 miles from Vire by 2nd August, which was on the American side of the inter-army boundary. There was confusion as to who had the rights to use certain roads and the British attack was restricted and diverted south-east. George was killed two days later on 4th August.

23rd Hussars August 1944

George was buried in grave XXVI. F. 18 in the Bayeux War Cemetery There was little actual fighting in Bayeux although it was the first French town of importance to be liberated. Bayeux War Cemetery is the largest Commonwealth cemetery of the Second World War in France and contains burials brought in from the surrounding districts and from hospitals that were located nearby. The Bayeux Memorial stands opposite the cemetery and bears the names of more than 1,800 men of the Commonwealth land forces who died in the early stages of the campaign and have no known grave. They died during the landings in Normandy, during the intense fighting in Normandy itself, and during the advance to the River Seine in August.

Commonwealth War Grave for Serjeant G. Beresford Bayeux War Cemetery, Normandy.

'We shall meet in God's Summerland to live together eternally.'

(Wording on George Henry Beresford's grave.)

Photo: Author

Charles William Bullock: 24th Lancers, Royal Armoured Corps

Date of Death: 11th September 1944

Commemorated on Alsager War Memorial

Charles William Bullock was born on 5th May 1909 in Burslem, Staffordshire, son of Frederick and Lillian Bullock. His father was a clerk. The family moved to Birmingham in 1911 before returning to live in Alsager.

In the early 1930s Charles moved to North Yorkshire to work in the Easterby horse racing stables. He trained as a jockey and raced in the 1930s for Easterby. In 1932 he raced at Thirsk and later that year at Ripon. Charles William met Violet Marne Hird from North Yorkshire and they married in 1934. They had four children, Robert, Cliff, Lillian, and Joy. Charles' father died in a Cheshire mental hospital in 1939 following injuries sustained in the Western Front in 1917. Following his father's death Charles returned to live in Alsager. They lived at 53 Crewe Road and according to the *1939 Register*, Charles William Bullock was employed as a groom at a racing stable. His mother, Lillian, worked as a draper from her shop at 53 Crewe Road.

Following the outbreak of war Charles enlisted as a Trooper, service number 7918820, in the 24th Lancers, Royal Armoured Corps. With the 8th Armoured Brigade, the regiment landed on Gold Beach, in the second wave of the Operation Overlord landings, supporting the 50th (Northumbrian) Infantry Division. The regiment landed on 7th June 1944 (D Day plus one). They were equipped with Sherman tanks, and shortly after landing the regiment was involved in the fighting around Putot-en-Bessin and Villers Bocage.

After intensive action in the Tilly-sur-Seulles, Fontenay-le-Pesnel, Tessel Wood and Rauray areas, the regiment was disbanded towards the end of July 1944 due to heavy casualties and limited available reinforcements, and its personnel were transferred to other regiments. Most of these men went to the 23rd Hussars or other units of the 8th Armoured Brigade, or the 29th

Armoured Brigade in the 11th Armoured Division. Since D-Day the 24th Lancers had lost forty-one officers and men killed in action, along with ninety eight wounded or missing.

Trooper Charles William Bullock

Charles was wounded on 5th September 1944 at Avelin near Lille and taken to a dressing station, then a hospital, where he died on 11th September. His commanding officer, Major A.E W Henderson, wrote to Charles' widow on 11th October to express his squadron's sympathy on her husband's death. The regiment were progressing through France towards Belgium and came to a place called Avelin. The Brigade headquarters was to be established there in the chateau, but the enemy were found to be still in the area. Charles, a dispatch rider, was shot in the neck. A doctor with the column gave him treatment at once before he was evacuated by ambulance to a dressing station. Charles' regiment had to push on and it was October, and one hundred and fifty miles away, before Henderson, his commanding officer, found out Charles had died. Henderson recalled that Charles had acted as his Brigadier's batman and because both Brigadier and Charles loved horses they had developed a rapport. Henderson wrote of Charles Bullock, *'He was a most fearless and keen dispatch rider who did his job thoroughly and fearlessly. I believe he was happy in his job.'*

From the Alsager Times 1944

Charles is buried at St Severs Cemetery Extension, Rouen, France, block 'S' plot 1, row N grave 16. Violet Bullock, his wife, moved to 85 Station Road, Alsager during the war. After Charles' death she later married Reginald Bailey in 1960.

St Severs Cemetery Extension, Rouen

On his grave was inscribed, *'For us he gave his all. Loved and remembered always by wife Vi, and children.'*

Signalman Henry Middling: Royal Corps of Signals 1st Airborne Div. Sigs

Date of Death: 24th August 1944

Commemorated on Wheelock War Memorial

Henry Middling was the only son of Mr & Mrs J Middling of *Lunt Cottages*, Hassall Green. He was part of the 1st Airborne Division which landed at Arnhem on 24th September 1944. He enlisted in the South Staffordshire Regiment and served over five years in India. He landed in France on D Day when he was slightly wounded in the leg. He recovered and went with his unit across France. His grandfather was the late Frederick Edwards who was in charge of Hassall Mission Church. Henry is buried at Arnhem Oosterbeek War Cemetery grave reference 2. C. 7.

Photo: Crewe Chronicle

Private Peter Hart:

The Oxfordshire and Buckinghamshire Light Infantry

Date of Death: 27th September 1944

Commemorated on Alsager War Memorial

Peter was the son of Thomas and Ivy Sarah Ellen Hart (*nee* Bottril) who were married in 1923 in Leicester. Peter Hart was born in Staffordshire in 1924. In his youth he was a Baden Powell Scout. His father, Thomas Hart died in Leicester in 1950.

Peter Hart saw action with the 8th Battalion in Tunisia and Italy, taking part in the Anzio and Salerno landings. The regiment took part in the battles of Enfidaville Salerno, the Volturno Camino and Garigliano Anzio, and then Montefiore Gemmano Sensoli and the Ceriano.

Peter Hart, service number 14325789, was killed, on 27th September 1944 and is buried in the Cesena War Cemetery which lies in the Commune of Cesena, in the Province of Forli, Italy. His death was recorded on Casualty List No. 1580. Technically, the Oxford and Bucks Light Infantry had been disbanded on 23rd September because of reduction in numbers. It was merged into the Queen's Brigade. The regimental cadre moved out of the battle area on 30th September 1944.

Most of those buried in the Cesena cemetery died during the advance from Rimini to Forli and beyond in September to November 1944, an advance across one flooded river after another in atrocious autumn weather. The cemetery site was selected in November 1944 and burials were brought in from the surrounding battlefields.

On his headstone, it reads:

B.P Scout

Of whom it was said

'He was a gentleman.'

Alsager in 1945

1945: Timeline of the war. (history)

The New Year saw the Soviet liberation of Auschwitz, and more camps were liberated in the following months. The Soviet army continued its offensive from the east, while from the west the Allies established a bridge across the Rhine at Remagen, in March.

While the bombing campaigns of the Blitz were over, German V1 and V2 rockets continued to drop on London. The return bombing raids on Dresden, which devastated the city in a huge firestorm, have often been considered misguided.

Meanwhile, the Western Allies raced the Russians to be the first into Berlin. The Russians won, reaching the capital on 21st April. Hitler killed himself on the 30th, two days after Mussolini had been captured and hanged by Italian partisans. Germany surrendered unconditionally on 7th May, and the following day was celebrated as VE Day (Victory in Europe). The war in Europe was over.

In the Pacific, however, it had continued to rage throughout this time. The British advanced further in Burma, and in February the Americans had invaded Iwo Jima. The Philippines and Okinawa followed, and Japanese forces began to withdraw from China.

Plans were being prepared for an Allied invasion of Japan, but fears of fierce resistance and massive casualties prompted Harry Truman - the new American president following Roosevelt's death in April - to sanction the use of an atomic bomb against Japan. Japan surrendered on August 14th.

In Alsager

In December 1944, the Home Guard had been stood down nationally and the Alsager Home Guard was disbanded. On 1st February 1945, part-time members of the National Fire Service were stood down in Alsager. This followed a national instruction.

Alsager news was not always comfortable reading for supporters of the war effort.

'Alsager Soldier's Wife Warned', was a heading in the *Crewe Chronicle* in April 1945. Looking at the story from 2017 it has elements of racial discrimination, and different standards towards the safety of children. The

case was brought to the Magistrates Court via the National Society for the Prevention of Cruelty to Children (NSPCC) Witnesses claimed Mrs X (I have omitted her name), went out at night and left her five young children alone in their home, and *'bringing men into the house'*. The NSPCC Official visited Mrs X and she was reluctant to show him her bedroom. *'Eventually two coloured soldiers came downstairs'*, testified the official. The children were found to be clean and satisfactory and the defendant admitted she had left the children unattended. The official warned the woman by bringing men into her home she was putting the children in moral danger. On another occasion when the official visited he found a young sailor in the defendant's kitchen. The defending solicitor said the only complaint was that the *'woman goes out occasionally'*. On another occasion, the police entered the house because of light flickering in the defendant's living room. The policeman found the children asleep and alone in the house and the coal fire in dangerous condition with a shirt drying near it. The defendant returned at 11.30 pm with a Royal Marine saying she had been to a dance and had been drinking in the *Mere Inn*. The defendant agreed she went out four or five times a week but that her children were clean. *'She denied she had misconducted herself with two coloured American soldiers'*. The defendant was bound over for twelve months not to visit dances and public houses and the children to be looked after by a competent person. Her place was in *'the home'*, said the Magistrate.

The case points out the stereotyping of black people in the 1940s and problems associated with families facing separation in wartime. The court discussed alleged misconduct by the defendant with *'two coloured American Soldiers'*. It did not infer misconduct with the Royal Marines found to be visiting the woman. Although the defendant was bound over for twelve months, in 2017, the consequences of the defendant leaving her children alone on a regular basis may have led to them being taken into care. The physical dangers children faced were considered less important than 'moral' considerations.

On 1st May 1945, the local Civil Defence Service was also stood down. Two days later the Women's Section of Alsager British Legion complained that food rations for German prisoners of war were greater than for British subjects. 125% of bacon rations and 200% of cheese rations were given to German POWs. Mrs Hurd, from the Alsager Legion, did acknowledge that the ration quotas for POWs were controlled by international law, but she did not think the *'despicable enemy'*, should have better rations. Some people were hungry and could not understand why the level of rations given to prisoners of war was greater than they received.

Meanwhile black marketeering continued. Later that month Peter Roach of *Heathlands*, Hassall Road, Alsager, was sentenced to three months imprisonment for *'black marketeering'*. At Worcester, he was convicted of selling clothing without surrendering coupons for them. He pleaded guilty. Roach had been selling clothing to workers at the Morgan Crucible Works, Norton, Worcester before being sacked. He also owned a café in Birmingham where he had been approached by a Greek called *'John'*, to sell clothing without coupons. Roach was probably living in the small men's hostel at *Heathside*, not *Heathlands* and had found a job at Radway Green. How he managed to conduct his businesses and illegal trading from Alsager is a mystery.

In 1945, an Alsager boy, Ronald Dillon, of Longview Avenue, was sent to a Borstal (Approved School) for theft from Alsager houses. He was a deserter from the Coldstream Guards, and had returned to his own village and broken into two properties. In one of these he threatened the occupier, Mr Fare, saying, *'If you come an inch nearer I'll knife you'*. Dillon had previously been in a Borstal school for house breaking but had joined the Guards after finishing his sentence. He pleaded guilty and asked for another case to be taken into consideration. He was given 21 days imprisonment and would be recalled to Borstal. He is the only known case of a deserter from Alsager. Such people were vilified by those whose relatives were serving at the front.

VE Day

Following the cessation of hostilities in Europe a service of thanksgiving was celebrated in St Mary's Church on Sunday afternoon, on 13th May. Councillor J Edwards thanked local people who had helped in the Civil Defence and WVS and other organisations. Some functions continued despite the peace: the local administration of food and fuel, encouraging the production of food, fostering the savings movement and the recovery of salvage. He announced that land had been acquired for a hundred new houses in Alsager. This included land in Well Lane. Sir Francis Joseph had made available some of his land for new housing.

In the evening of VE Day, a large crowd stood outside the Council Offices to listen to a broadcast of the King's speech to the nation. The broadcasting equipment was provided by Radway Green. Alsager Cadet Band led a procession from the council offices down the main road then

Hassall Road to the Marl Pit (situated near *Heathside hostel*) where a *'huge'* bonfire was lit by two schoolchildren and speeches were made by councillor James Edwards, Lt Col Webber RM, and Mr L.S Flatman of Radway Green.

The official civic celebration of victory in Europe was a street parade on Sunday after D Day. A detachment from the Royal Marines led the way, followed by Alsager Army Cadets under Lieutenant R. McKie who marched to St Mary's church for a combined service of thanksgiving. The council encouraged residents to put up flags and bunting and many streets were decorated. A collection was made for churches in England requiring repair for damage caused in the war.

Picture: Alsager Army Cadets

A feature of the street decorations in Alsager was the floodlighting of the Council Offices. Floodlighting buildings was still a novelty after the years of blackout restrictions.

The victory was celebrated on 16th June by the Longview Avenue Social Club on the new *'Radway Estate'* by the Residents' Association throwing a party for children. The outdoor event was captured by the *Weekly Sentinel* photographer. The event demonstrates the large number of young children living in Alsager on the new estate. The party was for four hundred children. Many of them would have attended the new school on the estate which had to be soon expanded using temporary buildings (which were still being used in the 1980s).

Longview Avenue VE Day celebrations June 1945: photo Weekly Sentinel.

Local VE Celebrations

(And Sentinel newspaper self-promotion!)

The old social centre in Longview Avenue, photograph from the 1960s with the 'new' social club behind it.

On 16th June 1945 the Family Allowances Act was passed. Mothers received a tax-free cash payment for each child in their care. This is the first time in Britain that a state payment has gone directly to a wife rather than her husband.

At the end of June, the Alsager British Legion held its annual fair with concerts and dancing displays and themed the event as an *'Old English Fayre'*. Funds raised were for British Legion funds and large crowds attended the event on the Parsonage Field. The fair was opened by Miss Ida Harding.

In July Sir Francis Joseph and his wife gave a tea party for one hundred and forty mothers, babies and local children at an annexe of his home, *'The Hall'*. The guests were all associated with Alsager Welfare Centre of which Lady Joseph was president. Councillor Dorothy Harpur thanked their hosts for their hospitality in a speech, on their behalf.

Also in July, *Heathside hostel,* still occupied by munition workers despite the war in Europe having ended, was still putting on concerts for its residents. The war in the Far East was still raging and production remained high. The hostel would soon close but ENSA groups like the one from Possil School, Scotland, visited *Heathside* in that month. Mrs Wyatt, the warden, gave the children a tour of the site. It appears Mrs Wyatt laid on porridge for her Scottish guests! Later in the summer of 1945 it was announced that Radway Green would still be a permanent small arms factory employing between four and five thousand people but would remain in a higher production capacity until the end of the *'Japanese war'*, as the *Staffordshire Advertiser* stated in an article called *'Peacetime Production'*.

On 5th July 1945, a General Election took place in Britain. The ballots were sealed for three weeks to allow the collection and counting of overseas service votes. Getting the ballot papers to servicemen proved a problem. Driver F. Steele of Woodside Avenue Alsager wrote to newspapers say he had completed a proxy voting form but had not received the ballot form as he had moved into another army unit. He said servicemen could not rely on their wives voting how they intended! He said lots of comrades were in the same position. Servicemen and women were sent pictures of candidates and short written statements to promote their cause. On 26th July 1945, the Labour Party were declared winners of the general election with a historic landslide. Clement Attlee became Prime Minister and formed a new government. Alsager, in Crewe constituency, was won by Sydney Scholefield Allen, a gain from the Conservative's Sir Donald Somerville.

On 27th August, the *Daily Mirror* (DailyMirror) printed an embarrassing article blaming The Ministry of Supply for leaving over twenty new houses empty in Alsager since December 1944. They said they had no need for them with the end of the war and they were no longer needed by the Royal Marines at *HMS Excalibur*. The council had no powers to requisition them. There must have been some political manoeuvring because it was revealed by the *Mirror* on 27th August that twenty-four houses were now going to be tenanted and were being decorated.

In early September, the 13 Club, the *'ROF Club House'*, by *Milton House*, put on a garden party and Victory celebration for one hundred and fifty adults and children, employees of Radway Green *'their wives and families'*. Tea was served in the dining room. There were sideshows, games, and a display of conjuring given. There were sports for children.

Alsager was the subject of a murder investigation in November 1945. Thomas Roycroft, aged 73, a retired miner of *The Cottage*, Hall Drive, Alsager, murdered his wife by slitting her throat, and then committed suicide by cutting his own throat. *The Cottage* was close to Sir Francis Joseph's home and was next to the Crewe to Alsager railway line. Their bodies were discovered by daughter Doris Robinson, Thomas's daughter from a previous marriage, who worked at Radway Green. The police broke into their home after Mrs Robinson raised the alarm. They found Thomas still alive, but he died soon afterwards in hospital in Stoke-on-

Trent. The couple had only married in July 1944. Thy both had grown up families from a previous marriage.

Society Engagement

The youngest daughter of Sir Francis Joseph, Cynthia, became engaged at the end of December 1945. She was in the WRNS in the war. She met Captain Peter Dean, Suffolk Regiment, after he had been evacuated from Dunkirk in 1940. Shortly afterwards he was sent on duty to the Far East where he was captured after the fall of Singapore and imprisoned in Thailand and Japan until his release by American troops. When they married in Alsager in 1946 they had an escort of Royal Marines on motorcycles from Excalibur. There was criticism of the public expense of providing this escort.

Service Personnel who made the news in 1945

Award of the Military Cross to Captain John Arrowsmith. M.C

John was the only son of Mr & Mrs Robert Sudlow Arrowsmith, of *Far Heath*, Hassall Road, Alsager. He was born 1921 in Alsager. His father was Managing Director of Messrs T. Arrowsmith Ltd of Burslem and a former member of Alsager Urban District Council.

Robert Arrowsmith-photo from the Sentinel

MICHAELMAS TERM, 1934

8817 **Arrowsmith, John** (SH) 1 1939. Second War, Major, Duke of Lancaster's Yeo. Egypt, Italy. MC. Desp. Chmn: and Man: Dir: T. Arrowsmith and Sons Ltd, Stoke-on-Trent, Goddard Engineering Ltd, Staffs; and other cos.

Shrewsbury School record of Arowsmith's career. (Shr)

John went to Shrewsbury School. Before joining the army, he was employed by Messrs. J Gimson Ltd of Fenton, *'stilt and thimble'* manufacturers. He joined the army in the ranks in 1941 and was commissioned with the Duke of Lancaster's Own Yeomanry in February 1942, service number 22490. Eleven months later he went overseas to North Africa and then on to Italy. He won the Military Cross for distinguished conduct in the Italian campaign in 1945 when he was serving with the 78 Medium Royal Regiment of Artillery. *The Liverpool Echo* reported on 13th October 1945 of John's award of the Military Cross: *'He showed outstanding qualities of courage, resource and initiative and had on many occasions, by his own volition, had moved forward his observation post at great personal risk in order to obtain better observation.'*

He was also Mentioned in Despatches on 19th July 1945. He was promoted Captain and then Adjutant. After the war, after serving with the Central Mediterranean Forces, he was appointed General Staff Officer 11 RA., on the Thirteenth Corps in the Allied-occupied Forces in Venezia Guilla, Italy. In September 1945, he was awarded the British Empire Medal for his services in Italy. After the War, he returned to Alsager and worked for Messrs T Arrowsmith and for Goddard Engineering

Corporal Robert Wilberforce Fisher: Award of DCM in 1945

Born on 27th January 1923, Robert Wilberforce Fisher was the son of Arthur Fisher, dental surgeon, and his former wife Grace, *nee* Head. In 1939, he lived with his father in The Avenue, Alsager. Before the war he was a law student. He was articled to Messrs Hayes and son, Solicitors, Hanley. His father had served in the Great War. Robert enlisted in the army and joined the Royal Armoured Corps, Service number 14201807. The *Alsager Times* published an article in June about the recce or reconnaissance function in the army. Corporal R. Fisher of 14 The Avenue, Alsager was in Italy in 1944 and working in reconnaissance for the Armoured Division going out on foot patrols to observe the German enemy near Caragliano. *'He stayed all night observing them. With his Colonel and Major Preen he also did an interesting patrol in a jeep along the sand dunes and then they walked until they were spotted, and shells landed near them. They were forced to creep away due to being sniped at by the enemy.'* The war around Caragliano became static with both sides unable to see one another while patrolling was on foot on the volcanic rocks. But as they did manage to progress there were instances of humour. He reported back to the Sappers saying there was *'a large crater at such and such a position which is causing a diversion. Can you deal with it?'* The Sappers looked at the map and found it pinpointed the crater on Vesuvius. There is no record of their reply to the recce.

Fisher was promoted Sergeant. On 11th December 1945, he was awarded the Distinguished Conduct Medal for his bravery during the battle for Italy. After the death of his troop commander he held a dangerous position until the York's and Lancs' Regiment could follow through and take the position.

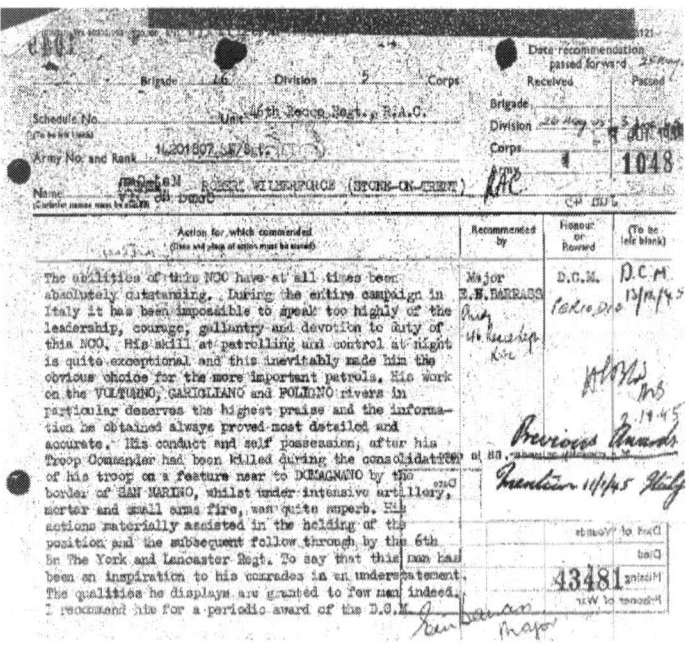

After the war he lived in Lodge Road, Alsager and practised as a solicitor from 20 Moorland Road, Burslem in a partnership with Howard Mellor, and Graham Clowes in the firm *Norris & Mellor*. He died in Stoke-on-Trent in 1975.

Corporal Victor Holmes Royal Engineers

His home was in *Grove House*, Sandbach Road. Alsager. He was the son of Francis Graeme Holmes, a Civil Engineer and Marion Holmes, *nee* Brandwood. Victor was born in 1919 and before the war was a pupil in Mr Lynam's surveying department in Alsager Urban District Council. He joined the Royal Signals, service number 2360689. Victor Holmes was *Mentioned in Despatches* in 1945 serving as a Corporal, and Alsager Council wrote to him to offer their congratulations. He married Marjorie Cloud in 1951. He lived in Rode Heath in later years and died in 1993.

Sergeant Cyril Rothwell M.M

Cyril Rothwell, from 5 Oak Street, Thurlwood, was awarded a Military Medal by Field Marshal Montgomery in 1945. The award was published in the *London Gazette* on 31st August 1945. The award was included in 'Normandy List no. 1.' He served in the 5th Regiment Royal Horse Artillery, service number 794566 enlisted in August 1929 aged 17. He served in 'G' Battery, Mercer's Troop. On returning home he was presented with a tea service at the *Royal Oak*. He was born in Stoke-on-Trent in 1912 and married Alice Bott in 1938. Although demobbed in 1946, records indicate he finally retired from the army in 1955 on reaching the age limit for service. He died in 1983.

Lieutenant Richard John Bailey

Richard married Marcia Webb in January 1945 at St Marys Church Alsager

Richard John Bailey was born in 1923 in Scholar Green.

He was the son of Phillip Bailey of *Ramsdell Hall,* Scholar Green, the Director of Ridgeway Pottery.

In 1942, at the age of nineteen, Richard John Bailey joined the Royal Navy, and was commissioned one year later, and served on British destroyers until 1946. He served July 1943 to October 1944 on *HMS Vigilant* (destroyer.) His ship was involved in the support of troops during the D Day landings. On arrival at the beachhead his ship began to bombard enemy positions and provide naval gunfire support for troops landing on the Juno Beaches. The ship was then deployed in the Task Force area on patrol, and convoy defence work.

From January 1945 to April 1946 he served on *HMS Hotspur* (destroyer). The ship had a refit early in 1945 and afterwards in April it carried out anti-submarine operations in Irish Sea and SW Approaches. In May it transferred to Rosyth Escort Force for patrol and escort in North Sea, and June to August it was deployed in the North Sea in support of re-occupation operations.

After the war Richard Bailey became managing director of the Royal Doulton Group when it included names such as Minton, Royal Crown Derby, Royal Albert, Paragon and Ridgway as well as Royal Doulton. He was knighted for his work.

He died in 2011 aged 87.

Geoffrey Frank White

The young RAF Recruit in 1943

Geoff White has had a long association with Alsager. He was born in Newton-Le-Willows on 15th February 1926 and attended Ashton-in-Makerfield Boys Central School from 1936 to 1940. (White)

One week after leaving school he joined Caulfields, Bleachers and Dyers Ltd, but continued his education by attending Newton-Le-Willows Technical School three nights a week studying drawing, mathematics and science.

In 1942 he joined the ATC (Air Training Corps) aged 16 and the following year on 22nd July 1943, in Wigan, he volunteered to join the RAF. He was attested on 1st September 1943 and undertook his eight-week basic training at RAF Cardington, Bedfordshire. Cardington was the home of the RAF Meteorological research balloons training unit. After this he was sent to the Northern Royal Polytechnic in London to train on a Radio Mechanics course.

In London he lodged in Holloway and one day, while he was studying, his digs were bombed out by the Luftwaffe. Shortly after moving to new digs he went down with peritonitis in early 1944 and was admitted to the medical centre which had taken over one of the South Kensington Science museums. They transferred him to Mary Abbott's Hospital in London and conveyed him there on a Greenline Bus converted into an ambulance. As a patient he was convalescing on a ground floor ward when German aircraft bombed the hospital. Luckily all the ground floor windows had been bricked up to lessen the possibility of injury. He was evacuated to the West Middlesex in Isleworth where he recovered from illness.

He was selected to attend a ground radar course early in 1944 in Yatesbury, Wiltshire. Radar was in its infancy and it was crucial Britain trained enough operatives to use the technology, but at the end of training Geoff was told there were too many trained men for the available jobs. He was given the option of working down a coalmine or joining the army. He opted to join the Royal Corps of Signals Regiment because of his experience in radio mechanics and radar. He underwent a short course as an OWL (Operator Wireless and Line operator). OWL operators were capable of sending and receiving Morse at twenty plus words per minute, and operate "19" and "22" wireless sets (the former, the standard set in most armoured vehicles). They were also skilled in the use of field telephones, switchboards, and *Fullerphones* (a machine for sending Morse by line, named after its inventor).

Graduates of this course were selected for active service abroad. Men with early alphabet surnames were sent to the Far East, middle alphabet surnames went to the Middle East, and names at the end of the alphabet (including Geoff) went to Europe.

Geoff, although part of the Royal Corps of Signals, was assigned to work with the 3rd Tank Regiment, 7th Armoured Division Brigade, (the Desert Rats) as they assumed responsibility as part of the British Army of the Rhine. As a radio operator he worked in a communications vehicle.

Geoff (Royal Corps Signals Regiment 1944)

Geoff White, 1945. Serving with the 7th Armoured Brigade (The Desert Rats) Note the U.S. markings

With the occupation of Germany, Geoff was mainly based in the Hamburg and Lüneburg areas and saw a great deal of the result of the destruction of German towns. Geoff recalls that the Germans were very effective however in clearing debris from town centres using improvised conveyor belt systems to remove rubble. They were far more efficient at clearing up damaged areas than their British counterparts at home. He saw many severely wounded and scarred Germans. In post-war Germany he obtained his own jeep and gained a degree of independence to visit places of interest and did not want his army career to end. Geoff did not leave Germany until 1947, finishing his career in Flensburg on the German/Danish border. He was officially a WS (War Service) Corporal, which meant he could not be demobbed on a lesser rank. In fact, Geoff was working as Acting Sergeant at the time of his release from the Royal Corps of Signals.

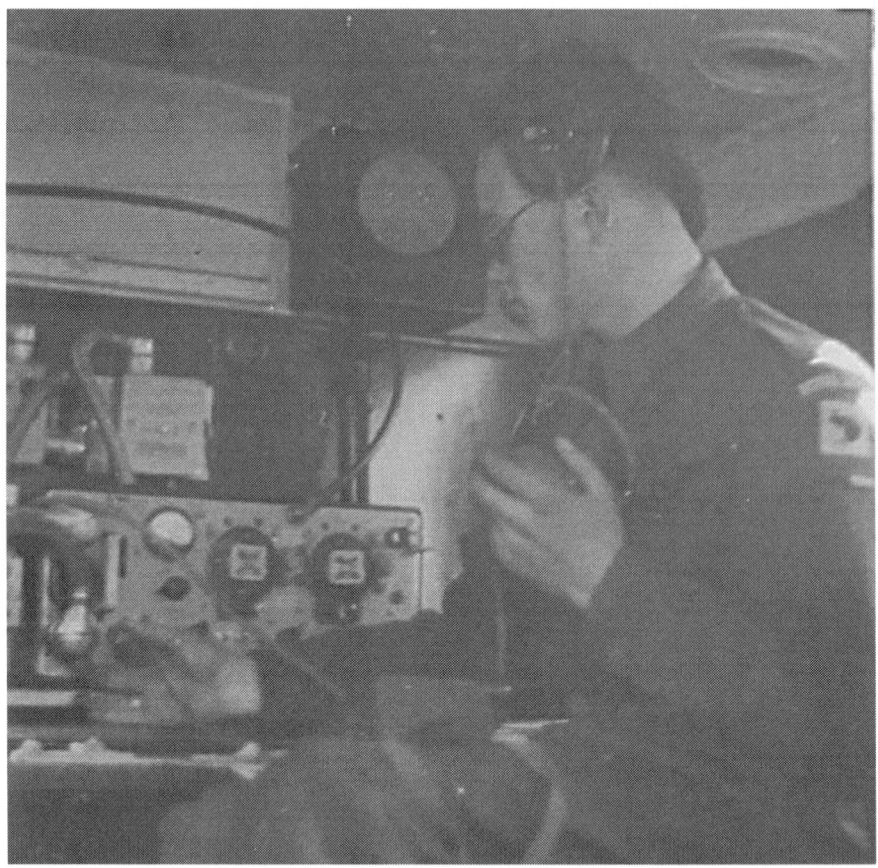

After being demobbed he took a teaching qualification at Loughborough Training College and went on to teach at several schools including Boteler Grammar School Warrington. In 1960 he was appointed Lecturer in Handicraft at Alsager College of Education. Geoff recalls that many of the World War Two buildings were still in use at the college in 1960. The old hall in the bomb-proof administrative building was still used for plays. Geoff recalls that the old *Heathside Hostel* huts were still in use as accommodation.

Deaths of Servicemen in 1945

Private Bertram Shortland: South Wales Borderers

Date of Death: 31st January 1945

Commemorated on Alsager War Memorial

Born in Stoke-on-Trent in 1912 to Richard & Margaret Shortland, (*nee* Ball), his father was an engine driver. He had a brother born in 1894, a sister Ida, born in 1906, and a sister Margaret, born in 1900. Bertram's family moved to Alsager, living at 91 Crewe Road. In 1940 Bertram was attested with the Royal Artillery, service number, 1778932. He married Florence Ena Hunt in 1944 in Hartismere, Suffolk. Bertram was transferred to the 2nd Battalion of South Wales Borderers on 20th September 1944.

The South Wales Borderers, pushing eastwards after the D Day landings, reached Abbeville, Ypres, Alost and Turnout by 25th September 1944. By late October after several months of continuous fighting, the battalion was in Holland. They spent an arduous and miserable winter on the *'island'*, a waterlogged area of land between Arnhem and Nijmegen overlooked by the enemy from higher ground to the north. The enemy was only twenty yards from the forward troops whose positions could often only be reached by boats. Clothes, bedding and feet were wet most of the time and patrolling often had to be done in boats They then reached Antwerp and Willemstad by 7th November. On 12th November the regiment was allocated to 49th (West Riding) Infantry Division and reached Helmond Venlo on 22nd to 25th November. On 30th November, it reached Nijmegen then Zetten. The Netherlands had fallen to the Germans in May 1940 and was not re-entered by Allied forces until September 1944. It was a severe winter and the Dutch landscape was snow-covered. In January 1945 Zetten was virtually destroyed when the Germans counter-attacked on the island. The vicious tank and infantry battle continued for several weeks before the Germans finally gave up and withdrew.

Near Zetten the battalion set out to dislodge the Germans from the *'castle'*, a stone building surrounded by a moat. The infantry attacked but drew heavy fire and the battalion's carriers, with much courage, went right up to the building and sprayed it with small arms fire from a stationary position, in spite of the rain of armour-piercing ammunition fired by the enemy. Guns and tanks continued the bombardment, but the building did not catch fire until Major Gillespie from the South Wales Borderers had the bright idea of using mortar smoke bombs. This caused a blaze and the next day the castle was taken. But Zetten fell to the enemy while the battalion was resting, and the castle had to be re-taken by the 24th January.

Bertram Shortland was killed in continued fighting on 31st January 1945. His death was reported to the War Office Casualty Branch for the twenty four hours ending at 09:00 hours on 13th February 1945, Casualty List No. 1680.

He is buried in grave 7. G. 5 in Jonkerbos War Cemetery, Nijmegen, Holland. The cemetery, which was created by No. 3 Casualty Clearing station, is in a wooded area known as Jinkers Bosch, from which it took its name.

The inscription on his grave:

The Dawn is not distant

Nor is the night starless

Love is eternal.

In his will, his widow Florence Ena Shortland, living in Ipswich, was left assets worth £268.11s 3d.

Ernest Coveney Tanton

Jeanetta Tanton

Brian Geoffrey Tanton

Date of Death: 10th February 1945

Commemorated on the Church Lawton War Memorial

The Tanton family on the Church Lawton War Memorial are buried in Leyton Municipal Cemetery in London.

They were killed when a flying bomb hit their house, 12 Lemna Road, Leytonstone. The bomb also destroyed a school in Kirkdale Road, Leytonstone. Ernest and Jeanetta's daughter, Dorothy, survived the attack, though she was hospitalised. The family are commemorated in Church Lawton because Ernest Tanton was the Methodist Minister earlier in his career for the Tunstall circuit which included Lawton and Alsager. Ernest was born in Dover in 1891 the son of James Tanton and his wife, Rosa Tanton (*nee* Coveney,) He had an older sister, Lilian, and a younger sister, Hilda. His father was a gold jeweller. He was educated at Dover Grammar School from 1904 to 1910 and later at Headingley College. He was ordained in the Methodist Church and firstly served in Bristol and Portsmouth Methodist circuits before gaining a commission to serve as an Army Chaplain in the Royal Army Chaplain's Department the Great War. His commission was published in the *London Gazette*.

Ernest served in Mesopotamia and Persia during the Great War and was awarded the Victory Medal and British War Medal. He married Mary, the daughter of the Rev Kinnings in Darlington on 27th June 1917, when Ernest was working in Worksop, Nottinghamshire, but his young wife and daughter, Betty, died in 1921 during childbirth.

> **V-BOMB VICTIMS**
>
> Many friends in the Potteries have learned with regret of the deaths as the result of enemy air action in Southern England of the Rev. and Mrs. Ernest C. Tanton and their young son, Brian. Dorothy, their 15-years-old daughter, who was injured and is in hospital, was the only member of the family to survive. The Rev. E. C. Tanton was minister at Wesley Place Methodist Church, Tunstall, from 1919 to 1922, and married Miss Frith, a native of Tunstall, whose mother lives at Scholar Green. Mr. Tanton served as an Army chaplain in the last war. At the time of his death he was superintendent of a Methodist circuit in the south.

After the Great War Ernest moved to Stoke-on-Trent to take responsibility for the Tunstall circuit. In 1926 Ernest married Jeanetta Frith in Stoke-on-Trent. Jeanetta Frith was born in 1902 in Goldenhill, Stoke-on-Trent. She was the daughter of Lucy and William Frith. Her father was a pawnbroker. Ernest then served in numerous places for the Methodist church including Liverpool, Blackpool and Brighton and Hove. He was the author of *Imitators of Christ*, and with the Rev Frank C. Raynor, *The Fight for Faith*.

Brian Tanton was born in 1934 and was eleven when he was killed on 10th February 1945.

Lance Corporal William Jesse John Wise:
1ˢᵗ Battalion Herefordshire Regiment &
King's Shropshire Light Infantry
Date of Death: 27ᵗʰ February 1945
Commemorated on Odd Rode War Memorial

William was the son of William Jesse and Gladys Wise, *nee* Mould, and was born in December 1919 in Scholar Green. The family lived at *'The Views'*, Scholar Green. William's father was a *'General Labourer'*. William's sister Evangeline was born in 1929.

William married Gladys Stubbs in Newcastle under Lyme in 1943. They lived in Biddulph. Before her marriage Gladys was a towel weaver.

William enlisted in the 1ˢᵗ Battalion Herefordshire Regiment. His service number was 4036308. The 1ˢᵗ Battalion had landed on the beaches of Normandy six days after D Day and for twelve months had fought through France, Belgium and Holland, before crossing the Rhine into Germany and advancing close to the Danish border near Flensburg.

The battles had been hard – particularly the breakout from Normandy, the liberation of Antwerp and the fighting on the Tuetoberger Ridge in Germany – and more than two hundred men had been killed.

On the northern flank of the Allied front in north west Europe the British XXX Corps and the 1ˢᵗ Canadian Army now launched a massive assault on the German lines. Operation Veritable pushed south east to join up with the US Ninth Army and force the Germans up against the Rhine. The month-long battle was intended to coincide with Operation Grenade, the US Ninth Army pushing north west in a pincer movement. However, after the Germans flooded the ground in front of the Americans, preventing any attack in the south, Operation Veritable went ahead anyway. The British and Canadians found themselves constricted by the terrain of the Reichswald Forest and progress was slower than expected over the wet, muddy battlefield. Sir Brian Horrocks wrote of the battle,

> *'Thirty Corps was 200,000 strong that day, and we were attacking with five divisions in line supported by 1400 guns. It soon became clear that the enemy was completely bemused as a result of our colossal bombardment; their resistance was slight. The main trouble was mines —and mud, particularly*

mud. I am certain that this must be the chief memory of everyone who fought in the Reichswald battle. Mud and still more mud. It was so bad that after the first hour every tank going across country was bogged down, and the infantry had to struggle forward on their own. The chief enemy resistance came from the cellars in the villages'.

Troops in the Reichswald Forest February 1945.

William was killed on the last day of the battle. He is buried in plot 46. E. 6. Cemetery in the Reichswald Forest War Cemetery in the town of Kleve, which lies in Nordrhein-Westfalen in the west of Germany close to the Dutch border, approximately 130 kilometres to the north west of Cologne, and approximately 25 kilometres to the south east of Nijmegen. William died in the advance through Reichswald Forest in February 1945. He was reburied at Reichswald on 14th November 1946 from Udem Cemetery, Germany.

The words on his gravestone; *'In heavenly love abiding. Until we meet again.'*

Sergeant Thomas Arnold Lawton:

Royal Air Force Volunteer Reserve 207 Squadron

Date of Death: 21st March 1945

Commemorated on Odd Rode War Memorial

Thomas Arnold Lawton

Thomas Arnold Lawton was born in June 1920 to John Thomas Lawton and Sarah Lawton, *nee* Murphy, in Scholar Green. The family lived in Spring Terrace and Thomas's father was a machinist in a colliery. His brother, Robert, born in 1917, was in the Regular Army.

According David Nicholls, a family friend, Arnold, being the youngest son of the family, was particularly inspired by his elder brother Stan who served at Dunkirk. He too wanted to make his contribution and so volunteered for active service in the RAF and became a valued member of 207 Squadron. Arnold became a great source of pride not only to his parents and brother Stan but also to his friends, in particular his old school-mate Dick Carman, who retired as Squadron Leader in the RAF. He continues to be fondly remembered to this day through sister-in-law Irene, nephews Graham and Raymond, Sandra (Ray's wife) and great nephew John (Ray's son).

Thomas, who preferred to be called Arnold, joined the RAF Reserve and served with 207 Squadron, service number 2222713 based at RAF Spilsby. He trained as a rear gunner and in 1945 served on Lancaster bomber Mk1 PA196 EM-D.

Sergeant Thomas Arnold Lawton (bottom right) with his crew

L-R back: CJ Dewdney F/E - RA Lewis, Pilot - W Judd, WOp - John Smith, Nav

Front: H Collin M/U - Gerald Masumoto B/A TA Lawton RG

Operations on the Lancaster bomber Mk1 PA196 EM-D.

date (all 1945)	crew	a/c	target	5 Gp force	raid comments
2/3 Feb	as above	PB764	Karlsruhe	250/15 lost	Complete cloud cover resulted in poor target marking and operation was a failure
7/8 Feb	as above	PB764	Ladbergen	177/3 lost	Later recce showed canal banks had not been breached bombs having fallen in nearby fields

Date	Aircraft	Target	Force/Lost	Notes
8/9 Feb	as above	PB764 Politz	475/12 lost	Port inner engine became u/s and Captain aborted after jettisoning part load of bombs
13/14 Feb	as above	PB764 Dresden	244/6 lost	Force attacked in two phases, the first being led by 5 Group. 8 Group followed in second phase and USAAF followed on 14 Feb in daylight
14/15 Feb	as above	PB764 Rositz	244/4 lost	This was a small oil refinery near Leipzig. Once again trouble with port inner engine and Captain aborted
3/4 Mar	as above	PB764 Ladbergen	212/7 lost	Aqueduct breached in two places and put out of action
5/6 Mar	as above	PB764 Bohlen	248/4 lost	Bohlen was a synthetic oil plant. Cloud cover resulted in poor target marking but some damage
6/7 Mar	as above	PB764 Sassnitz	191/1 lost	Sassnitz was a small port on the island of Rugen in the Baltic. Considerable damage. 3 ships sunk in harbour.
12/13 Mar	as above	RF144 Dortmund	n/a	A big raid with only 2 lost out of the total force of 1108. A record effort on a single target. Engineering production stopped, and post war assessment indicates that it would have been many months before industry would have got back to normal.
14 Mar	as above	PD220 Wurzburg	n/a	No details available.
20/21 Mar	as above	PA196 Bohlen FTR	224/9 lost	Very accurate bombing putting refinery completely out of action.

Arnold is commemorated on Panel 275 Runneymede Memorial

Together with the rest of his crew, based at RAF Spilsby in Lincolnshire, Arnold failed to return from an attack on the synthetic oil plant at Bohlen, near Leipzig on the night of 20th/21st March 1945. The plane was lost without trace. All the crew are commemorated on the Runnymede Memorial. Their average age was 22.

224 Lancasters and 11 Mosquitoes of 5 Group attacked the synthetic oil plant. This accurate attack put the plant out of action and it was still inactive when captured by American troops several weeks later. Nine Lancasters were lost. With the Lancaster, No. 207 Squadron ranged as far afield as Italy and Gdynia, Poland. Its raids on enemy territory were sometimes costly and in May 1943, and March 1944, two No. 207 Squadron COs - Wing Commanders TAB Parselle and VJ Wheeler - did not return from raids on Düsseldorf and Frankfurt respectively.

On D Day the squadron's Lancasters attacked Caen in support of the Normandy landings. The squadron's last operational mission, on 25th April 1945, was against the SS Barracks at Berchtesgaden. In its five hundred and forty operations in the Second World War, the squadron lost one hundred and fifty-four crews. Seven DSOs, 115 DFCs and 92 DFMs were won by its members. *Sources:*

WR Chorley, Midland Counties Publishing, 1998)
The Bomber Command War Diaries - An operational reference book: 1939-1945 (Middlebrook & Everitt, Penguin, 1990) (W.R, 1990)

Gunner Edwin Farrington: Royal Artillery

Date of Death: 1st April 1945

Commemorated on Barthomley and Balterley

War Memorial, St Bertoline's Church, Barthomley

Edwin Farrington was born in Audley, Staffordshire in March 1918 to Thomas Matthew and Margaret Ellen Farrington, (*nee* Darlington). Edwin's brother, John was born in 1912. Another brother Thomas Farrington was born in 1920. His mother died on 26th February 1930. His father remarried to Annie Maydew in 1930. In 1939 the family were living in *Balterley Green House*, Balterley, a rural hamlet near Audley but historically in the parish of Barthomley. His father was a coal hewer and his brother Thomas was a horseman on a farm. Edwin's father became a War Department Constable during the war.

Edwin joined the 25th Field Regiment, Royal Artillery, service number 964015.

25th Field Regiment during World War II

25th Field Regiment fought in Africa as part of the 4th Indian Infantry Division. They took part in the East African Campaign, a series of battles fought in East Africa by the British and Allies against Italian forces from June 1940 to November 1941. The 4th Indian Division fought in Egypt and took part in Operation Compass in December 1940. The division was involved in the decisive battles of that campaign in the camps around Sidi Barrani. In December 1940, the division was rushed to British Sudan to join with the 5th Indian Infantry Division to prevent the Italian forces from threatening Red Sea supply routes to Egypt, as well as Egypt and the Suez Canal itself. In June 1942, they were at the Gazala Line at Tobruk. In September 1942 at the fall of Tobruk Edwin Farrington was captured and became a prisoner of war.

Edwin was transported back to Europe and was eventually incarcerated at Stalag VIIIB Lamsdorf, in Poland. The camp, later renumbered Stalag 344 was located near the small town of Lamsdorf (now called Lambinowice, in Poland) in what was then known as Upper Silesia.

Location of Stalag 344 POW Camp

Today on the site of the camp is the Polish Central Prisoner of War Museum. The camp initially comprised barracks built to house British and French prisoners in the First World War. More than one hundred thousand prisoners from Australia, Belgium, Britain, Canada, France, Greece, New Zealand, the Netherlands, Poland, South Africa, the Soviet Union, Yugoslavia and the United States passed through this camp. In 1941 a separate camp, Stalag VIIIF was set up close by to house the Soviet and Polish prisoners. In 1943, the Lamsdorf camp was split up, and many of the prisoners (and Working Parties/Arbeitskommandos) were transferred to two new base camps: Stalag VIIIC Sagan and Stalag VIIID Teschen, which became VIIIB. The camps at Lamsdorf, VIIIB and VIIIF were re-numbered Stalag 344.

Stalag 344 Lamsdorf before the forced march to Germany, January 1945.

Edwin's Royal Artillery records show his status as a prisoner of war: *E Farrington. Rank: Gunner. Army Number: 964015. Regiment: Royal Artillery, POW Number:220496. Camp Type: Stalag. Camp Number: 344. Camp Location: Lambinowice, Poland*

In January 1945, as the Soviet armies resumed their offensive and advanced into Germany, many of the prisoners including Edwin Farrington were marched westward in groups of two to three hundred in the so-called *Long March*. Many of them died from the bitter cold and exhaustion. In the depths of winter under freezing conditions, with minimal food, the men walked hundreds of kilometres, between January and March 1945 with the Lamsdorf men heading north.

It was an exhausting, hazardous and debilitating experience for the men, drawing on reserves of strength both physical and mental. The general route of the column from Stalag VIIIB and its work detachments, as well as many of those from Stalag 344, was west through the southern tip of Upper Silesia, across the mountain ranges of eastern Sudetenland to Germany. For most columns the rations received from the Germans were meagre and irregular issues of bread, tinned meat and potatoes, and there was a constant struggle to get enough food to keep going. Fortunately, most of them benefited from gifts of bread and often of hot food and firewood in the smaller Czech towns and villages. Later groups coming on the heels of many thousands of other prisoners did not fare as well as the first parties to pass through the Czechoslovakian countryside, and eventually the Germans forbade the giving of food to prisoners of war since the Czechs refused it to German civilian refugees. The Commonwealth War Grave record indicated Edwin Farrington died on 1st April 1945 and was buried in Gefrees cemetery, a town in the district of Bayreuth, Germany. It is situated in the Fichtelgebirge, 21 km northeast of Bayreuth.

Gefrees, Germany.

This is probably where Farrington died on his long march into Germany. On 18th September 1947, his body was transferred to Durbach Commonwealth War Graves cemetery, Grave Reference: 3. D. 5. Durbach is in the south of Germany approximately 45 kilometres south of Munich.

Edwin's Royal Artillery records show his death. The initials M.E record the theatre of war in which Edwin served not where he died, the Middle East (Tobruk). His attestation file records his fate.

E. Farrington's grave

Edwin is also commemorated in the Betley War Memorial.

Part of the beautiful Betley War Memorial window

Private Raymond Ecclestone:

The Highland Light Infantry (City of Glasgow Regt 1st Battalion-Glasgow Highlanders)

Date of Death: 14th April 1945

Commemorated on Odd Rode War Memorial

Raymond Ecclestone was born on 5th June 1926 to Mary Hannah Ecclestone, *nee* Williams, and John Bertie Ecclestone. In 1911 his parents lived in Chapel Street, Mow Cop with a family; Winifred, born 1904, John Hugh, born 1906, and James, born 1909. Raymond's father was a yardman for a railway company. In 1939 Raymond lived at 3 Chapel Street Kidsgrove. His widowed mother ran a shop at the address. In 1939 Raymond was still at school but by 1945 was old enough to enlist. He served in the Highland Light Infantry (City of Glasgow Regt 1st Battalion-Glasgow Highlanders) service number 14794833. 1st Battalion, Highland Light Infantry went to France in 1939 as part of the BEF, fighting during the withdrawal to Dunkirk and was eventually evacuated. After four years in Britain it returned to France as part of the 53rd (Welsh) Division, landing in Normandy towards the end of June 1944. Battles included the crossing of the Odon, the Ardennes, the Reichswald and the final advance into Germany. The Battalion War Diary describes the failure to take Häuslingen at 19:00 hours on 13th April when Raymond was probably killed.

Raymond is buried in Becklingen War Cemetery, grave reference 2.F 7. He was reburied in this cemetery on 2nd August 1946 from Groß Häuslingen. The small village of Becklingen lies in the north of Germany approximately 85kms north of Hannover. The site of Becklingen War Cemetery was chosen for its position on a hillside overlooking Luneburg Heath. Luneburg Heath was where, on 4th May 1945, Field-Marshal Montgomery accepted the German surrender from Admiral Doenitz. Burials were brought into the cemetery from isolated sites in the countryside, small German cemeteries and prisoner of war camps cemeteries, including the Fallingbostel cemetery, within a radius of about 80 kilometres. Most of those buried in the cemetery died during the last two months of the war. Becklingen War Cemetery contains over two thousand Commonwealth burials of the Second World War, ninety-seven of them unidentified. There are also twenty-seven war graves of other nationalities, many of them Polish. There are several other men from Raymond's Battalion buried in adjacent plots.

Becklingen War Cemetery

Trooper Joseph Henry Lowe: Royal Tank Regiment RAC 44th

Date of Death: 19th April 1945

Commemorated on Odd Rode War Memorial

Joseph Henry Lowe was the son of Joseph Henry and Bertha Lowe, *nee* Buckley, and was born in May 1923 in Rode Heath. The Army Roll of Honour incorrectly gives his birth as being in Hampshire. His father was a builder and died in 1935 in Stoke-on-Trent. In 1939 he lived with his widowed mother at 2 Bibby Street Rode Heath. His mother worked in *'Paid Domestic Duties'*. He was an only son and he drove for Hollinshead's coaches.

Joseph joined the Royal Tank Regiment RAC 44th service number 7959089. The regiment served in Italy and then returned to Britain. Whilst we have few biographical details for Joseph we do have an extensive record of his military career. The following is an extract from a Brief History of the 44th Royal Tank Regiment 1939 – 1945 to illustrate the extensive fighting Joseph was involved in:

'The months of March, April and May 1944 were spent in preparation for the D Day Landings. On 4th June the regiment moved from Worthing to Portsmouth and sailed from Gosport on the 8th June landing in France on the 9th June, concentrating on the village of Amblie. On the 25th June the regiment was joined by 'F' Battery, 4th Royal Horse Artillery and 'B' Company 2nd /60th Kings Royal Rifle Corp and were to remain a group until the end of the war…'

After months of campaigning the regiment had reached Germany:

'The main push through Germany now started with the Regiment taking part in 'Operation Swan' which started on the 30th March, advancing through Winterswisk, Verdun and Octroi. On 3rd April the regiment rested the day at Lindenhurst and then moved to a defensive position at Ohno. On the 6th they crossed the Dortmond-Ems canal after first clearing the west bank of enemy opposition. The regiment now began to come across very stiff opposition from small determined groups of Germans. Advancing through Hogsten and reaching Haltered on the 8th. Then through Recue and across the Weser canal and on north. On the 9th April encountered heavy defences south of Neuenkirchen manned by students of the German Officer Training Unit. The regiment suffered twelve killed but many hundreds of Germans were killed.

On the 10th advanced again across the Ems canal through Osnabrück and North East towards Broman, arriving 20 miles south of the city in the early hours of the 11th. On the 11th the Regiment crossed the Weser and soon made contact with the German 2nd Marine Diva and with the 2nd /60th Rifles advanced slowly clearing the village of Gt Eldora on the 15th. The next day capturing Sud-Kamden taking 3 officers and 260 men prisoner. The Regiment continued to advance and fight, taking Kirchwalselde and Rahnhorst. On the 19th April the regiment was concentrated around Scharnhorst to prepare for the capture of Bremen. The advance on the city started with considerable fighting, the regiment in support of the 52nd Lowland Div and by the 22nd April the regiment was in position for the final assault on the city and a massive air raid by the Royal Airforce taking place on the 23rd.

Joseph was killed on 19th April in the battle for Bremen. He is buried in plot 2 C 11 in Becklingen War Cemetery, Germany.

Marine John Hanahoe: Royal Marines

Date of Death: 15th July 1945

A Second World War serviceman associated with H.M.S Excalibur who is not on a local War Memorial but buried in a Commonwealth War Grave in Christ Church, Alsager.

John Hanahoe was born in West Hartlepool on 24th September 1902 to Emily and John Hanahoe. His father was a labourer originally from County Mayo. Ireland. His sister, Mary Agnes Hanahoe was born in 1902, and sister Margaret Hanahoe in 1904. In 1911 the family were living at 47 Randolph Street, Middlesbrough. In the 1939 Register John was living with his father at 12 Grovedale Road, Islington London. He was a meat porter.

John's service number was CH/X106139. He was based at Chatham Division Royal Marine. Kent but at the time of his death was based at *H.M.S Excalibur* Alsager. His Time at *H.M.S Excalibur* was spent on gunnery, torpedoes, engineering, discipline, and *'power-of-command'*. He was accidentally killed in Alsager: according to Army records he fractured the base of his skull in a road accident in Lawton Road, Alsager. Because of his age (the recruits at the base were between 17 and 23 years old) John Hanahoe must have been on the staff at *the Brunds*. He was 42 years old at the time of his death and unmarried.

Probate details state his address was 15 Princes Avenue, Finchley Middlesex, and that he died on *'war service'* on 15th July 1945. Probate of £318.16s.4d was granted to his sister, Margaret Hanahoe.

Radway Green Royal Ordnance Factory 1940 to 1947

Radway Green Royal Ordnance Factory, Photo BAE Systems

The need for a new munitions factory

Britain needed a large supply of munitions to fight the war. The decision to build a munitions factory for small armaments at Radway Green in 1939 fundamentally changed Alsager. The site was chosen because it was adjacent to a railway line and in a rural location between the urban areas of Stoke-on-Trent and Crewe and so thought to be less vulnerable to attack from enemy aircraft. The site was partially sheltered from enemy aircraft by being near Mow Cop hill. Radway Green was also selected because it was planned to twin production at the new factory with Royal Ordnance Factory Swynnerton, south of Stoke-on-Trent. There was availability of workers within reasonable travelling distance to both factories. A large supply of pottery workers in Stoke-on-Trent could be transferred to munitions production from the pottery industry, which was non-essential to the war effort.

Prior to the 1930s Britain's ordnance manufacturing capability had been concentrated within the Royal Arsenal, Woolwich. In the late nineteenth century, the term *'Royal Ordnance Factories'* began to be used collectively of the manufacturing departments of the Arsenal (principally the Royal Laboratory, Royal Gun Factory and Royal Carriage Works) which, though they shared the same site, operated independently of one another.

Radway Green ordnance factory was the largest of the five new munitions factories to be built in Second World War. From a greenfield site it became a factory employing fourteen thousand workers by 1943.

It is reported that Alsager Urban District Council spent an *'agonised'* almost *'all night sitting'*, before they decided to vote in favour of building the factory; *'Patriotism took precedence over real feelings'*. The council were concerned that an explosion at the factory would kill large numbers of residents in Alsager. (AP&P, 1999)

In December 1939 Norman Hill, a surveyor for the government's construction contractor, Trollope and Colls, attended a meeting at a makeshift compound adjacent to Radway Green railway halt. (Hill, 1998)

At the meeting were officials from Woolwich Arsenal, which was selected to oversee munitions production, local surveyors including H.V Lynam from Alsager Council, and senior administration for the new factory. They were joined by local farmers including Mr Barker and Mr Siddall, whose land was requisitioned by compulsory purchase. The remit was for the factory to be in partial production by 31st May 1940. It was to produce small calibre rifle ammunition and twenty-millimetre cannon shells. The initial contract with Trollope and Colls was for two years by which time the factory should have met its full production potential. A production block and administrative offices were to be built first. The command staff, all from Woolwich Arsenal, included R.W. Knowles, Resident Engineer, Bill Lennox, Clerk of Works, and Bill Oldham, Quantity Surveyor. Norman Hill recalls he took lodgings at *Lane Ends Farm* with the Siddall family. (*Lane Ends Farm* is now the *Holly Trees Hotel* in 2017.)

Trollope & Colls, a London firm, were paid £900,000 for the contract. There was resentment from Cheshire and Staffordshire builders that they had not been offered the work. The Trollope and Colls team was led by G.S. Mitchell, Manager, and John Morley, Accountant, and three principal engineers; Jacobs, Webber and Rigby. Norman Hill was their Surveyor. Building began in December 1939 and almost immediately the contractors had to contend with many engineering problems caused by the harshest winter in living memory.

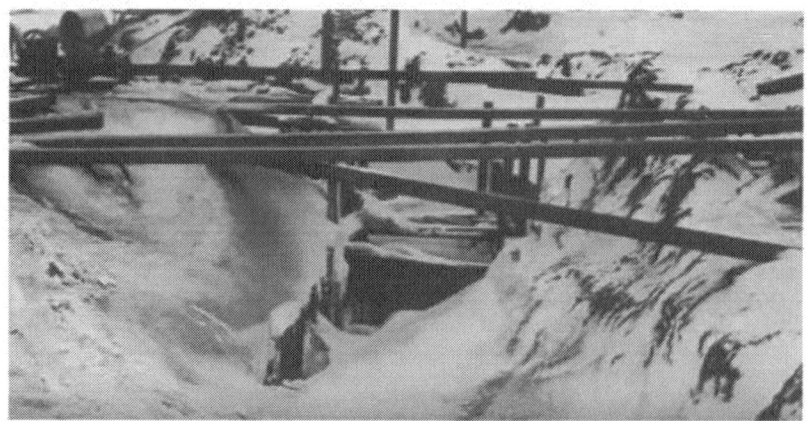

Winter 1940 and there were early construction problems at Radway Green. There were snow drifts up to five feet thick and heavy frosts in Alsager that winter.

Construction

Trollope and Colls had to bring in vast numbers of workers to build the factory. Accommodation for construction workers, who came from far and wide, was lacking and some lodged in local farms and even slept in haylofts.

The undulating land was unsuitable for a factory, so blasting was necessary to level it. The discovery of a vein of sand during the excavation of the foundations nearly led to the abandonment of the project and the search for an alternative site. The site was difficult. A stream had to be culverted, ponds drained, and some specially reinforced concrete foundations completed. During construction steam was injected from mobile boilers into the ground to facilitate the mixing of concrete in freezing weather. Men with excavators had to be diverted to clear huge snowdrifts blocking Alsager's roads. Because the ground for the new B Block was so hard excavators could not break it, so explosives were used six feet apart and two feet six inches deep. (AP&P, 1999) The builders persisted and gradually the factory took shape.

A new road was constructed to improve communications to Crewe. (This is the road which today runs under the M6 motorway.) Before this road the route to Crewe was via a winding lane over the brook and railway line and back over the railway line over Siddall's land.

Vast diggers and machinery 'trundled' through the village. We had never seen anything like it.' (Margaret Bebbington.)

The vehicles taking building workers and raw materials to the new factory considerably increased the amount of traffic through Alsager after 1940.

The original access to the factory was past *Alsager Mill* and *Hall Farm*. (Testimony of Mr Peter Barker 2017) A more direct route was made later via a new land further down off the main road which can still be seen today. (Between the *Alsager Mill* and the *Plough Inn*.) A workers' bus park was created at the top of Mill Lane.

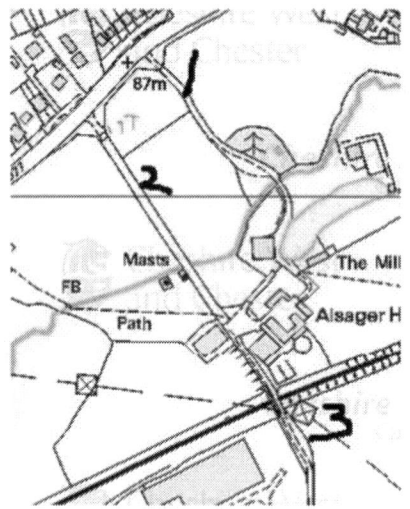

Access to the new factory

1. *First route into Radway Green 1940 via Mill Lane past rear of Hall Farm. The bus park was at the entrance of Mill Lane.*
2. *Second Route more direct from Crewe Road.*
3. *Railway Bridge reinforced 1940 to take heavy traffic. The first production facility is shown to the left of figure 3. The roadworks were undertaken by subcontractors, Hasphaltic.*

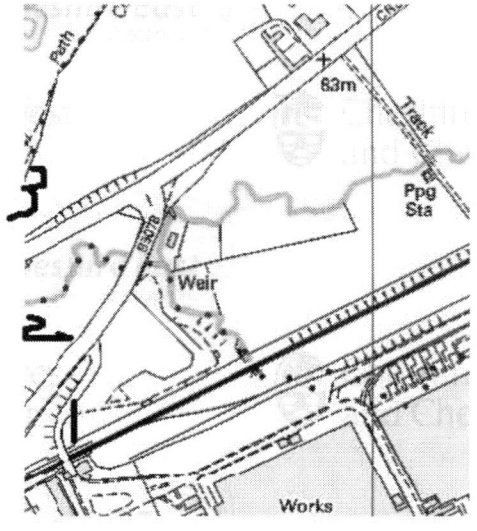

Second access to the factory from Crewe Road 1940 (Radway traffic lights in 2017)

1. Final constructed entrance to ROF Radway Green 1940
2. Original road to Crewe was over level crossing before it doubled back to Oakhanger
3. New road to Crewe

Norman Hill, the surveyor, negotiated sub-contracts with local builders for the erection of staff houses and carried out improvements to the local waterworks and sewage beds. Essential sewers and roads had been laid.

Construction site

Steel frame construction: The sub-contractors for steelwork were Dorman Long.

Mains and electrical power were brought into the site and by mid-May 1940 the production block and administrative office were nearly complete. The original production plan was to use components from Royal Ordnance Factory Swynnerton and for Radway to be a finishing plant but after a bomb destroyed the Woolwich Arsenal filling factory in September 1940 the loading and filling of shells was added to Radway's production capability. The original plan was for the factory to take two years to build but as early as May 1940 a pilot project directed by A.T. Barnard was up and running to manufacture .303 Mark V11 ammunition using old machinery from the Great War. Norman Hill, writing in 1998, said the first two production machines were imported from the USA by convoy, and that some other machines which did not reach Radway Green were destroyed when Allied ships were sunk by U-boats.

A.G. Barnard was the country's foremost expert on small arms manufacture. Workers made ammunition under tarpaulin sheets until the roof was completed. Dozens of lorries took factory waste materials and clay from the construction site to Barker's sand quarry and tipped the spoil there. Radway Green had a problem with the disposal of waste products. Peter Barker remembered the constant stream of lorries carrying copper bin products up Station Road, creating a mess. Some was buried on the outskirts of Alsager near the *Brunds* and the Marl Pits (Hassall Road).

Factory foremen were recruited from Woolwich Arsenal to supervise predominantly local labour. Most of the skilled workers also were transferred from the Woolwich Arsenal though there was a shortage of housing accommodation for them. Initially, digs were found with local families and several large properties acquired and adapted. In 1941 a new manager was recruited; Leonard Samuel Flatman.

Leonard Samuel Flatman-(left) General Manager ROF Radway Green at his son Peter's wedding.

Leonard Flatman was born on 30th April 1897 in Plumstead. Leonard worked at ROF Woolwich before becoming manager of a Royal Ordnance factory in Durham before the war. He was a member of the Institute of Mechanical Engineers. He married Barbara Lyon in 1921. Part of his secret work in the war was to travel to the United States for meetings with the United States military. He travelled to the States in 1942 and 1943, sometimes travelling by a circuitous route via Lisbon, Brazil, and Puerto Rico. Leonard was awarded an OBE in 1957 when he was Director of Ordnance Factories (Ammunition.) He died in 1963 in Cheltenham.

Summary of the acquisition of property by the Ministry of Supply for Radway Green and military personnel

Kelly's Directory (Kelly's, 1939) lists the occupiers of the following large houses in Alsager:

The Hall: Captain Francis (Estrange) Joseph K.B E. DL. J.P. *The Gables:* William Walker J.P *The Cedars:* Mr Aische; *Milton House:* Mrs Wheaton-Smith.

The Second World War brought about the acquisition in Alsager of *The Gables*, *Milton House,* and *The Cedars* for use as hostels by the Ministry of Supply. Only *The Hall* remained in private hands. These properties were acquired principally to provide billeting for the Royal Ordnance Factory, Radway Green, which grew from nothing to a workforce of fourteen thousand, and a consequential need to construct or acquire more housing and schools for the increased population. These acquisitions fundamentally changed Alsager. In addition, several farms were requisitioned, and other villas taken to billet soldiers.

Other large houses outside Alsager with traditional landowners in the villages were not requisitioned by the Ministry of Supply. *Kelly's Directory* lists the principal landowner as Sir Phillip Baker-Wilbraham J.P of *Rode Hall*. In the Great War *Rode Hall* became a hospital but in the Second World War the property was not used for the war effort. *Ramsdell Hall,* in Scholar Green, the home of Phillip Bailey, was not requisitioned but it was partially used for divisional Air Raid Precautions (ARP) work. *The Old*

Rectory in Barthomley was turned over for military use by American troops later in the war.

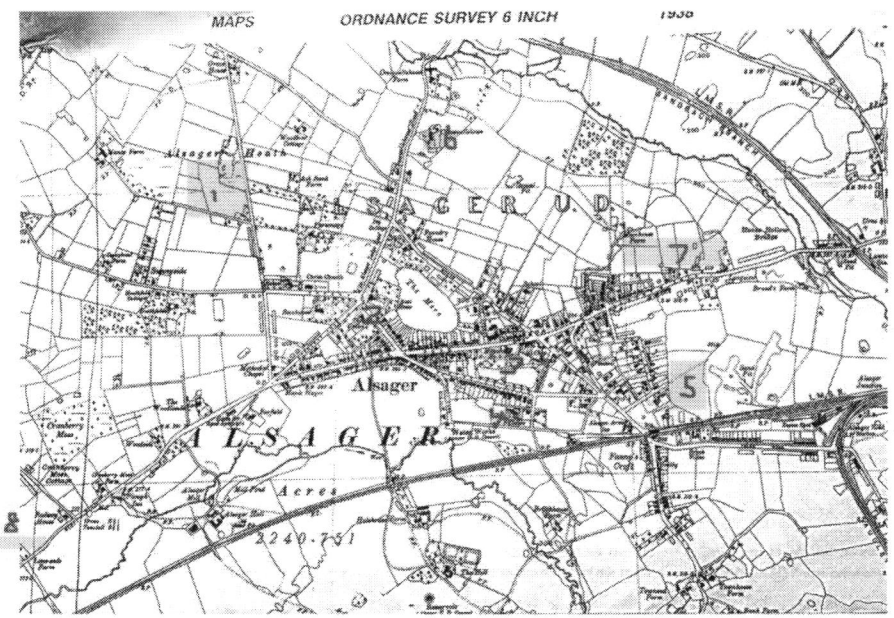

Some of the property requisitioned by the government 1939-45 in Alsager for Radway Green

1. *Heath Farm* for Heathside Munitions Hostel
2. *The Gables* for accommodation
3. *Milton House* for accommodation
4. *The Cedars* for military uses
5. *The Brunds* for male hostel then Royal Navy and then *HMS Excalibur*
6. *Creswellshawe House*-evacuees then planned-use for elderly accommodation
7. *Moorhouse Farm* for new housing estate for ROF Workers and a new school.
8. *Farming land* for ROF Radway Green

In addition:

Houses were requisitioned in Station Road for billeting of soldiers.

The Mere was used by the Navy for training.

St Mary's Schoolroom was used to assist evacuees.

The Council offices: *Prospect House*, and *Fairview House*, used by Civil Defence.

Other property such as *Oak Villa* was used for Rest Centres or for evacuees.

In 1940, *Milton House* was partitioned into separate dwelling units by Trollope and Colls, who added an annexe and games room for ROF personnel. In addition, the eight acres of grounds were used for the construction of huts for personnel. In 1941 the Ministry of Supply acquired the Victorian mansion, *The Gables*, in Church Road where two flats were created, the upper unit used for the Ministry of Food and Agriculture. Accommodation was needed for the management of the new factory. The acquisition of *The Gables*, a large Victorian villa, was made possible by the death of its owner William Walker, aged seventy-two. The incoming residents must have been surprised by the opulence of *The Gables* with its extensive grounds. Its first resident in 1941 was Leonard Flatman,

Outside Alsager, *Lawton Hall*, a hotel since 1906, was turned into a Civil Defence Reserve Camp. It was used for training but also for temporary accommodation, meals for visiting executives, and for socials.

Radway Green Production (Labbatt, 1999)

From June 1940 the factory machinery operated twelve hours a day for seven days a week. By the autumn it could supply ammunition to the Royal Air Force during the Battle of Britain. A foundry and rolling mill was added to Radway's capacity. By the end of 1941 the factory was self-sufficient apart from the supply of raw materials for explosives. By 1941 there were seven thousand workers rising to fourteen thousand in 1943.

The new factory

By October 1943 the factory consisted of 7 main blocks.

	Block	Size in Acres	
1.	Administrative Block.	floor space	0.47
2.	Foundry and rolling mill	floor space	3.72
3.	Press shop small arms components	floor space	4.72
4.	Examination block and tool shop	floor space	3.18
5.	Automatic machine shop…shell making	floor space	4.65
6.	Loading factory	floor space	0.96
7.	Maintenance and stores	floor space	1.71

In 1942 Trollope and Colls completed a large gas plant and added the Filling Factory to the site.

Inside the works. Each block was given a letter to identify it, starting with block 'A.'

Railway sidings were added so the completed shells could be transported to Crewe to the packing sheds. Ammunition was then transferred to the ROF storage facilities in Nesscliffe near Shrewsbury. A new station at Millway also provided a facility for workers to commute to Radway from Stoke-on-Trent. The railways in Britain were nationalised during the war.

Radway Green workers at their machines. There were four main processes in the manufacture of ammunition: A standard round a brass case was tapered and detonator was fitted with mercury fulminate. Cordite was introduced and finally a small nickel lead bullet fitted and sealed into the tapered end of the case. There were twenty individual operations in the manufacture of a .303 shell.

By the autumn of 1943 the factory was producing fifteen million rounds of .303 and eleven million rounds of 20mm cannon per week.

Ammunition produced at Radway Green during WW2: .303

Mark V11 Standard ball cartridge with lead core bullet and cordite load

Mark V111E Streamlined bullet with solid lead core loaded with nitro-cellulose powder.

B. Mark X11 Carries incendiary bullet and case loaded with nitro-cellulose powder.

V Mark 1 Armour piercing bullet with steel or tungsten core. Standard cordite cartridge.

C Mark 11 and 1V Tracer bullet with cordite. Phosphorus compound to assist gunner's aim.

20mm cannon shell. Ball, tracer, and High Explosive. This ordnance had greater destructive power than the .303.

1943 was to be the peak of production at Radway Green: weekly output of fifteen million .303 bullets and one million 20 mm aircraft cannon. Difficulties in recruiting staff were exacerbated by a Cabinet decision in December 1943 when ROF factories lost their priority to recruit workers. Armed services recruitment took precedence in preparation for the invasion of France. Some workers were transferred out of Radway in 1944 back to ROF Swynnerton to meet their manufacturing requirements.

The Workers at Radway Green

Workers came from Alsager and all the surrounding urban areas to work at the factory. Getting to Radway Green by train was precarious in the bad winter of 1940. On one occasion, a train was stuck in snowdrifts near *Alsager Hall Farm*. (Crisford, 1992) The train was virtually buried. They kept the steam heating on and a snow plough arrived by mid-morning and soldiers dug the sides of the train out. Four trains per shift took the day shift workers into the railway stop at Millway (Radway Green Station was just down the line.) These four trains would return at 1:30 pm with the afternoon shift and take the early shift home. The trains had two steam engines each because all of the ten coaches were packed with workers. The trains had to load and offload workers quickly to get clear of trains behind. Following these workers' trains on the timetable were three express trains though Alsager, only one of which set down and collected in Alsager.

Most Alsager residents travelled to Radway by cycle or car. Many workers were bussed in from Stoke-on-Trent in fleets of specially chartered buses. Shifts started as early as 6 am. Alsager was suddenly inundated with heavy traffic and local people were upset. Local residents had to join long queues for buses. Many Alsager residents were co-opted to work at Radway. Local men like Jack Smith of Station Road Alsager, a bank manager with Barclays, was appointed to Radway to lend his financial acumen to the payroll function with the firm. Jack Smith also served in the Alsager Home Guard. Radway did not import all its technical staff from Woolwich, though most of the munitions experts came from London.

Double decker buses and coaches were used to transport workers to Radway Green. One factory bus stop was at the entrance of Mill Lane (Alsager Mill—Old Mill 2017) until later in the war when a bus park was built closer to the factory near where the Radway level crossing is today. From the original bus park workers had a long walk to the factory. There were many complaints by Radway Green management that buses were often late which was disruptive to production and to the shift system.

Petrol supplies on their way to Radway

Civil Defence at the factory

The factory recruited from its own ranks a platoon of Local Defence Volunteers to patrol the area, but recruitment of full time police proved difficult because of low pay. Frank Harrison-Barker was appointed Air Raid Protection Officer in 1940. He came from Woolwich Arsenal and had great experience in civil defence of munitions factories. He also organised the factory's ambulance station and the siting of air raid shelters.

Site of two of the four ack-ack guns and searchlights protecting ROF Radway Green after construction. (marked with an X) One positioned between the Mill Lane entrance and the newer Hall Farm entrance. The second was above the factory in the fields.

Management was forced to persuade the Director of Ordnance to transfer police staff from other factories and to call upon a detachment of Royal Engineers billeted at *Crewe Hall* to act as cover in an emergency. In May 1940, rumours spread in the factory there had been an attack by German paratroopers and the Local Defence Volunteers ran out brandishing sticks and heavy objects to defend the factory. The rumours were unfounded. By June 1940 the factory had forty members in its LDV and twenty-eight Special Constables. They only had twelve rifles which were allocated to the Special Constables. By 1941 the LDV had been transformed into a Home Guard with additional defence provided by the War Office Constabulary. Armed response was significantly improved. The War Office Constabulary were responsible for the security of the inner core of the factory while the Home Guard patrolled two outer rings. Communication was via field telephone. Norman Hill and other contract staff, despite their busy jobs, were recruited into the factory Home Guard. Norman was also given First Aid work to supervise in the Ambulance Block. On Home Guard duty he would patrol the flat roof of the factory with his Sten Gun and telescope.

The factory had its own Auxiliary Fire service with twelve staff. The Chief Fire Officer was Mr Welsh. The firemen lived in six specially built houses at the back of the factory. The buildings were camouflaged, and the roofs turfed with grass. By September 1940 air raid shelters were well established. The air raid shelters were situated in reinforced cloakrooms on both sides of each workshop. For females in the cupping and case shops each shelter had seven bays and seventy persons could be accommodated in total in each shelter if the klaxon sounded. Aircraft spotters were placed on the roof and production continued in the factory until the workers reported a *'take cover'* warning. The fire precautions' procedure was extensive and comprehensive. If the factory exploded due to fire not only the factory personnel would be at risk; it was likely Alsager would have been severely damaged too. Twelve men from each shift in the bullet making department had to report for first aid and stretcher bearing duties in an emergency to go out with the Rescue and Decontamination squads. There were twenty-seven men in these squads. Twelve men from each shift were also detailed to become internal fire watchers in the case shops and another twelve for the bullet shop. Four men from each section patrolled the cupping shop. Forty external fire watchers were also appointed for each shift to patrol all key parts of the outside of the factory. The ROF Police force were armed with revolvers.

Bombing Raids over Radway Green and Alsager and district

The Royal Ordnance Factory, Radway Green, the town of Alsager, and the surrounding district, were lucky not to be severely damaged by bombing in the Second World War, but there are interesting stories relating to bombing incidents.

The munitions factory had a night decoy system designed to prevent air attacks on it. This was situated at an air ministry-owned site at Chorlton, five miles to the south of Radway (site of Wychwood Park near Crewe). Most decoy sites in Britain were constructed around four miles (6.4 kilometres) from their protection target, and at least one mile (1.6 kilometres) from any other settlement. They consisted of elaborate light arrays and fires, controlled from a nearby bunker and laid out to simulate a fire-bombed town. By the end of the war there were two hundred and thirty-seven decoys protecting eighty one towns and cities around the country.

Inside the munitions factory modifications were made to minimize the effects of bombing. Glass panels were replaced by eight feet high brick partitions to protect workers.

The factory was nearly hit by a bombing raid by enemy aircraft. Norman Hill, (Hill, 1998), remembers an incendiary bomb dropped by a lone enemy aircraft into the orchard at *Lane Ends Farm* where he was lodging in 1940. The farm was only a few hundred yards from the factory. The six residents at the farm were evacuated to the nearby *Plough Inn* managed by Jack Parkes that night. A heavy bomb was dropped near *Lane Ends Farm* on another evening which created a large crater. Lone aircraft were often spotted and were monitored from Crewe Rolls Royce which had a large civil defence presence.

The following is reproduced from *Alsager in World War Two* (Mary Morris)

'Two days before Christmas 1940, on a bitterly cold evening, Audrey Cartwright and her mother were setting the table for two R.O.F. Workers living with them, who were expected home from the factory. The sirens were wailing. Suddenly there was a terrific explosion outside, the sound of rushing water and the light of flares dropping all around. There was a lovely white tablecloth all set out for the R.O.F. workers coming home. My mother and I had a roast in the oven for them and in the centre of the table was a table lamp. We had cleaned up and scrubbed the farm for Christmas and

everything was looking beautifully polished. There was a beautiful fire roaring away in the chimney. There was a bitterly cold night outside when all of a sudden there was a terrific bang …and the beautiful tablecloth was covered in soot which blew down the chimney. The blast toppled the mantle lamp. It scorched the side of my face, but I saved the lamp, which would have set the place on fire. The bomb blew the windows out of the farmhouse and the shippon, and killed two cows. It made a huge crater, big enough to have buried a house in. It burst the banks of the big brook which flooded the land, but saved us. It saved lives. People came from miles round, for months and months to see it, from Hanley, Stoke and Burslem, and my father received mail for months, afterwards addressed to 'Bomb Farm.'

One family felt the blast at home in Audley Road and the ceiling at home later collapsed. Some of the houses in Audley Road were structurally damaged by the explosion. Mr Peter Barker recalls that when this bomb landed it lit up the whole sky. Another incendiary bomb fell by Alsager marl pits in Hassall Road. The marl pits were the former site of the Alsager Council tip.

A parachute bomb falls to earth. Photo: South Cheshire Archives, Crewe.

December 29th, 1940

On December 29th, 1940, Mr Bill Evans of Smallwood was standing outside his home in Back Lane when he spotted a German plane in broad daylight flying very low overhead. He was a schoolboy at the nearby Smallwood School. To his relief the plane carried on in the Crewe direction. Mr John Gallimore was working in an office at Crewe Rolls Royce Works and spotted the plane, a Messerschmitt, approaching. The plane saw the factory and turned towards it and released two bombs onto it. Fourteen people were killed in the bombing. There had been no air raid warnings and the barrage balloons were in place. The plane had not been seen by local civil defence staff.

Around that time bombs fell near to Hassall Green narrowly missing the canal. Another fell near to the *Boarded Barn* in Scholar Green. Early in 1941 incendiary bombs dropped in the wood near to Rode Park cricket ground. It is thought the bombers confused Lawton Mere with Alsager Mere when looking for the Radway Green munitions factory. The bombs killed a cow.

One lady remembers as a child cycling to Oakhanger the day Chesterton was hit by bombing. She was picking walnuts from a tree to supplement rations when she heard the boom of the bombing seven miles away in Chesterton. She quickly cycled home where her mother was waiting by the door, worried about her.

Bomb damage:

Photo: FHS Cheshire

Lester Crisford, (Crisford, 1992) remembered the bomb dropped at the edge of Cranberry Moss, and a few days later a parachute land mine drifted within yards of the bomb and there was an enormous explosion.

Lester Crisford:

photo: family archive.

No one could hear the parachute bombs coming. One Air Raid Warden and a policeman watched one come down over Wheelock and could do nothing about it. Lester witnessed three bombers over Alsager during the Battle of Britain, strays from the south of England. Later in the winter of 1940/1 the sirens would go off about 8 pm and the bombers would come over on their way to Manchester or towards shipping on the Mersey. Lester could see a glow in the sky after bombing. Search lights were positioned in the fields just beyond where the *Manor Hotel* is today. Anti-aircraft guns would be firing. He had to take cover because when the Crewe guns fired shrapnel fell over Alsager. He remembers walking up Merelake Road; barrage balloons in Crewe could be seen from there. Local fields were strewn with silver paper dropped by the bombers to try to jam the radar. Lester recalled that during one incident in the winter of 1940/1 a bomb fell close to the stud farm in Oakhanger where there were twenty race horses. The horses panicked, jumped the hedge and ran along the road through Alsager. They kept going towards Kidsgrove, up

Goldenhill Bank and stopped exhausted in Swan Square Burslem when dawn broke. There were up to forty barrage balloons based at Crewe and occasionally they would break their cabling and drift over Alsager. Soldiers would shoot them down. On a good day Lester Crisford could watch the sky from the Alsager Golf Club and see dozens of barrage balloons in the far distance in Crewe.

He recalled the last time bombers flew over Alsager was a winter night in 1944. They had released V1 flying bombs before reaching Alsager.

These bombers were a surprise. He had been ignoring recent air raid sirens because he thought they were just practices. But when he heard the Heinkel's throbbing engines he knew the planes were real enemy aircraft.

Luckily there was no major accident or bombing at Radway Green during the war but there were many hours spent in the air raid shelters including a stretch of ten hours on 22nd December 1940 (alert warning), and seven hours two days before on 20th December (take cover warning).

On that evening, there was widespread attack by high explosive and incendiary bombs over a wide area of Staffordshire and the Shelton Steel Works was hit. Radway Green remained unscathed although up to two hundred incendiary bombs landed in fields above the factory. Some railway trains took shelter in the old Harecastle tunnel until the threat of an air raid was over. (Smith, 2017) Another bombing raid of large land mines landed harmlessly onto White Moss.

A chart shows that air raid shelters at ROF Radway Green were used most in 1940/1 and as the war progressed the threat from enemy aircraft declined.

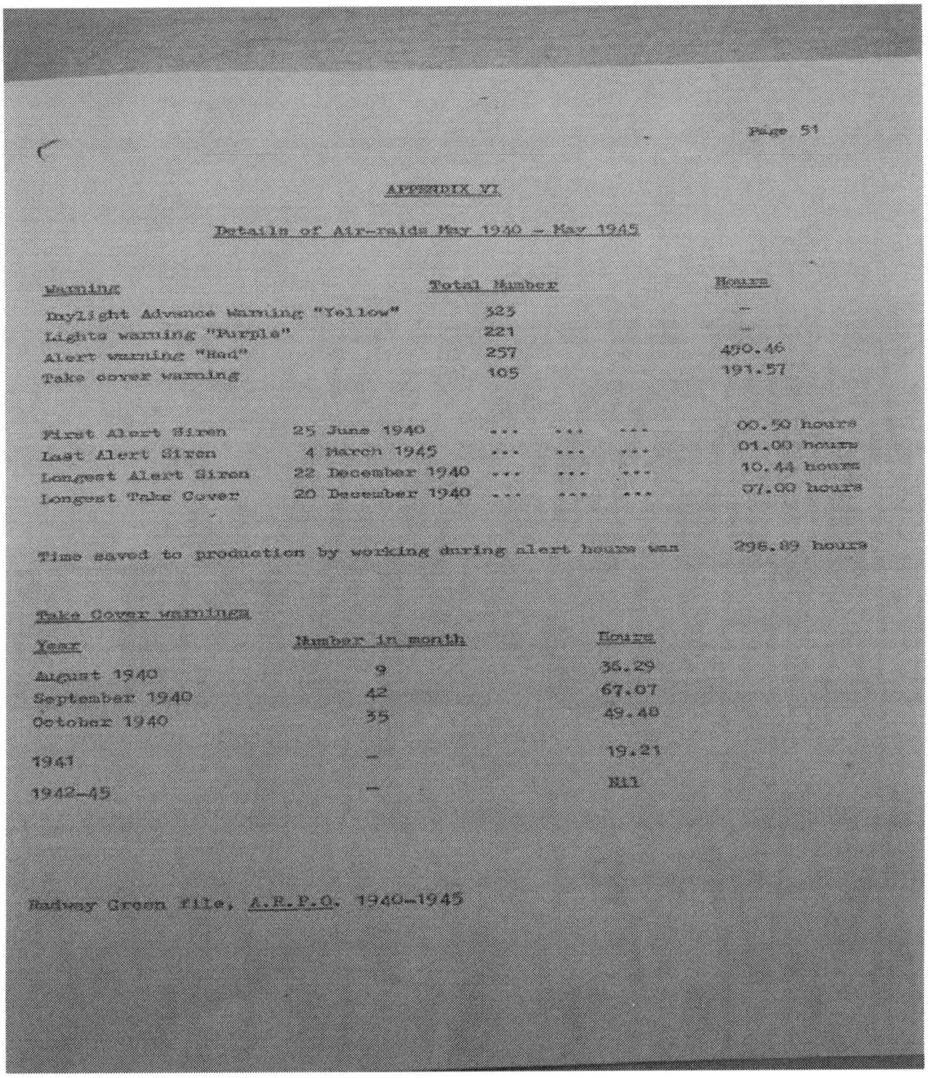

```
                                                                    Page 51

                        APPENDIX VI

                 Details of Air-raids May 1940 - May 1945

Warning                              Total Number         Hours
Daylight Advance Warning "Yellow"        325                -
Lights warning "Purple"                  221                -
Alert warning "Red"                      257              450.46
Take cover warning                       105              191.57

First Alert Siren        25 June 1940     ...   ...   ...   00.50 hours
Last Alert Siren         4 March 1945     ...   ...   ...   01.00 hours
Longest Alert Siren      22 December 1940 ...   ...   ...   10.44 hours
Longest Take Cover       20 December 1940 ...   ...   ...   07.00 hours

Time saved to production by working during alert hours was   296.89 hours


Take Cover warnings
Year                 Number in month            Hours
August 1940                  9                  36.29
September 1940              42                  67.07
October 1940                35                  49.48

1941                         -                  19.21
1942-45                      -                   Nil


Radway Green file; A.R.P.O. 1940-1945
```

Aid Raid warnings ROF Radway Green 1940-45

Crewe was less lucky. Five miles up the railway line bombing damaged engines and track, and buildings.

Bombing in Crewe.

(FHSCheshire)

Working Conditions at Radway Green

While there was a good pool of unskilled labour recruited locally and from all over Britain and Ireland there was a shortage of skilled operatives in the tool room. The Director had to re-deploy semi-skilled toolmakers where he could to more difficult work. Training sessions were provided for those who worked lathes and grinders. Tool making workers were in short supply. In 1942 six hundred disabled staff were recruited to boost staff numbers.

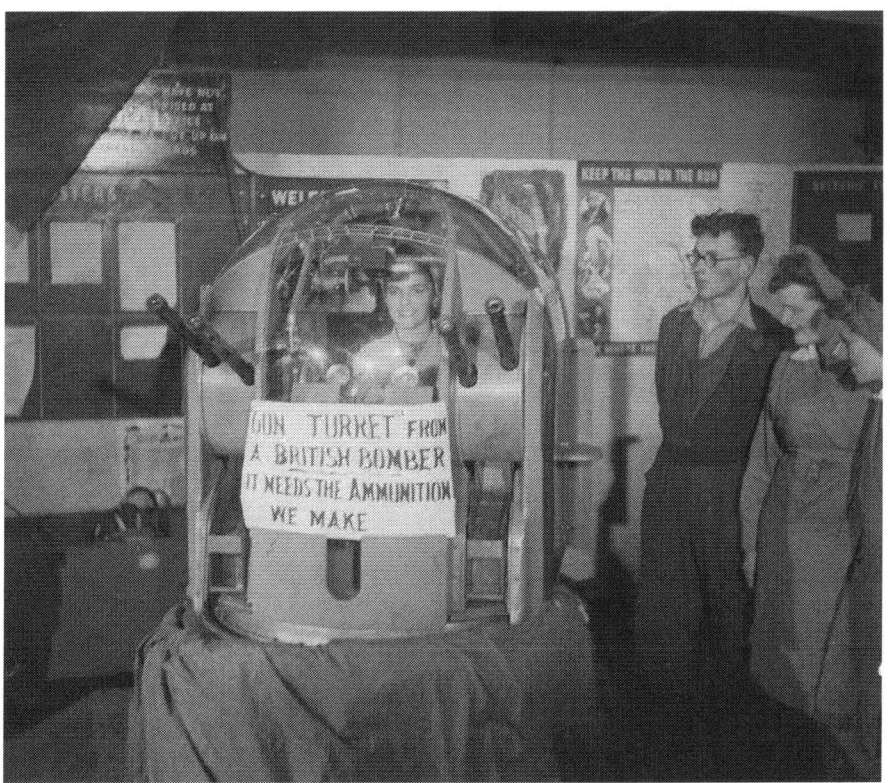

Part of the morale boosting exercise at Radway in 1943 where workers could sit in a mock-up of a cockpit. Photo Imperial War Museum

Absenteeism was a problem at Radway Green particularly with staff who had to travel a long way to work. The factory introduced competitions to improve attendance and embarked on publicity campaigns in 1943 called 'Spring Attack'. Transport arrangements were improved to decrease absenteeism. The system of blacking out factory windows was causing a decrease in morale and this was altered, and shutters introduced to allow more natural light. Food quality was improved and better internal broadcasting equipment to relay radio programmes.

Target blackboard for Radway Green at the time of Duncan Sandys' visit for the Spring Attack campaign to improve absenteeism and production performance. Photo Imperial War Museum.

Duncan Sandys, Parliamentary Secretary for Defence, toured the factory in April 1943 to boost morale by addressing workers in the canteen and inspecting workshops. The visit coincided with the anniversary of the founding of the RAF and workers were shown plane cockpits and could sit in them. Duncan Sandys told the workers that *'Spring Offensive'* was the first of such campaigns and if successful they would be rolled out in other factories. The campaign was focussed on reducing absenteeism and improving production performance. Sandys said that when he toured the Western Desert in 1941 it became evident to him that the supply of small arms ammunition, and 20-millimetre shells fired from British aircraft, was crucial in the victory. Of the millions of rounds fired many would have come from Radway Green.

During *'Spring Attack'*, incoming workers were treated to martial music and there were displays by the Army Physical Training Corps. There were radio broadcasts on Worker's Playtime on the Home Service from the factory, but Radway Green was never mentioned by name, the announcer saying, from a *'factory somewhere in England'*. People listened to broadcasts on crystal sets or by wireless using accumulator wet batteries. The accumulator was rather like a large square shaped glass bottle with a handle on the top for carrying it. Inside were the components that made the wireless work surrounded in acid.

Duncan Sandys M.P addresses workers at Radway Green. Note the dance band on stage to entertain workers. Photo Imperial War Museum.

By the end of the campaign workers from the foundry were the best attendees. The workers with the best attendance records were invited to the Odeon Cinema in Hanley and presented with medals from the Mayor of Stoke-on-Trent.

In 1944 there was a slogan competition to improve morale at the factory. There were three thousand entries, and the winner received £5 in National Savings Certificates, for the winning slogan, **'Never absent, never late, we're the chaps the Nazis hate.'**

In the Sentinel publication *'The Way We Were'*, in 1992 it was recalled that the bulk of the workers recruited for Radway Green were from Stoke-on-Trent where there were twenty-two thousand unemployed adults in December 1939, but many had previously worked in the pottery industry and had no experience of engineering. In 1941 there was a two-shift system of twelve hours which was leading to stress and absenteeism.

'It was a potentially dangerous job for women who risked their lives daily filling bomb and shell cases with explosives. Inevitably there were deaths and serious injuries. In Radway they worked twelve hour shifts seven days a week when the factory opened in 1940. They had to be trained from scratch to do engineering jobs.'

In 1941 the factory introduced a three-shift system for men.

There is no evidence to back up these claims of deaths at Radway Green. When Andrew Alston discovered two Radway Green Accident books from 1944 the list contains the first and last names of the injured party and their address. Most of the injuries recorded were of a minor nature.

In her study of Radway Green in *'Alsager, the Place and its People'*, Mary Morris described the working conditions endured by workers. Loudspeakers were installed were installed so workers could listen to Workers Playtime and I.T.M.A and concerts on the radio. There was a distribution of stockings, cosmetics, chocolates, and cigarettes, and E.N.S.A shows were put on to which villagers were invited. There was a dispute over wages for skilled women workers in 1944 between the Ministry of Supply and the TWGU which was resolved with better rates of pay for women.

The safety rules were strict. Workers were not allowed to take everyday items into the factory. This was called *'contraband'*. This included matches, lighters, cigarettes, and jewellery, hairclips, and even sweets -eating sweets with fingers which had touched explosives was risky. The factory clothes were overalls or white jackets and trousers with no metal fastenings. Regulation footwear containing no metal was mandatory. Women wore a turban or turban-style headscarf. Outfits were made of cotton and were provided for each new shift, workers having to change into them in specially designated rooms. Before entering the factory, workers showed their passes to security.

In line with the recommendations of the Industrial Health Board, a three-shift system was introduced. Women had their hours reduced to fifty hours a week, and men to sixty with Saturday morning off. But such was the strenuous nature of work in the foundry it was necessary to reduce their hours to forty-eight per week in 1942. When hours were reduced to sixty in other parts of the factory the managers were astonished to find production did not fall, but the introduction of semi-automatic machinery helped and allowed more time for machine maintenance. In June 1941, a few women who were employed as slingers, crane drivers, and lorry drivers, work usually done by men, were paid the same rates of pay as their male counterparts, but women in other parts of the factory received a lower basic wage than men. This could be increased through a complex bonus system. Earnings could reach £3. 12s a week but overseers and examiners only earned £3. 7s a week. Finally, in 1942 these all skilled workers working with piece workers received the same bonus pay.

The influx of workers was not altogether welcomed in Alsager. Morris quotes one resident as saying:

> *'The village filled up with Southerners. We didn't like them very much. They took over. They took control. They established themselves in the '13 Club'. They played*

hockey on the Parsonage Field. Young people resented this. The older people resented this.'

The '13 Club' was a social club for ROF workers erected in the grounds of *Milton House*. It was situated at the *'Bank Corner end of Milton House'*. It was called the '13 Club' was called this because Radway Green was designated 'Royal Ordnance Factory 13.' The *'Southerners'* referred to in the quotation would have been the workers brought from Woolwich, predominantly skilled munition workers, to start production. They formed many of the supervisors and managers at the factory. According to a 1992 interview conducted by Mrs Skinner with *'Mrs S' 'the wives of the Woolwich Arsenal workers thought Alsager was rural and primitive.'*

The concerns of Alsager people were understandable as pressure was placed on housing, schools, and roads but most of the incoming workers from London were of a high calibre and essential to the success of Radway Green.

Sidney Lake: Recollections of his daughter, Christianne (Morris, 2017)

An example of the excellent calibre of person coming into Alsager was Sidney Lake. Many of the people who came to Alsager were not just experts in the field of munitions but had already served their country in both World Wars. Alsager was enriched by the experience and participation of such men and women.

Sidney in the Great War where he worked in 'intelligence' on the front line. Photographs: Family archive.

Sidney Lionel Lake, a British subject born in London, lived in Paris before the Great War working for WH Smiths, and was a fluent French speaker. His language skills were most useful when he joined the 6th Wiltshire Regiment on returning to Britain in 1914. He was employed as a despatch rider and could translate items when required. Later as a Sergeant in the Royal Fusiliers he was involved in intelligence work because of his knowledge of France and the language. (His Service Card has the words *'intelligence'* on it.)

Before the Second World War he provided intelligence reports to the British Government before he and his French wife were forced to escape in June 1940. He boarded the last cargo ship out of Bordeaux. The Dutch owners were unhappy to let the ship depart until persuaded at gunpoint by the Royal Navy to take the fleeing people! Returning to England Sidney came to work in munitions at Radway Green during the Second World War in a technical capacity. He was the manager of four hundred female staff. He raised a family in East Court, Alsager and remained in the town for the rest of his life.

Ernest Valentine Skeates (1907-1966)

Before working for munitions in Liverpool Ernest served in the British Army. He was born in Stoke Newington, London. He brought management experience of the munitions industry when he came to Radway Green.

Ernest Skeates in uniform. Family archive

Ernest Skeates (right wearing pocket handkerchief) post war photo with ROF staff Family archive.

Interviews with ROF Workers regarding their experiences

Roy Dale - Factory Worker 1940-1980

Roy came to work at Radway Green in 1940 and remembers how quickly the factory was built. Many old farmers were still using horses and carts around the area before the factory was built. He was a local man. He remembers the loading factory being built in the harsh winter. In 1941 he left Radway to build Mulberry harbours for the war effort and then served four years in the Royal Navy before returning home to get married and continue working at Radway Green until 1980. Seventy years after first joining Radway Roy returned to visit the factory invited by BAE systems. The technology had changed but the end product was virtually the same, the shells for rifles, aircraft and cannon. Roy said in an interview with BAE journalists, *'It was a good life. I enjoyed it anyway.'*

Source of interview and photo: BAE Systems.

Interviews taken by Mrs J. M Skinner, B.Ed. Alsager College of Education Exploring History assignment 1992.

Flossie Band

'I just left. The pressure was too much, I hated women who were from all over the place in my shed. The supervisors were awful. So, I just walked out and joined my husband in Cornwall. They caught up with me and I had to attend a disciplinary hearing. They found me another job because I refused to go back to Radway Green.'

On medical resources; *'If a man was to break or sprain his arm or a leg then the medical team at Radway Green were well equipped to x-ray and plaster these injuries so that less time was wasted, and the injured person could return to work as soon as he was able.'*

Workers' disused footpath over railway to ROF Radway Green near to Alsager Hall Farm. Photo Author 2017.

Mrs Walsh: Entertainment at ROF Radway Green

'Radio was installed with loudspeaker to each part of the factory. It enabled management to speak to workers, advise them of air raids or fire drills, and pure entertainment. Gramophone records, radio plays, comedy were broadcast over the radio. The Radway Green concert party was formed and artists from ENSA paid visits to the factory performing on the canteen stage.'

An offer from the Workers Educational Association to talk to workers about politics was initially declined by the Superintendent as being potentially subversive until persuaded otherwise by the Chief Security Officer!

In April 1942 following a grant from the Ministry of Supply of £325, a Sports Association was formed. Unused land by the car park became a sports field with a full-time groundsman. Cricket and football pitches were built, and teams were soon competing against other factories.

All ROF factories had to have a canteen and these were standardized by a controller. The dining rooms were large halls filled with well-lit long tables. One end of the room was given over to a long counter where dishes were passed straight from the kitchen. At the other end was the stage for theatrical entertainment. In the morning they made bacon sandwiches and tea for workers beginning a shift. All drivers and security men received tea at regular intervals. Lunches were in two sittings and constituted a three-course meal which cost the equivalent of ten pence. Radway Green also had a manager's dining room. The Ministry of Food gave permits and points to bolster the food rations for munitions workers.

A dentist visited three times a week and in March 1942 a nursery was opened as part of a national scheme to allow mothers with children to work. Radway Green provided a laundry service so every worker was supplied with a clean outfit at the beginning of every shift. They provided free face cream, and make-up for women. The face cream was to alleviate the drying of skin caused by toxic jaundice or anaemia which many workers suffered from.

Some of the explosive substances used in manufacture such as cordite, a low explosive accelerant consisting of nitro-cellulose and nitro-glycerine were considered *'safe'*. But the substances that made up detonators, the small copper shells for the triggering process, was made up of lead azide. This looked like castor sugar but was highly toxic and could cause injury to hands during the filling process. Fulminate of mercury, as it was sensitive to heat, could also cause problems leading to poisoning and *'mood swings'*. An explosive component in pellets, tetryl, was a highly sensitive chemical which could cause skin to turn yellow, leading some women to be called *'canaries'*. Tetryl could cause accidents and explosions. All safety rules were handed out in booklet form and workers were dismissed for breaking rules such as smoking.

In December 1942 and 15th March 1943 there were two separate incidents of theft from Radway Green by employees. Two women were fined £5 and a man £15 for the theft of towels, soap, flakes, clogs, and overalls from the factory. (Radway Police Reports file)

Radway Green workers, despite the burden of the shift system and the hard work contributed £25,000 to the North Staffordshire Royal Infirmary through fundraising events associated with the Sports and Social Club.

About two thousand employees were still working at Radway Green by December 1945 and one of the priorities was to dispose of surplus ammunition and weapons shipped in from the war zones, and by December 1946 over a million rounds of ammunition and fifty-five tons of weapons were being neutralised and turned into raw products a week.

Radway Green transformed itself into a factory not only producing small arms but also washing machines and cookers. Many years later it provided the blanks for decimal coinage. The factory is today a modern, well equipped, and successful munitions company owned by BAE Systems.

New Use for Radway Green Cannon Shell Factory

The Story of *'Heathside'* Hostel for Munitions Workers, Alsager

The *Heathside hostel* was a partial solution to the lack of accommodation for munitions workers in Alsager. With the need to recruit more women workers it was becoming increasingly difficult to employ women from Stoke-on-Trent, partly because the Swynnerton factory, south of Stoke, was taking in the bulk of surplus labour.

Heathside came to be built on farming land at *Heath Farm* owned by the Bennion family. Mr Charles Bennion, interviewed in 1992, described how the farm was acquired.

Mrs C. Skinner interviewing Mr C. Bennion in 1992 (J.W.Skinner, 1992)

> *'In August 1940 the Ministry of Supply representatives arrived during the first week of August and said it was the best area for them to build cottages for the workers of Radway Green.*
>
> *They came in on Thursday at 4pm in the afternoon. They were back on Friday morning. A car and a van came. They got their theodolite and measuring equipment out on our land without any agreement. The Ministry of Supply told my father he would have to sell the farm within three weeks. My father pleaded with them to choose another site. But nowhere else was suitable. We had to sell all the crops growing. My grandfather was asked to keep an eye open on it for them. But there was a nine-month delay before they started.'*
>
> *'Compulsory purchase was put on the farm and the whole of the farm was sold off. Building did not start until 1941, April. This brought workers from Scotland, Ireland, and all over the place.'*

Heath Farm was situated by Hassall Road (previously called Chapel Lane.) The farm track led to a cottage before reaching the farm itself. All of the area was open fields. Opposite the farm entrance in Hassall Road was a lane leading through to *The Parsonage*. The farm according to Mr C Bennion, *'was a successful dairy farm with a prize-winning Ayrshire herd. Our cow 'Buttons' was the champion milker in the country'*.

Heath Farm with Mr Bennion and 'Buttons' the Ayrshire cow.

Photograph Bennion family.

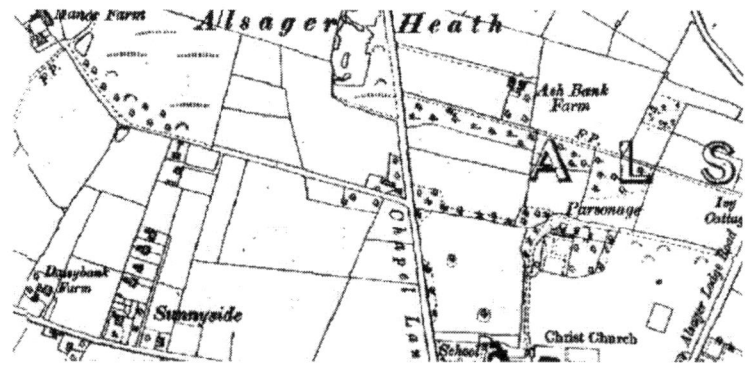

O.S Map 1911. Map of Alsager showing Manor Farm and its geographical location. The lane to the Parsonage is where Alsager School is today located. The Heathside site eventually became a College of Education after the war.

> **HEATH FARM, ALSAGER, FARM STOCK DISPERSAL.**
>
> Exceptional interest was shown in the dispersal of Mr. C. H. Bennion's farm stock at Heath Farm, Alsager, conducted by Messrs. Henry Manley and Sons on Wednesday last week. Despite being the off-season for farm stock dispersals, the unusually large attendance of buyers contributed to a record sale. Over 250 lots of implements, poultry, dairy effects, and furniture found buyers in keen opposition, and the following excellent prices were returned: Car trailer, £13 10s.; balance plough, £8 10s.; drill plough, £5 15s.; poultry houses to £15; water bowls, £7 10s.; water tank, £6 5s.; weighing machine, £6 12s. 6d.; refrigerator, £7 15s.; Lister pump, £8, etc. Pullets realised to 8s. 6d. each; cockerels 4s.

Heath Farm's stock was sold off in August 1940 and aroused a great deal of interest from local farmers as reported in the Chester Chronicle.

The design and building of *Heathside*

Heathside was built by Ministry of Supply contractors J&S Seddon in 1941. It was planned to accommodate over seven hundred workers. After completion it housed over one thousand workers, mainly women, who were brought into Alsager from all parts of the country. Only the main administrative buildings, sick bay, and boiler houses were brick built, the remainder beings huts. The main administrative building and boiler houses had very thick walls to restrict possible bomb damage. The main administrative building also had a basement.

Heathside Administrative buildings completed in 1942. Photograph from film by J, C. Christopher 1947. (Christopher, 1947)

Former entrance to main administrative building which was built in 1941/2. Photo: author 2017

Original metal window design and radiators

Most roof design was flat roofed but there was some asbestos pitched roofing. Photo: Author 2017

Brick was sourced locally in Stoke-on-Trent. Photo: Author 2017

*Boiler House WW2.
Photo by Author 2017*

There were ten boiler houses on Heathside. If one was destroyed by bombing the others could continue independently

Boiler house detail. Coal feed into boiler and ashes tray

Photo: Author 2017

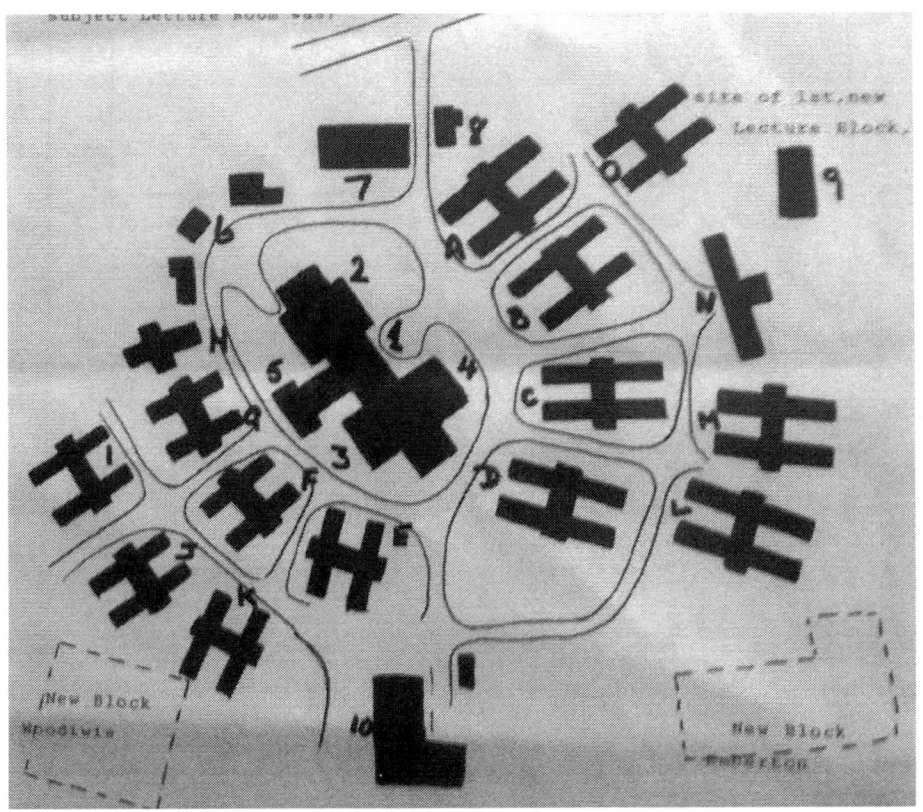

A plan for from Alsager Teacher's Training College 1947 but with the essential Heathside Hostel plan unchanged. The main administrative building was in the centre of the development (1) Here were situated the Hall used for films and shows (2) Dining Rooms (3) kitchens, shop/post office waiting room. Each of the 12 accommodation blocks were connected with brick built toilets, a laundry and store room. In 1947 when the hostel became a teacher training college the huts were named after Poets.

Heathside. The original buildings shortly after refurbishment for Alsager Teacher's Training College.. Photograph from film by J.C Christopher 1947.

The huts were of *'Laing'* design. Alsager Council was responsible for infrastructure services such as water supply and sewage disposal. The heating for the hostel consisted of ten separate boiler houses each containing two boilers. This was because the administrators were worried about a bomb hitting a large boiler and the destructive consequences of that. The boilers were coke fired with hot water piped throughout the site. There were twelve huts, the original design of which was modelled on the design in the early *Butlin's* Holiday camps. The *Laing* hut consisted of standard prefabricated lightweight timber wall sections bolted together. The walls were lined both inside and out with plasterboard and additionally the outside covered with felt. The brick-built central section of each 'H' pattern consisted of the bathrooms, store, airing room and laundry. Each girl was asked to share a room, which comprised of two single beds, two chests, and two wardrobes, and a wash hand basin with cold water supply. The main building in the centre of the site held several public rooms. These consisted of a waiting room, a sitting room, a library, and a small shop with a post office incorporated, and of course a sick bay. A week's board and lodging which included three meals a day and laundry would cost twenty-six shillings and sixpence.

Laing hut design 1940s at RAF Malbis. The Alsager huts were camouflaged in brown and green.

Heathside. Main Buildings. Photograph from film by J.C. Christopher 1947.

The hostel was built to accommodate over one thousand single women munitions workers aged between nineteen and thirty and transport was laid on to ROF Radway Green and back by bus. Meals were taken in the main building where entertainment was provided in the way of film shows and live entertainment. *Heathside* had its own Fire Brigade.

Administration and Support

Administration and support facilities at *Heathside* included its own Civil Defence team, its own fire service, and catering staff. The hostel was initially due to be patrolled by Alsager Home Guard but because of their commitments Lawton Home Guard fulfilled this function.

The hostel provided its own entertainment for its residents. At the Alsager Fete on 25th September 1942 held at *Heathside*, the Heathside Fire Service put on a fire and rescue display. There was also entertainment provided by clowns and tumblers. The event also included a sports event for children, a gymnastic display by Service personnel, and an exhibition of Hungarian Dances by the Christ Church juvenile dancers supervised by Miss Bingham.

Children from the Senior School could watch films at *Heathside* after school on a Monday afternoon provided they were accompanied by an adult. Films were usually Cowboys and Indians with Gene Autry and Roy Rogers; comedy with Arthur Askey, George Formby, Old Mother Riley; and a few war films. Detective films shown were Sherlock Holmes with Basil Rathbone. There was a later evening performance for adults. Films were preceded by newsreels complete with war propaganda.

Elderly residents allege that the ROF dumped faulty .303 cartridges, bullets, and pom pom shell parts in the marl pits near *Heathside*. Schoolboys, it is said, although it was prohibited, would scavenge to collect these shells, and try to reassemble constituent parts.

Lester Crisford (Crisford, 1992) recalls the weekly film shows on a Wednesday evening at *Heathfields*. Queuing was necessary because admittance was on a first come first serve basis and the shows were popular. The hall only held three hundred people. The shows in Alsager were preferred because of the problem of getting to Crewe or Hanley by bus. If you couldn't get on a full bus you had to wait an hour. Trains were invariably late, but they did at least turn up. Arriving outside a cinema in Crewe or Hanley meant another queue, and one still had to get home. Crisford used to cycle to Crewe to go to the cinema but because bicycle theft was common people had to lock them up in a cottage near Crewe station. Bikes were not easily replaced as they were not manufactured in the war.

Alsager Auxiliary Fire Service WW2. The AAFS gave demonstrations at village fairs. They placed high stands with moveable discs 50-100 yards from their appliances and hosed water at the discs to make them turn. Photo FHS Crewe. (FHSCheshire)

In June 1943, a performance of *The Master Builder* by Henrik Ibsen was put on at *Heathside* by *The Community Players of Stoke*. *The Sentinel* reported *'The large audience thoroughly enjoyed the performance which was in aid of the Friends' War Victims' Relief Services, an organisation that is doing excellent work in organising hostels and relief squads during and after air raids.'* Fundraising was a feature of most entertainment at *Heathside* during the war. One of the celebrities who appeared at *Heathside* was Violet Carson who later starred as Ena Sharples in Coronation Street. In 1942 Violet was a regular singer on radio programmes.

Violet Carson, singer and entertainer.

The Heathside Fire Brigade commenced a Widows and Orphan's Fund and promoted dances which were popular. One such dance was held in February 1943. *Heathside* also had its own Dance Band.

In October 1943, the focus of the fundraising effort was for the Red Cross when the Northern Express Concert Party came to *Heathside*. They were assisted by the *Rattigan School of Dancing*. The audience sat on folding wooden seats.

In March 1944 a J.B. Priestley play was performed at Heathside which can be seen in the Alsager Times Review

Priestley play: A performance of "Eden End," a three-act play by J. B. Priestley, was given to a large audience at Heathside last night, by the Community players. The cast included Geoffrey Wilde, Winifred Metcalfe, Eunice Mellor, M. Shufflebotham, Arthur Robinson, Cecil Scrimgeour and Reginald Banks. The play was produced by Ernest Kershaw. Proceeds are for the Friends Relief Service, an organisation which relieves wartime suffering in this country.

'False Pretences.'

Staff lodging in Alsager's hostels were eligible for lodging allowances in some circumstances. In July 1943 Leslie Sutch, of *Heathside Hostel*, was summoned to Sandbach Sessions for falsely claiming lodging allowances of £1.4s. 6d. from the Ministry of Labour. He pleaded not guilty. The prosecutor said Sutch had moved from Worcester to Alsager and made a claim on the understanding he had a wife and children and he was maintaining them. However, Sutch was separated from his wife and had agreed to pay them £2.15s a week but he was £27-£30 in arrears of the payments. Kidsgrove Labour exchange had discovered the discrepancy and brought forward a prosecution.

Heathside had its own religious organisations including a Young Women's Christian Association branch. On 15th September 1943 they held a garden party and fete to raise money for overseas based YMCA canteen and comforts facilities for service personnel. The Queen had agreed to hold a reception for the scheme. Four nominees were put forward for one woman to be chosen to be present at the Royal occasion. Going forward for the final ballot were Nurse Barningham, Miss Margaret Bearsden, Miss Madge Cockayne, and Miss Freda Mitchell. It was estimated the final proceeds would be significantly higher than the original target of £250.

The Roman Catholic church held masses at the hostel as there was no local Catholic church in Alsager.

The Alsager Times reported a large and unusual event in August 1944 at *Heathside*. It was called *'Pro Patria'*, and took the form of a cavalcade *'of the first five years of the war'* described in story, poetry, and music to represent the Allied countries, the Services, and war workers in procession. Mr E.H.W. Goff, Civil Defence Officer at *Heathside*, did the writing, production and directing of the event. Music was provided by the *Pims in the Prize* band conducted by Mr T. Marginson. Poems were recited by Mrs Marsden, and the Glee Club Singers were led on piano by Miss Dunnamore. The vocalist was Mr Mindy. One tableau depicted a wounded Tommy with a Red Cross Nurse attending to him. In the same tableau was a hospital bed with bandage dressings. *Heathside's* target for its contribution to *'Salute the Soldier Week'*, was £2,300 for the provision of clothing and surgical facilities for a field hospital. In fact, their target was surpassed and £3,000 was raised. Many of the acts put on at *Heathside* were organised by ENSA (Entertainments National Service Association) who would tour different hostel establishments for munition workers.

The following report in the *Scottish Daily Record* in July 1945 indicated the Scottish Possil School and Woodside children's' groups visited Crewe, Alsager and ROF Swynnerton. It is interesting to note the Warden of *Heathside* was a woman, Mrs Wyatt.

The hostel provided a comprehensive service to residents including a sick bay.

Sick bay building from WW2. Photo by Author 2017

Original Heathside building. Demolished 2017. Photo: author 2017

Transition to Teachers' Training College

Sign erected outside redundant hostel 1946

With the end of the war in 1945 *Heathside* Hostel became redundant. The workforce at ROF Radway Green significantly reduced and the hostel was closed. The original owners of the farm, the Bennion family were not offered the site back. Instead Cheshire County Council held discussions with the Ministry of Education for the site to become an emergency Teachers' Training College to be managed by Cheshire County Council. Work commenced to transform the buildings in September 1946. The man who was responsible for opening of the college was Jim Collorick. The first Principal was Mr S.W. Woodiwiss.

Jim Collorick (Collorick, 2017) Royal Navy. Born 1922

Jim Collorick 1942 First Administrator and later Bursar of Alsager College

Jim Collorick was born in Chester on 3rd March 1922. He attended the Central School Chester and left school aged 14. He entered employment as a clerk in a Solicitor's office and in 1936 was earning 7s 6d a week. On 3rd September 1939 he was camping with friends and on hearing about the declaration of war on Germany struck camp and cycled to Chester to enlist. Because he was under age he was forced to join the Home Guard until March 1940 when he was 18. After basic training as a radio operator he served on *HMS Hesperus*, an 'H' class destroyer built in 1939 originally for the Brazilian navy but commandeered by the Royal Navy when war was declared. In late 1941, she was assigned to guard North Atlantic convoys; a role she undertook for three years. In 1942 the U-boats were hunting in packs and were a serious threat to the convoys. On 26th December 1942 *Hesperus* rammed a U-boat, sinking her, but this did considerable damage to the ship and she was forced to undertake repairs in dry dock and subsequently in 1943 she was converted to an escort destroyer. *Hesperus* sank two other U-boats in the war with depth charges.

Jim Collorick's role as radio operator was to communicate via Morse code to other ships. Jim also took down intercepted messages in code from enemy U-boats. He would then pass the code to a Code Breaker sitting next to him to decipher, but it was not until Alan Turing at *Bletchley Park* broke the German code system that the convoys knew when they were being followed.

With *Hesperus* in dry dock for repairs Jim married Joyce Martin in Chester on 9th January 1943. He was not to gain leave for another three years. He was transferred to Inverary, Scotland, and joined Combined Forces, a mixture of army and navy organisation. They were tasked to train for the invasion of Europe in 1943, which was postponed owing to the request of the Soviet Union, and instead the force took part in the invasion of Sicily on 11th July 1943. Jim's troops were tasked to establish the landing area for the 1st Canadian Regiment. They travelled in landing craft from the *Circassia*, a peace time liner converted into a troop ship. After securing the beachhead Jim's regiment was withdrawn after eight days to Malta. He then re-joined the navy on *HMS Wolborough*, escorting convoys between Alexandra, Egypt via the Suez Canal to Gibraltar, the ships carrying cargo.

Jim Collorick married Joyce Martin on 9th January 1943.

Jim was transferred off convoy duty to re-join Combined Operations to take part in the liberation of Greece in October 1944. After the successful landing, Jim was based in the port of Piraeus, a dangerous posting as a civil war was underway between the Royalist Greek government, EAM, the left wing National Liberation Front, and ELAS, the Greek People's Liberation Army, who were communists.

In March 1945 Jim was transferred back to convoy work but then with the end of the war in Europe was ordered to prepare for service with the Pacific Fleet. His orders were cancelled with the end of the war with Japan in August 1945. Jim returned to Britain being based in Devonport until he was demobbed on the 25th February 1946.

Jim Collorick photographed in 2013 with a framed painting of HMS Hesperus.

Jim Collorick became the first Administrator and later Bursar of Alsager College. In a 2017 interview with the author Jim explained what the site was like in 1946 when he saw it for the first time. *'In February 1946 on being demobbed I returned to my old job as a solicitor's clerk. Feeling undervalued I applied for a job advertised in the Cheshire Observer with Cheshire County Council. The salary was £7 a week and the job was Administrative Assistant for a Temporary Project, the setting up of an Emergency Teachers' Training Scheme, a proposed college for teachers in Alsager on the old Heathside munitions workers' hostel site. I was successful in getting the job. When I first saw the accommodation, it was derelict, and the buildings were covered in camouflage paint. My job was to act as the coordinator between the Cheshire County Council and the Ministry of Works and Ministry of Supply to renovate the buildings so they could be transferred to Cheshire's ownership by 1st January 1947.* 'On 1st September 1946, I was given a blue folder. In it contained a letter from Colonel Joseph from the Ministry of Education in London saying in five years' time no new teachers would be available. The Ministry went around all Army Camps and sites and Alsager Heathside had been selected for an Emergency Teachers' Training College. On 1st January 1947 three hundred male students were the first intake into the new college. Among them were ex-Squadron Leaders and former British prisoners of war. The ex-servicemen preferred the huts to live in, they felt at home in them and did not want to move to more modern accommodation.'

After thirteen months of commuting by train to Alsager from Chester Jim moved to Alsager and took up residence in one of the former munitions workers' huts. Jim commenced his career in Alsager, a career which would continue for the rest of his working life. The hostel buildings were converted into college accommodation. He was to remain in employment with Alsager College from 1947 until his retirement.

He has had a long association with Alsager and is a member of Alsager British Legion.

The Royal Naval Training Establishment, and The *Brunds* Hostel

(Excalibur) 1942-1947

Original 'blister hut' at the Brunds-a Royal Marines clothing storeroom

Background

The Government requisitioned part of *Brunds Farm* adjacent to Fields Road, Alsager, in 1942 as land for a hostel for ROF Radway Green. To build the hostel access to the site was made via Barker's sand quarry. The hostel was built with *'Laing'* hut construction as at *Heathside*. The hostel opened in May 1942, the work by Hall and Robinson Ltd having commenced in December 1940. The amount of hostel accommodation needed for men and women at Radway Green had been difficult to estimate and the accommodation was found to be superfluous. The internal design, including the washroom layout, was also changed several times.

Entrance to the Brunds

The Royal Marines

The amount of hostel accommodation required for Radway Green had been overestimated and in 1943 The *Brunds* was transferred to the Admiralty for accommodation for the Royal Navy as a dry land training base for the Royal Marines. It was a land-based establishment but with a facility on Alsager Mere for six cutters which were used for rowing. The first command was held by Captain H. Hammond-Chambers D.S.O. The base was managed as if it were a sailing ship, so if recruits did not return to the Guard Gate House at the designated time they had *'missed the boat'*, and had to wait for the next one. Locals always called the base the *'Ship'*, though it was officially called *Excalibur* after Arthurian legend, a name conjured up by base officers. Sailors such as Leslie Neal from London trained at there. He later took part in the D Day landings.

Leslie Arthur Neal, Photo: War Time Memories BBC (Project)

Access to the Mere for rowing was gained via the *Pinewood* private school or Mrs Holland's garden in Sandbach Road. *Excalibur* became the responsibility of the Fleet Air Arm to train 17-year-old marines for a six week period before further training in other establishments. Mrs Susan Walley *nee* Hammersley of The Avenue, Alsager, remembers the Marines marching down Sandbach Road towards the Mere singing their songs. The landing stage for the cutters was a large affair, the remnant posts of which could still be seen in the 1960s. Susan Walley's father Leslie Hammersley used to invite marines to his house. They would babysit for him whilst he attended dances and social occasions at the *'ship'* HMS *Excalibur*. Social occasions with the marines at the house in the Avenue would involve Leslie Hammersley inviting the Marines to pull a large roller of the cricket variety through his house to the rear garden, perhaps for competitions or feats of endurance. Leslie Hammersley, as a member of the Alsager British Legion, held a close link with the Marines from *Excalibur*. Leslie Hammersley was an ARP Warden and would cycle to different locations in Alsager and beyond where he was on duty. His responsibilities included fire watching where he would be on the lookout for fires started by enemy incendiary bombs. He often cycled as far as the *Salamanca Inn* near Smallwood, an ARP meeting point.

In May 1942 Arthur Hampton and his band played to a packed audience who were raising money for the Radway Green *'Spitfire Fund'*. The camp often put on concerts, film shows, and entertainment to which the local residents were invited.

It was no holiday camp and there were occasions when personnel went absent without leave. In April 1946 the Staffordshire Advertiser reported Marine W.R. Buckley had been discovered hiding in a cellar at 41 Waterloo Road Burslem, the home of Mrs Elsie Broster. He had been absent from camp without permission for five weeks. Mrs Broster was sent to prison for three months despite pleading she had a fifteen-year-old son to look after. The Marine was court marshalled.

In 1946 *Excalibur* became a New Entry Training Establishment (1944) for training *'regular'* peace-time adult sailors. The regulations for new recruits were spelled out in a guide book. The Rating Pilots were regular servicemen as opposed to those called up for National Service.

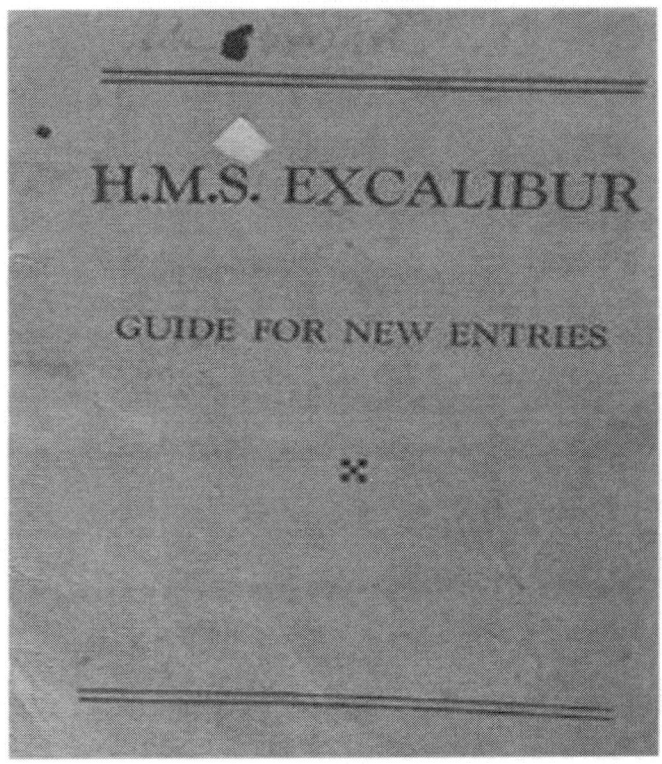

Excalibur was a training unit for most Royal Navy trades including the *'non-seaman'* branches such as cooks, stewards, telegraphists, and air mechanics. They were formed into classes according to the trade they specialised in. They were trained in seamanship, rifle drill, marching, PT and divisional organisation. They had regular kit inspections and were required to keep a journal of their stay on vacation.

In 1946 Captain Cuthbert was awarded the CBE at the same time as his wife, Betty Cuthbert, who was given the honour for her work as chief woman fire officer with The National Fire Service. In Alsager Captain Cuthbert was responsible for seven hundred recruits between the ages of seventeen and twenty-three who underwent training in seamanship, swimming, and physical training. John Cuthbert had previously served on *H.M.S Ajax* in the Mediterranean and Greek campaigns.

The Cuthberts were resident in Alsager in 1946 when they were presented with their awards at Buckingham Palace by the King.

Excalibur, 1946, *with a view of accommodation in the rear ground.*

E.D. Rutherford M.B., B.Ch.

The son of Dr Robert A. Rutherford J.P., who practised at Manorhamilton, Co. Leitrim, for over fifty years, Ernest Davis Rutherford was born on 16th August 1877, and was educated at Portora Royal School, Enniskillen. He studied medicine at the former Queen's College, Belfast, and graduated M.B., B.Ch. in the Royal University of Ireland in 1902. He served in the Great War as a Lieutenant Surgeon in the Royal Navy. Though elderly he was recalled to serve again on the outbreak of the Second World War. In 1943 and 1944 he was the doctor at *Excalibur*.

The establishment had its own dance band or blues orchestra which toured other towns and cities as can be seen in this advertisement from the *Hull Daily Mail*

Ship's Bell H.M.S Excalibur which is now situated at Fort St George, Scotland.

The last commander of *HMS Excalibur* was Captain R.H Wright D.S.C who took over from Captain Cuthbert in April 1947. He served with distinction in command of destroyers. Captain Cuthbert left Alsager to take up a post in the Royal Naval College, Greenwich, in London. Sir Francis and Lady Joseph organised a private luncheon at the *North Stafford Hotel* for Captain Wright on taking up his position.

Chief Petty Officer George William Anderson 18th February 1902 – 31st August 1946 Photo: Family archive. (Archive)

A death recorded in association with *H.M.S Excalibur* took place in 1946. William Anderson was born in Shadwell, London. As a boy sailor he trained in February 1918 on *HMS Impregnable* and in 1919 on *HMS Dauntless*. In 1926 serving as a Chief Petty Officer, he was slightly wounded with a bullet in action against Chinese troops on *HMS Mantis*. In 1928 he married Rosina May Smith in London. In 1946 he was recalled to service and was working as a Chief Petty Officer at *HMS Excalibur*. He was found hanging at the base on 31st August 1946 and an inquest concluded death was due to asphyxia due to strangulation (suicide) but no further action due to lack of evidence. A sad footnote to the history of *H.M.S Excalibur*.

Excalibur Displaced Person's Camp

In 1948 *HMS Excalibur* was decommissioned as a naval base and it became a displaced person's hostel for war refugees from Latvia, Lithuania, Estonia and the Ukraine who were fleeing from the Soviet

Union. The British Red Cross facilitated the immigration of the refugees to Britain. Many men from these countries had fought on the side of the Germans in order to try and regain independence, and they were afraid to return to their countries of origin, as many who had returned were executed by the Russians. A school was set up for the education of their children whose only common language when they arrived was German. The school continued to exist for many years in the same set of wooden huts under the name *'Excalibur School'*. Lessons were conducted in English by Mr Fielding and Mrs Hughes who both could speak German. Meals were taken in the former Marines Canteen and the laundry and clinic was based in a separate building. The first Roman Catholic Church in Alsager was one of the wooden huts and was attended mainly by the Lithuanians, most of whom were Roman Catholic. The camp, which accommodated up to three hundred persons, was occupied only by women and children. Residents lived in twenty-four rooms in one long building. Each family had their own room. Men could only visit at weekends.

The refugees included Richard and Endla Tulp. In their obituaries in 2010 in the *Guardian*, their daughter, Hele Lakin described the extraordinary story. (Lakin)

> *'My father, Richard Tulp, who has died aged 92, and my mother, Endla, who has died aged 90, were two of the many people whose lives were turned upside down by the Second World War. Born and brought up in Estonia, they left their country in August 1944 with the German forces, after the invasion of Estonia by the Soviet Union. They eventually settled in Britain, and were unable to visit their homeland again until Estonia declared independence nearly 50 years later. Richard was born while his father Johann was away fighting in the First World War. Johann never returned, and Richard was brought up by his mother Lisabet and grandparents on a farm. After military service, he worked as a bookkeeper for the Estonian Cooperative Society. From 1940 Estonia was occupied by the Soviet Union. When the country was invaded by Germany the following year, Richard's employers were still under the authority of the Russians, and all Estonian men were being conscripted into the Red Army. Richard fled to Riga, in Latvia, and found work with the German air force, maintaining aircraft. In 1945 he was posted to Wuppertal on the Rhine. Following the Allied invasion of Germany, he went with a group of compatriots to France looking for work.*

They were employed by American forces to take care of German prisoners, and for a time were well paid and well fed. But when all of Richard's money was stolen, the group was imprisoned. One of the party spoke some French and managed to secure their release. Then they tried to join the French Foreign Legion, but were rejected. For the next year, Richard travelled around France and the Rhineland looking for work. Eventually, he returned to Wuppertal and there he met and married Endla.

Daughter of Vassil and Emilie Kallivere, Endla was born into a middle-class family in Tartu, Estonia's second city, and educated at the local grammar school. She subsequently enrolled at Tartu University to study economics. At the start of her third year, the Soviets invaded, and she moved to the capital Tallinn, enrolling at the technical school there. She supported herself by undertaking secretarial work as well as completing her studies and learning Russian. I was born in 1946, and two years later Richard travelled to England to look for work; Endla and I followed him some 18 months later. We were sent to a camp in Hull, Yorkshire, while Richard was doing farm work in Northamptonshire, and it was difficult for my parents to meet. But eventually they were able to settle together in Alsager, Cheshire, at first in a displaced persons camp called Excalibur. Richard found work in the potteries and the family grew with the birth of my brother Toivo and, later, twins Rick and Tom.

Despite being a multilingual economist, my mother, a self-taught seamstress, made her living creating clothes for local people. Richard worked at the Enoch Wedgwood pottery until, in 1976, he was knocked off his scooter and severely injured. After hip replacements, despite his physical strength he was unable to walk without a stick. Richard continued an active life despite almost constant pain. Endla carried on with her sewing. Our family was sustained by their strength of character.

Endla Tulp, left at Excalibur Displace Persons Hostel 1948 photo: South Cheshire FHS

The Acquisition of *Milton House* in Alsager for the War Effort

Photograph of Milton House: Author

In the Second World War, *Milton House*, a large Victorian property built in 1866, was to be an important source of accommodation for staff from Radway Green. The census (1939Reg) gives insight into the interesting people living in *Milton House* before the war and the part they played in the conflict is worth noting.

In 1939 Ernestine Wheaton-Smith (1888-1976), her husband, Franklin Wheaton-Smith, (1880-1946), and their daughter, Barbara, were living in *Milton House* as can be seen in the 1939 Register entry. Ernestine's cousin, Charles W.T Craig and his wife, Anne Marie were lodging with them. There were also three servants, Frank and Miriam Coxley and Joyce Spence. It shows Ernestine working with the WVS as the war began and her daughter working as an ambulance attendant.

Shortly after this survey in September 1939 the Wheaton-Smith and Craig families left *Milton House* and it was requisitioned by the Ministry of Fuel and Supply and turned into a hostel, the Wheaton-Smith family moving away from Alsager to *The Manor*, Pilton, Somerset. One of the reasons why the family may have abandoned *Milton House* were the large death duties paid in 1939 for Ernestine Wheaton-Smith's mother. The Liverpool Evening Express reported on March 13th:

1939 Estate duty of £72,658 has been paid. Dame Anna Eliza Craig, of Milton House, Alsager. Cheshire, daughter of the late James McKay, of Pittsburg, U.S.A., and widow of Sir Ernest Craig, Bart., for many years M.P. for Crewe, gross: £18,761, net £13.

Anna Ernestine Craig 1888-1976

Anna Ernestine Craig was born in Denver Colorado in 1888 when her father, Ernest, was working in gold mining. By 1891 she was living in Alsager. In 1912 she took the journey back to the North America where she married Franklin Wheaton-Smith in Canada. He was, like his father-in-law, an adventurer and mining explorer.

Despite spending most of their time in the States the Wheaton-Smiths did come to *Milton House* to take up residence in the 1930s.

Franklin Wheaton-Smith in New Mexico and his passport picture

Charles Craig

Who was the Charles Thurlow Craig in *Milton House* in the 1939 Register?

Charles Thurlow Craig was born on 14th September 1901 in Gresford, Wrexham, the son of the Colliery Director from Denbighshire, Donald Craig, brother of Sir Ernest Craig. In 1939 Charles W.T Craig was lodging along with his French wife, Anne Marie, with his cousin in *Milton House*. Thurlow, as he later was known, had served as a Midshipman entering Osbourne Naval College in 1917, and he later saw action on *HMS Temeaiere* in the Arctic Ocean. After the Great War, wanting adventure, he travelled in 1922 to Buenos Aires, Argentina, with the intention of becoming a gaucho, a South American cowboy. He lived in Argentina, Paraguay, and Brazil, as a farmer and gaucho, and became an accomplished horse rider. In 1932 he became involved in the Constitutionalists Revolution in Brazil which inspired him to write his novel, *A Rebel for a Horse* in 1934.

Returning from South America Thurlow became briefly involved in the Spanish Civil War before meeting his future wife Anne Marie, 'Mitzi,' and returning to England to lodge at *Milton House*. He was actively writing novels while in Alsager, producing *The Changed Face*, and *Plague over London* (Hutchinson & Co 1939.) According to the 1939 Register, Thurlow's French wife, '*was seeking work*', in 1939. The commencement of hostilities in September 1939 changed everything.

With Thurlow's expertise in languages and his naval experience he was recruited by Naval Intelligence for the war effort and served incognito in Belgium assisting the resistance. His wife, Anne Marie, worked as an undercover agent of the Bureau des Menées Antinationales on behalf of the Free French and received the Croix de Guerre for her heroism.

After the War, C. W. Thurlow Craig and his wife lived at *Can Blaenau*, Rhyd-Cymerau, Llandeilo, Carmarthenshire, Wales, where Craig continued to write, most notably the Sunday Express column '*Up Country*', and books on fishing and shooting.

Craig Wheaton-Smith

When Franklin and Ernestine Wheaton-Smith were living in *Milton House* in 1939 their son Craig, born in 1917, was living with them. He was born in Pittsburgh, USA, his grandmother's home city. In the 1920s he lived in Santa Barbara, California. He returned to Britain to live with his mother in *Milton House* in the 1930s and amongst his friends was Roy Palfreyman from Station Road. (A D Day veteran who is still alive and remembers Craig- 2017). In 1938 Craig Wheaton-Smith returned to the United States but returned in 1939 before the outbreak of war.

In July 1943 he married Princess Tatiana, daughter of Serge Vincent de Bolotoff, Prince Wiasemsky and Rosalie de Bolotoff (Selfridge). She was the granddaughter of the founder of *Selfridges*, Harry Gordon Selfridge

Harry Gordon Selfridge

Princess Tatiana Rosemary de Bolotoff Wiasemsky was a well-known society debutante and the marriage gained a great deal of press coverage. They married in the chapel of the *Savoy Hotel* on 19th June 1943.

In December 1943 Craig Wheaton Smith resigned his commission in the British Army to take a commission in the United States Army as recorded in The London Gazette of 24th December 1943.

Craig Wheaton-Smith served in France with the United States Army. In 1945, and now promoted to Major, he was responsible for the security of a secret Nazi dynamite factory which had been discovered in the forests. Tatiana and Craig were divorced after the war. He continued to live in Somerset, where he farmed, and in the USA. He died in Vermont in 2002.

Craig Wheaton Smith

In late 1939 the ROF Contractors Trollope and Colls did the partitioning work to create bed-sitting rooms at *Milton House* also completing an annexe to it. *Milton House* was converted for the Ministry of Fuel and Supply and brick buildings built in the gardens for Royal Ordnance Factory workers.

Milton House during the war

Ted White born 1924: Merchant Navy - resident of Milton House in the war

Ted White (who lodged in the hostel from 1944. Photographed 2016) Ted's room was located above the portico (pictured below)

Ted White had lived in Alsager since he was left the navy in 1944 on medical grounds. He was born on 15th March 1924 in Glasgow, the son of a Turf Accountant. His brother William was born in 1917. He attended Morrison's Academy, Crieff, Perthshire, Scotland, as a boarder, staying at the home of one of the masters.

In 1939 he moved to Brighton to be with his mother and attended Brighton & Hove Grammar School.

'I made a mistake of wearing a kilt on my first day at the school for which I was ridiculed by other boys. The teacher said, "Hadrian's Wall was constructed to keep rabble out".

'When I struck out at a boy who was teasing me I got worse back, and I went on to be flogged by the Head to make it worse.'

He was still at school when in 1940 he joined the Merchant Navy. His first post was in the *Alderamin*, in 1941, a Dutch vessel taking cargo

between Hull and the west coast of Africa for the war effort. It was 7, 886 tons and had been built in 1920 and principally carried 10,000 tons of oil seeds, rubber and general cargo.

It was part of a convoy which included two destroyers. They unloaded and loaded at Lagos and similar ports. Occasionally there was time for relaxation on shore swimming in the sea. Ted once witnessed a man being attacked by a shark. Years later he was surprised to hear that Dr George Bates from Alsager, who was in the RAF at the time, was playing golf nearby and was called to assist the shark victim.

S.S Alderamin: photograph-Wikipedia

In 1942 Ted White contracted malaria on board the *Alderamin* and was brought ashore for treatment in West Africa. He never re-joined the *Alderamin*. Another crew member Edward Ford writes of an incident while the ship was in Free Town in 1942:

'Loaded with supplies for the army we set off in convoy bound for west Africa, three days out we left the convoy and made our way to Free Town where we unloaded. This took some time as all the unloading was into barges and done with our own derricks but in the end the job was done, and we set off down the coast to Lagos where we were to load peanuts. This port and loading had to be seen to be believed, there was a long wharf on the mouth of the river, with the Naval anchorage about ½ a mile inland then further upstream was a ship repair yard and above that was an oil terminal. The method of loading must have dated back to the days of sailing ships when only a few hundred tons were loaded at a time. Two gangways were placed to the fore deck and two aft, then there was a continuous stream of men with a sack of nuts on their backs running up one gangway tipping the contents down the hold and taking the empty sack down the other. The process was continuous, I think they were paid by the number of sacks they did in a day as they were running all the time.

Disaster came one day in the form of a fire, we had been smelling oil all morning, it seems that there was a leak from the oil terminal. How the fire started I don't know but from the repair yard down to the Naval anchorage the river was one mass of flame. All the men loading us disappeared the moment the fire started, one moment our deck was crowded and the next empty. There were three minesweepers in the anchorage that were engulfed in the fire when the depth charges exploded and put out the fire and the three ships, the anchorage was empty. We were able to get two survivors from the sweepers, they had jumped overboard before the fire had reached them, only to be put on a charge for abandoning ship before being ordered. We completed our loading around 8,000 tons of peanuts all loose in the holds, and went to the coal wharf to top up our bunkers. Just before Christmas we set sail for home with orders to go to Port of Spain in Trinidad to join a convoy to New York before joining a convoy across the Atlantic and home.'

A year later in March 1943 the ship was torpedoed by U-boat U-338 and sixty four crew were killed.

Ted White, lucky not to have remained on the *Alderamin*, was returned to Britain where he recovered. He was transferred to the Royal Navy as a merchant seaman under regulation T424X in 1943. (The Royal Navy needed experienced crew from the merchant navy. He was now on Royal Navy pay but remained a merchant seaman.) His next assignment was to be transferred to the USA and was based at *HMS Astbury Park*, a shore based establishment. He then took a train across the USA for three days to join his next posting on *HMS Khedive*, an escort carrier. It was built by the Seattle-Tacoma Shipbuilding Co. of Tacoma, Washington and originally called the *USS Cordova* before being transferred to the British.

The carrier had had a complement of six hundred and forty-six men and an overall length of 492 feet 3 inches (150.0 m). Ted worked as a steward on board the ship commissioned from 23rd August 1943.

HMS Khedhive 1943.

The maiden voyage as a British vessel was down the Pacific Coast to Panama, through the canal and across to Rosyth Scotland. It was carrying twelve Avenger and ten Corsair aircraft for passage to UK. After the voyage Ted transferred from the ship to join the *Compania*. She was built at *Harland & Wolff* shipyards in Belfast, Northern Ireland. When construction started in 1941 she was intended as a refrigerated cargo ship for transporting lamb and mutton from New Zealand, but was requisitioned by the British Government during construction and completed and launched as an escort carrier, entering service in early 1944. *Campania* operated escorting convoys and doing anti-submarine work in the Atlantic and Arctic theatres of war. In 1944 Ted White became ill and this was diagnosed as tuberculosis. He was discharged from the navy in Southport and went down to Hastings to be near his mother in a sanatorium. He recovered. T.B was usually a death sentence, but Ted overcame the illness.

His brother Bill visited him in late 1944. Bill had been discharged on medical grounds from the RAF and had married a girl from Kidsgrove Staffordshire and was working at Rolls Royce, Chesterton. Bill sent him a train ticket, so Ted came to visit him and decided to stay, early in 1945.

He took digs in Butt Lane but soon moved to Alsager. (He did not like the outside lavatory and the pig in the outbuilding in Butt Lane.) He obtained a job in Chesterton at the Rolls Royce works where his brother worked.

He obtained digs at *Heathside Hostel*, Alsager in June 1945. One of the buildings was designated for men with 12 single rooms. The remainder were for women munitions workers. It was a block with 12 single rooms. He was there for two months.

He took part in a play at *Heathside* theatre called *'Ghost Train'*. It ran for three or four nights. He played the male role in a courting couple. Playing opposite him was Hilda Garrett. Shortly afterwards Hilda travelled to Bristol and committed suicide from the Clifton Suspension Bridge. Ted was most shocked and upset and did not know why Miss Garrett should have taken her own life.

Ted recalls the main building of the hostel had a café and the entertainments manager was Ivor Newcombe. After two months at *Heathside* Ted obtained a room in *Milton House*, which had been requisitioned by the Ministry of Fuel and Power as a hostel. He was allocated a nice room by the front entrance. Here he enjoyed use of the tennis courts and on-site catering by Mrs Bayliss. There was even a guest building for visitors to stay.

When Rolls Royce at Chesterton closed and moved to Derby, Ted obtained at job at the Ministry of Fuel and Power depot at Bignall End and walked to work from Alsager across the fields. Sometimes he rode a bike and occasionally he had a lift back from work in a lorry. Ted would grade the coal and organise it to be shipped out from the railway sidings.

Ted says that Alsager was a very busy place especially with all the transport coming down Crewe Road to Radway Green. He says Sir Francis Joseph did not make himself popular because he tried to get the chip shop closed at the entrance of Hall Dive. In 1945 Ted met Eileen Newstead, who was originally from London. She was the wages clerk at ROF Radway Green and every week took a taxi to the bank in Alsager to bring back the munitions workers' wages. When Eileen and Ted married in July 1946 Eileen had to give up her job, as married women could not hold employment in the Civil Service.

Ted White marrying Eileen Newstead July 1946 St Mary's Church Alsager.

They obtained two rooms with friends in Woodside Avenue Alsager, but when the tenants moved to Blackpool Ted and Eileen were evicted by the council despite offering full rent. Luckily, they were allocated a house in The Butts, Alsager on the same day as their son was born. Ted went on to have a successful photography business in Alsager.

Milton House after World War Two

After the war Milton House remained a hostel for Radway Green and many of its features remained unchanged from the war years.

Sgt Bob Parish (Royal Signals) before his career at ROF Radway Green.

Robert, who was ROF Radway Green's first apprentice, had been demobbed from the army in the Middle East, and with the aim of becoming a professional mechanical engineer, applied to Radway Green and was successful. In 2017, Robert Parish, who lived in *Milton House* in 1948 described the accommodation. *'It was an imposing building, in very good condition, and it provided sumptuous conditions for its residents. There were two long narrow brick buildings in the grounds where the football pitch [Milton Park] is now. The bedrooms in those buildings were about the smallest rooms I have ever seen but they did accommodate a narrow bed, a combined chest of drawers and a wardrobe. The problem was one of where to stand to get dressed - the floor space was about a foot wide. I remember that the area between the brick buildings and the lovely pillared entrance to the house itself consisted of immaculate lawns and rose beds. One of the strictest rules of the house was that no one walked across the grass; so we had to use the paths around the edges. The main house had two lovely lounges and a morning room in addition to the dining room. The bedrooms here were spacious but not fitted with any washing facilities. These were in a central area known as the ablutions. I do not remember any leisure facilities. There was a resident Matron (she lived in a flat at the top of the house), cleaners and cooks of course, and a lovely old gardener who grew vegetables for the kitchens on the area of land somewhere about where the play area and fire station are now (2017). I remember here were some greenhouses, but these may have belonged to the old Urban District Council. The Matron was a very nice lady who looked after me somewhat, giving me advice on how to get on with senior staff, some of which had lived there years and did not take too kindly to a young apprentice living with them.'*

Robert remembered his board and lodging cost 10 shillings a week and in addition he gave Matron his ration book (which could have presented problems when he went home to Birmingham at weekends though his mother never complained.) After some months the senior staff left *Milton House* to be replaced by new post-graduate workers at Radway. The management of *Milton House* was transferred to the YMCA, the Matron left and was replaced by a manager who lived in. Robert now gained a bedroom in the main house, *'a nice room too, looking out onto the rear lawns'*. The doors were closed at 10pm which presented difficulties when Robert wanted to play darts in the *Mere Inn*.

Sergeant Bob Parish, Royal Signal Regiment.

In 1948/9 there was a stagnant, derelict, fish pool at *Milton House*. Today this is called the *'Sunken Garden'*. A few of the residents of *Milton House* decided to dig it out by hand with the intention of creating a swimming pool. Mr Flatman, the Superintendent of Radway Green, took a lot of interest in his apprentices and provided an electrician and some pumps off old Grindley Ltd presses and had them installed in the well house, situated at the Crewe Road end of the grounds. Water was pumped from the well house to the hole which was filled for swimming. As water seeped out of the mud walls, the pool became dirty. The residents did use it for a while but soon gave it up.

The wooden building situated at the Bank Corner end of *Milton House* adjacent to a gate in the wall was the original *13 Club* provided for staff of Radway and was out of bounds to apprentices. It remained well after *Milton House* was closed in the early 1960s. The *13 Club* was initially relocated to the Radway estate before moving to its present location in Cedar Avenue

Residents of Milton House in WW2 were predominantly managers from ROF Radway Green.

There were women residents in Milton House. Evidence of this comes from the Crewe Chronicle. On 2nd July 1944, the Crewe Chronicle reported a female tenant living at Milton House, Josephine Clarke, was fined by the court for travelling on the railway with an outdated ticket. It is possible Ms Clarke was a resident member of staff.

Conclusion: The Post War Years

Alsager had to adapt to the post-war environment. Following demands for amenities the council acquired two points of accesses to the Mere for the public. Swimming by the public was not prohibited. *Northolme Gardens* was named after the house on Crewe Road opposite. It was created at a cost of £350. *Photo: Northolme Gradens 1946 from the Alsagr Times*

A member of the public writing to the *Alsager Times*, wanted the gardens to be the site of a new war memorial and a statue of Hermes and for *'unaccompanied children to be barred from the gardens'*. He was subject to sarcastic replies in the paper.

Problems occurred however when young people began to bathe naked in the mere. A council worker was employed to deter the practice.

"Modesty Adviser."

Because lake-side residents have complained that bathers at Alsager, Cheshire, are stripping for a swim in view of their houses, the council have appointed a demobbed ex-Serviceman as "modesty adviser."

Ex-corporal Fred Beech, 32, has got the job, and his duties, say the council, will be to:

"Be a diplomat, preserve the balance and see that bathers' conduct does not give offence."

There is no question of the council stopping bathing; they simply wish to avoid annoyance to the householders.

In March 1946 Alsager British Legion held their annual dinner. The photograph demonstrates how large the Alsager branch had become after the war. Ranks of men and women from the Second World War joined veterans from the Great War in St Mary's Schoolroom. Legion membership stood at two hundred and sixty-seven in 1946 of which one hundred and six were recent members. The Legion was still an organisation for ex-servicemen and women and this did not include

former members of the Home Guard, a rule which highly unpopular with former members of that organisation. (This exclusion would not have included members of the Home Guard who had fought in the Great War or had been regular members of the armed services.)

The question of a new war memorial in Alsager was the subject of consultation in the town. A large committee was formed to discuss the possibilities. Very few Alsager people responded to the consultation, the conclusion being the public did not see the need to replace the beautiful statue, their current cenotaph. Only £147. 10s 6d was collected from the public towards a new war memorial from eighty contributors. The bank balance for the fund eventually stood at £478 which included a £250 contribution from Alsager British Legion. The committee decided that some of the money should be used for a welcome home party for the troops. By January 1947 the names of the men killed in the Second World War were inscribed on a plaque and added to the Alsager War Memorial. Councillors had misread the public. The sum collected was called *'disgustedly low'*, by one councillor but the public thought the replacement of the existing war memorial was unnecessary.

The official welcome home celebrations for ex-servicemen and women did not take place in Alsager until 28th February 1947. Two hundred and twenty personnel attended the event which was held in the Assembly Rooms at *HMS Excalibur*. The commanding officer, Captain J.W Cuthbert, CBE RN officiated. The band of *HMS Excalibur* played at the event. Councillor Timmis said, *'We looked forward to the time you would be back among us, and now you are home again we are proud of you.'* Mr H.C. Mellor, on behalf of the service personnel, paid tribute to the people who had carried on so courageously under war conditions. Present were some of the men who received gallantry awards in the war: Sergeant Robert Fisher, and Bombardier Norman Frost. (Frost, service number 1636552, received the Belgium Croix de Guerre, 2nd Class with palm. Frost fought with the 118 Heavy Anti-Aircraft Regiment, Royal Artillery. He was awarded the medal on 8th December 1945. He was born in January 1915 in Alsager and died in 1989. He worked as a gardener and lived in Cross Street. He married Phyllis Dutton in 1936.)

The profound changes to Alsager during the Second World War were regretted by some but accepted by others. Some, like Leslie and Mary Hammersley missed the peace and quiet of pre-war Alsager. Others thought the changes brought to Alsager worth it.

Councillor Dorothy Harpur, M.B.E, Chairman of the Council three times, looking back at the war in 1971, said of the people who came to Alsager; *'You did us good … You came and brought your families. You brought fresh blood and fresh life. First with the evacuees from Liverpool. Then the munition workers, the Navy, the marines. After the war, it was the displaced persons, Poles and Lithuanians. And now we have the college students billeted on us. It's nicer to have more people and more facilities, even if the village is not as picturesque.'*

The new Secondary School did not arrive until 1954. No cinema was built to replace the temporary picture house at *Heathside*, but at least Radway Green ROF survived when many thought it would close after the war.

On 3rd August 1946 *Heathside Hostel* officially closed and was transferred to the Ministry of Education. *Alsager College*, as it became, was officially opened in May 1947 by Mr G.N Flemming, Under Secretary of State for Education. The first intake was three hundred and fifty-one students with an average age of thirty. The course lasted twelve months for teachers destined to work in primary and secondary modern schools.

In the same year, the Minister of Education declared the college to be *'permanent'*. The college later became part of a combined *Crewe and Alsager College*. The Alsager site closed in 2008 and is being redeveloped to include a sports hub to continue the tradition of sport and recreation on the former *Heathfields* and college site.

Work was in short supply and some ex-servicemen had to advertise for work in the post war years!

The *Alsager Times* reported in February 1948 Alsager was *'second place among all local authorities in the national housing progress chart'*. One hundred and forty-three new houses were built up to 31st December 1947, one new house for every thirty-two inhabitants. By comparison Stoke-on-Trent built one new house per two hundred and fifty-eight inhabitants in the same year.

Violet Bullock, right of picture, (war widow of Tpr. C.H Bullock) receives the keys to her new council house in 1946.

Left, is Councillor Mr R. Titmus. Centre is Mr H.V Lynam, UDC Surveyor

Alsager UDC achieved a great deal. It had coped with the increased pressures of sudden population increase by building more council houses. and updating civic amenities such as Fairview Park.

Councillor Dorothy Harpur said the building of ROF, Radway Green, had boosted Alsager in terms of providing more housing and jobs. The expansion and growth of the town was seen as a good thing. But the large houses requisitioned by the Ministry of Supply during the war were transferred for other uses or sold. Most have since been demolished.

Post-war austerity did prevent the introduction of amenities such as a new cinema. A proposed Secondary School was not included in the County Council building programme for 1949 as expected, but the council decided to keep the Parsonage Fields in reserve as it could be used by a new school. The Alsager Cricket Club were opposed to the building of a school next to the Parsonage Fields as it would lose its ground. A new secondary school was not achieved until the early 1950s. There had been letters to the *Alsager Times* demanding a Grammar School in Alsager. There were outline plans to use the former *HMS Excalibur* as a temporary secondary school but in the end, it was used to house displaced persons from abroad. To have converted *Excalibur* to a secondary school would not have provided a good permanent solution. The site was later used as an infant school in the 1950s after the closure of the dispersed persons' camp.

Local people had to adapt quickly to tough conditions during and after the War. They survived despite considerable military, economic, and social pressures.

The town and surrounding villages have grown considerable since the Second World War. Alsager has lost some of its village-like qualities. Most people knew one another in 1938. It was a quieter, more peaceful place, but it has thrived in many ways. It has a great range of social organizations which have continued the tradition of public participation and social care. We should celebrate its successes.

Dorothy Harpur (nee Goss) MBE

(1894-1972)

Picture from Cheshire Life May 1971

Nurse in France 1918, British War Medal, Victory Medal,

First Woman Councillor Alsager UDC/ Chairman 1943,

Coordinator in Civil Defence 1939-45

Appendix: Awards to Alsager and District men and women during the Second World War

Captain Charles William Kennerley Potts, West Kent Regiment, Military Cross 1942

Sir Francis Joseph K.B.E was created a Baronet June 1942

Commander William Hazlett Sayers, R.N. Distinguished Service Cross, 1943

Ruby Esther Stainton, MBE Services to Nursing in France and Middle East

Richard Goss, Grenadier Guards, MBE 1945

Pilot Officer Alexander Millar McKie. RAF, Distinguished Flying Medal 1944

Pilot Officer Nelson Arthur Bevans. RAF, Distinguished Flying Cross 1944

Flight Lieutenant Tom Cecil Scott, RAF, Distinguished Flying Cross 1944

Captain John Arrowsmith, Royal Artillery, Military Cross 1945

Corporal Robert Wilberforce Fisher, Reconnaissance Corps, Distinguished Conduct Medal, 1945

Corporal Victor Holmes, Royal Engineers, Mentioned in Despatches 1945

Sergeant Cyril Rothwell, Royal Horse Artillery, Military Cross, 1945

Captain J.W Cuthbert, Commander of HMS Excalibur, CBE 1946

Betty Cuthbert, for work with the National Fire Service, CBE 1946

Bombardier Norman Frost, Royal Artillery, Belgium Croix de Guerre, 2nd Class with palm. 1945

Private Roy Palfreyman. 4th Armoured Division, Légion d'Honneur France. Awarded 2017 for service in France 1944/5.

Index

13 Club, 349, 350, 398
1939 Register, 15, 17, 19, 28, 32, 84, 112, 139, 205, 246, 275, 319, 385, 387
Air raid shelters, 55, 76, 78, 337, 342
Air Transport Auxiliary, 29, 47
Aische, Dr Michael, 31, 32, 33, 328
allotments, 57, 65
Alsager, 5, 7, 8, 9, 13, 15, 17, 19, 20, 21, 22, 23, 24, 26, 27, 28, 29, 31, 32, 33, 37, 41, 42, 45, 52, 54, 55, 56, 57, 58, 59, 62, 64, 66, 70, 71, 78, 79, 80, 81, 86, 93, 95, 96, 97, 98, 100, 101, 102, 105, 108, 119, 120, 121, 122, 123, 124, 125, 126, 127, 128, 129, 130, 131, 132, 133, 152, 154, 155, 157, 160, 162, 164, 165, 166, 167, 168, 170, 171, 172, 173, 174, 177, 178, 180, 181, 184, 186, 188, 193, 196, 201, 202, 204, 208, 209, 210, 211, 212, 214, 215, 216, 217, 218, 219, 220, 222, 223, 224, 225, 226, 228, 229, 230, 236, 261, 262, 263, 275, 277, 280, 281, 282, 283, 287, 288, 290, 291, 292, 293, 299, 301, 319, 320, 322, 323, 327, 328, 329, 334, 337, 338, 339, 349, 350, 351, 353, 357, 363, 364, 365, 366, 367, 368, 369, 370, 372, 375, 376, 377, 378, 379, 382, 383, 384, 385, 386, 387, 390, 391, 394, 395, 399, 400, 401, 402, 405
Alsager British Legion, 15, 22, 28, 58, 71, 282, 287, 375, 378, 400
Alsager Hall Farm, 167
Alsager War Memorial, 86, 108, 152, 155, 157, 188, 193, 201, 261, 263, 275, 280, 299, 400
Anderson, George William, 382
ARP (Air Raid Precautions), 15, 16, 17, 18, 19, 21, 22, 23, 24, 26, 27, 33, 39, 48, 57, 63, 97, 124, 125, 181, 193, 328, 378
Arrowsmith, Capt, John, 290, 405
ATS (Auxillary Territoial Service), 46, 47, 187
Bailey, Lt Richard John, 293, 294
Bailey, Philip, 22
Baker Wilbraham, 51, 68, 215
Band, Flossie, 353
Band, Jack, 29
Band, LAC Gilbert, 212, 213
Barker, John, 12

Barker, Peter, 33, 56, 64, 67, 121, 218, 324, 327, 339
Barnard, A.T, 326
Barthomley, 7, 8, 162, 309, 329
Bates, George, 20, 391
Battle of Britain, 62, 82, 88, 89, 97, 98, 146, 330
Bebbington, Jo, 76
Bennion, Family, 356, 357, 372
Beresford, George Henry, 272, 274
Bevans, P/O Nelson Arthur, 229, 405
Bickertons Shop, 64
Blaney, Gordon, 185, 186
Bloch, Dr Walter, 33
Bloch, Frida, 33
Bloch, Robert, 33, 34
Boden Hall, 51, 172
Boffey, Edwin Archer, 19
Bosson, George, 240
Bourne, Charles, 77
Boyce Adams shop, 64, 65
Braddock, Mr W J, 166
Brant, Pilot Officer Harry, 112
British Army, 17, 26, 51, 67, 81, 84, 113, 117, 133, 160, 162, 180, 212, 218, 237, 238, 241, 243, 244, 246, 247, 248, 249, 250, 251, 254, 255, 256, 261, 272, 273, 291, 292, 293, 303, 309, 311, 317, 318, 351, 373, 401, 405
British Expeditionary Force, 53, 62, 80, 237, 244, 247, 259
Brookes, Ernest, 237
Brough, Thomas, 250, 251, 252
Broughton, Lady Vera, 71
Brufnell, Thomas, 28
Brunds, 36, 122, 319, 327, 329, 376, 377
Bullock, Charles William, 275
Bullock, Violet, 277, 402
C.A.G Pilots, 28
Carson, Violet, 367, 368
Cartwright, Audrey, 338
Cartwright, Private Wilfred Ernest, 84
Cedars, 31, 32, 328, 329
Chamberlain, Neville, 49, 54, 62
Christ Church Alsager, 56, 66, 81, 102, 121, 128, 131, 170, 188, 202, 215, 262, 319, 366
Church Lawton, 7, 8, 74, 112, 113, 114, 143, 162, 205, 210, 237, 250, 272, 301

Church Lawton War Memorial, 112, 113, 143, 205, 237, 250, 272, 301
Civil Defence, 15, 16, 17, 18, 24, 46, 48, 50, 57, 75, 99, 166, 282, 283, 330, 336, 366, 369
Clarke. June, 217
Clowes, James, 81, 217, 218
Collorick, Jim, 372, 373, 374, 375
Conlon, Benjamin, 92
conscientious objectors, 48
conscription, 46, 47, 48
Corfield, Moses, 22
Craig, Anna Ernestine, 386
Craig, Charles Thurlow, 387
Craig, Sir Ernest, 386, 387
Creswellshawe, 219, 329
Cummings, George, 18
Cuthbert, Betty, 379
Cuthbert, Captain, 379, 380, 382, 401, 405
D Day, 160, 181, 184, 213, 223, 251, 254, 261, 275, 294, 299, 317, 377, 388
Dale, Roy, 352
de Bolotoff- Wiazemsky, Tatiana, 36, 388, 389
Dig for Victory, 56
Dorothy Harpur, 5, 17, 40, 165, 168, 287, 401, 403, 404
Dudson, Helen, 21
Ecclestone, Raymond, 315
ENSA, 353
evacuees, 38, 39, 41, 44, 45, 54, 219, 329, 401
Evacuees, 38, 40, 219, 330
Evans, Lewys William, 264
Evans, Winifred, 167
Excalibur displaced person's hostel, 382
Fairview House, 330
Farrington, Edwin, 309, 311
Fire Service, 17, 25, 48, 97, 223, 281, 366, 367, 379, 405
Fisher, Cpl. Robert Wilberforce, 223, 291, 405
Flatman, Mr L S, 217, 225, 226, 284, 330, 397
Flemming. Mr G.N, 401
Forchheimer, Isle Sara, 35
Foreign Born Nationals in Alsager and district in 1939, 31
Frost, Norman, 401, 405
Gables, 328, 329, 330
Gibson, James Victor, 246, 249

Godwin, Claud Herbest, 102, 103, 104
Goss, Captain Richard, 188, 189, 190, 405
Goss, Huntley, 28
H.M.S Excalibur, 319, 381, 382
Hammersley, Leslie, 226, 378
Hanahoe, John, 319
Hancock's Shop, 64
Harpur, Dr Henry, 8
Hart, Peter, 280
Heath Farm, 329, 357, 358
Heathside, 20, 128, 165, 169, 214, 283, 284, 287, 329, 356, 357, 358, 361, 363, 364, 365, 366, 367, 368, 369, 371, 372, 375, 376, 394, 401
Holland, Lt. Reginald B., 83
Holland, Margaret (Bebbington), 44, 45
Holmes, Victor, 293, 405
Hulse, William, 254, 258
Jacobs, Captain George, 81
Jones, Bill, 17
Jones, Edwin Buckley, 259
Jones, Lt. Derrick H, 101
Jones, Rev William Thomas, 105
Joseph, Sir Francis, 14, 26, 42, 54, 55, 58, 60, 66, 67, 70, 93, 120, 130, 168, 170, 287, 288, 289, 394, 405
Lake, Sidney, 350
Lawton, Thomas Arnold, 305, 306
LDV, 52, 74, 75, 76, 77, 93, 100, 101, 181, 226, 337, 372, 400
Longshaw, Cyril Dennis, 267
Lowe, Joseph Henry, 317
Lynam, Harry Valentine, 13, 16, 24, 26, 27, 39, 57, 63, 98, 128, 129, 224, 225, 293
Maddock, Beatrice 'Bee', 36
Maddock, Fred, 191
Maddock, Grace, 36
Maddock, John Francis, 36
Martyn-Johns, Pilot Officer Colin Tremain, 113, 114
Mckie, Commander John C,, 222
McKie, Lt. Alexander Millar, 220, 221, 222, 405
Meiklejohn, John, 19
Mellor, Sgt Archie, 223
Middling, Henry, 279
Milton House, 36, 54, 63, 96, 128, 178, 288, 328, 329, 330, 350, 385, 386, 387, 388, 390, 394, 396, 397, 398

Ministry of Supply, 31, 63, 130, 224, 288, 328, 330, 349, 354, 356, 358, 375, 403
Morrow, Sapper R, 223
Moseley, Ernest, 201, 263
Moseley, L/Cl Alfred Eric, **201, 202, 203, 204, 263**
Moulton, Robert Bruce, 108
Nelson, John James, 7, 13, 72, 229, 230, 405
New, John, 243, 244
Nicholas, Rev Dan, 215
Nursing, 19, 21, 24, 26, 28, 79, 99, 405
Odd Rode War Memorial, 84, 92, 115, 139, 149, 187, 191, 240, 243, 254, 264, 267, 303, 305, 315, 317
Palfreyman, Mrs P.J, 40
Palfreyman, Roy, 178, 179, 180, 184, 388, 405
Palin, James, 17
Parish, Bob, 396, 397
Pfingst, Dora, 35
Pierpoint, Sgt Harry, 193, 194, 195, 196
Potts, Rev Charles Churton, 54, 59, 132, 209
Prospect House, 17, 224, 330
Queen Elizabeth, 79
Quinton, Major Joseph, 79, 80
Radway Green Royal Ordnance Factory, 14, 97, 122, 128, 129, 130, 157, 171, 210, 217, 226, 261, 283, 284, 287, 288, 320, 322, 324, 325, 327, 328, 329, 330, 333, 334, 335, 336, 342, 345, 346, 347, 348, 349, 350, 351, 352, 353, 354, 355, 356, 366, 372, 376, 377, 378, 385, 394, 396, 397, 398, 403
RAF, 20, 21, 22, 53, 82, 83, 86, 88, 89, 128, 131, 139, 141, 143, 144, 146, 147, 152, 153, 155, 156, 162, 163, 168, 195, 205, 210, 212, 215, 216, 220, 223, 230, 231, 232, 236, 262, 305, 306, 308, 346, 365, 391, 393, 405
RAFVR, 125, 139, 143, 145, 155, 162, 193, 205, 229, 231
Rationing, 52, 63, 64, 100, 171, 226
Red Cross, 15, 18, 19, 21, 58, 98, 123, 165, 171, 224, 226, 368, 369, 383
Richardson, John, 224
Rigby, Pilot Officer Robert Harold, 86
Rode Hall, 51, 68, 172, 328

Rode Heath, 7, 8, 52, 62, 64, 80, 81, 115, 117, 123, 168, 191, 212, 215, 243, 246, 264, 293, 317
Rothwell, Sgt. Cyril, 293, 405
Royal Air Force., 139, 152
Royal Navy, 82, 106, 108, 115, 117, 120, 149, 157, 160, 174, 267, 294, 329, 351, 352, 372, 373, 377, 379, 380, 392
Roycroft family, 288
Rutherford, Dr E.D., 380
Salute the Soldier campaign, 216, 217, 369
Sandys, Duncan, 346, 347
Savings Campaigns, 37, 58, 59, 70, 71, 121, 128, 168, 217, 218
Sayers, Commander William Hazlett, 174, 405
Sayers, Dr Mathew, 20
Scholar Green, 7, 8, 23, 51, 84, 92, 139, 168, 187, 240, 254, 294, 303, 305, 328
Scott, Ft/Lt Tom, 230, 233, 234, 235, 236
Settle Speakman, 14, 130
Shaw, Alec, 227
Shortland, Bertram, 299, 300
Skeetes, Ernest, 351, 352
Smith, Captain Robert George, 70
Smith, Sergeant Vincent George Louvaine, 205
Spite, Driver Norman, 210, 211, 212
St John's Ambulance, 17, 21, 24, 26, 78, 226
St Mary's Church, 44, 130, 283, 395
St Mary's schoolroom, 17, 66, 168, 217, 400
Stainton, Ruby Esther, 228, 405
Statham, Freda, 187
Swindells, Captain John, 75
Tantun family, 301, 302
Teacher's Training College, 363, 364, 372, 375
Territorial Army, 28, 46, 248
Timmis, Councillor, 57, 401
Tudor, L/AC Sidney J., 210
Tudor, W/O Frank, 210
Tulp, Endla, 383, 384
Urban District Council, 7, 17, 24, 78, 98, 122, 165, 172, 210, 290, 293, 321, 396
VE Day, 183, 281, 283, 285
Wetherby, Florence, 19
Wheaton-Smith, Craig, 36, 178, 388, 389
Wheaton-Smith, Ernestine, 385, 388
Wheaton-Smith, Franklin, 385, 386

White, Geoff, 295, 297
White, Ted, 390, 391, 392, 393, 395
Wilding, Owen, 223
Wilhelmina, Queen, 67
Wilshaw, Dennis, 128, 165
Wings Week, 168, 170
Wise, William Jesse John, 303
Women's Land Army, 48, 167
Woodcock, Richard Shiel, 261

Woodward, Able Seaman Alfred, 115, 117, 118
Woolwich Arsenal, 128, 326, 350
WRAAF, 47
WRNS, 46, 289
WVS (Women's Voluntary Service), 16, 20, 36, 98, 99, 219, 224, 283, 385
WVS (Women's Voluntary Service), 16
Yorke, Pte Leonard James, 218

Note on the Author

Rob Blaney was born in South Cheshire in 1952 and went to Alsager School and Sandbach School. He served with the 1/51st Highland Regiment in the British Army and taught English at the Collegiate School, Liverpool. He has worked as a Manager and a Director of a Housing Association. In 2009 he gained an MA in Creative Writing from Chester University. He has written Alsager in the First World War, and six novels, all obtainable from Amazon Books. His poems have been published in journals.

Citations and Sources

// Alsager Collection FHS Cheshire.

[Article] // Birmingham Post. - [s.l.] : Birmingham Post.

/ auth. Bristol BBC.

/ auth. Crisford L.P // Memories of Alsager. - 1992.

/ auth. Hill Norman G.. - [s.l.] : Lawton Heritage Society , 1998.

/ auth. Reports RAF Combat.

[Interview] / interv. Shaw Alec.

Alsager College Film / dir. Christopher J.C. - 1947.

Alsager Parish Magazine [Journal].

Alsager Times [Journal].

Alsager, the Place and its People [Book] / auth. AP&P Alsager. - [s.l.] : The Alsager History Research Group, 1999.

Census 1911 National Archives.

Chester Observer [Article]. - Ches Observer.

Coastal Command [Book] / auth. Campbell John.

Commonwealth War Graves Commission.

Crewe Chronicle [Article]. - Crewe Chronicle.

Daily Mirror [Journal].

Details of Robert Moulton [Interview] / interv. Munslow Angela. - 2017.

Dover Express [Journal].

Excalibur, Guide to New Entries [Article]. - 1944.

George William Anderson / auth. Archive Family.

Huzaren van de nacht [Book] / auth. Cornellissen.

Immigration and Naturalisation Record H.M Government [Case].

In a Separate Little War [Book] / auth. Bird Andrew D..

interview [Interview] / interv. Smith Sandra. - 2017.

interview 2017 [Interview] / interv. White Geoff.

Interview 2017 [Interview] / interv. Band Gilbert.

Interview 2017 [Interview] / interv. Palfreyman Roy.

Kelly's Directory [Book Section] / auth. Kelly's. - 1939.

Leslie Arthur Neal / auth. Project BBC Wartime Memories.

Liverpool Echo [Journal] // Liverpool Echo.

Liverpool Evening Express [Journal].

Liverpool Post [Journal].

London Gazette [Journal].

Manchester Evening News [Journal].

Memoirs and Diaries.

Naval-history.net; [Online].

Neville Chamberlain. - [s.l.] : www.history.com/speeches/chamberlain-declares-war-on-germany, 1939.

On the Bloody Road to Berlin [Book] / auth. Williams Rogers and.

Prisoner of War Records [Report]. - [s.l.] : National Archives.

Radway Green, a history of ROF Radway Green 1940-1999 [Book] / auth. Labbatt P.. - 1999.

RAF Bomber Command KLosses of WW2 [Book] / auth. W.R Chorley. - [s.l.] : Middlebrook & Elliot, 1990.

Recollecions of Sidney Lake [Interview] / interv. Morris Christianne. - 2017.

Recollection of the outbreak of War / auth. Joan Hamlett nee Bailey. - 1939.

Recollection Tony Finlow.

Recollections 1939-47 [Interview] / interv. Barker Peter. - 2017.

Recollections of Ernest Skeetes [Interview] / interv. Cheetham Angela. - 2017.

Recollections of Excalibur-Displaced Persons Hostel [Journal] / auth. Lakin Hele.

Recollections of Norman Ackroyd.

Recollections of the Second World War [Interview] / interv. Bennett Doug. - 2017.

Recollections of WW2 and formation of Alsager College [Interview] / interv. Collorick James. - 2017.

Sayers Family Archive / auth. Sayersarchive.

Sentinel [Article] // Sentinel and Weekly Sentinel newspapers.

Shrewsbury School Records.

Sinking of a torpedo / auth. Hoffman Ferdinand.

Soldier in the Sand [Book] / auth. Potts.

Staffordshire Advertiser [Journal]. - 1939-45.

Tatler Magazine [Journal].

The Black Bull [Book] / auth. Delaforce Patrick.

The Impact of World Wr Two on Alsager / auth. J.W.Skinner. - [s.l.] : B.Ed Alsager College, 1992.

Thurlwood, please drive slowly [Book] / auth. Westwood Phillip. - [s.l.] : Three Counties Publishing, 2009.

UK Gov National Corporate Register [Book Section]. - [s.l.] : UK Gov, 1939Reg.

United States Immigration Records [Report].

War Diaries British Army.

Wartime Britain 1939-1945 [Book] / auth. Gardiner Juliet.

Western Morning News [Journal].

www.bbc.co.uk/history/worldwars/wwtwo/ww2_summary_01.shtml [Online] / auth. history BBC.

www.iwm.org.uk/history/8-things-you-need-to-know-about-the-battle-of-britain [Online] / auth. Imperial War Museum. - 2017.

Made in the USA
Columbia, SC
02 November 2017